AN
INNOCENT
IN
*S*COTLAND

ALSO BY DAVID W. MCFADDEN

POETRY
Intense Pleasure, 1972
A Knight in Dried Plums, 1975
On the Road Again, 1978
My Body Was Eaten by Dogs, 1981
The Art of Darkness, 1984
Gypsy Guitar, 1987
Anonymity Suite, 1992
There'll Be Another, 1995

FICTION
Animal Spirits, 1983
Canadian Sunset, 1986

NON-FICTION
A Trip Around Lake Erie, 1981
A Trip Around Lake Huron, 1981
A Trip Around Lake Ontario, 1988
An Innocent in Ireland, 1995
Great Lakes Suite, 1997

AN
INNOCENT
IN
*S*COTLAND

More Curious Rambles and Singular Encounters

DAVID W. McFADDEN

M&S

Canadian Cataloguing in Publication Data

McFadden, David, 1940–
An innocent in Scotland

ISBN 0-7710-5528-5

1. McFadden, David, 1940– – Journeys – Scotland.
2. Scotland – Description and travel.   I. Title.

DA867.5.M24 1999   914.1104'859   C98-933035-4

We acknowledge the financial assistance of the Government of Canada through
the Book Publishing Industry Development Program for our publishing activities.
We further acknowledge the support of the Canada Council for the Arts and the
Ontario Arts Council for our publishing program.

Poems by Sorley Maclean, quoted on pp. 175 and 176, are from
Calum I. Maclean, *The Highlands* (London: B.T. Batsford, c. 1959).

Map by Visutronx
Typeset in Goudy by M&S, Toronto

Printed and bound in Canada

McClelland & Stewart Inc.
The Canadian Publishers
481 University Avenue
Toronto, Ontario
M5G 2E9

1 2 3 4 5   03 02 01 00 99

For Swallow Willow, Smoky the Weasel, and Cosmic Plan.
For the McConnell sisters – Skye, Hayley, and Sheena.
And for Amy, Ben, and Chloë, Owen, Galen, and Zoë.

"The traveller sees only what interests him; for example, Marco Polo never noticed Chinese women's small feet."
— Bertrand Russell, *In Praise of Idleness*

"I go everywhere twice. Once to get the wrong impression, once to strengthen it."
— Don DeLillo, *The Names*

"Indeed Cypriot manners at their worst never came near the stupidities and impertinences I endured from the Scots on my only visit to the Rump."
— Lawrence Durrell, *Bitter Lemons*

CONTENTS

1. Grey Sneakers / 1

2. Stepping on Snails / 10

3. Major Bill and Mr. Tingle / 20

4. Tattoos from Tip to Tail / 33

5. Deep Peace of the Shining Stars / 44

6. Miracle at Saint Ninian's Cave / 61

7. Beyond the Cheviot Hills / 69

8. The Great Collector and the Great Explorer / 78

9. A BritRail Pass for Life / 89

10. Morton Takes Over / 95

11. A Trip Around Loch Froachie / 106

12. Regicide at Lumphanan / 113

13. Somewhere a Duck Is Quacking / 127

14. Sueno's Stone / 139

15. The Pine Martens of Glengarry / 150

16. The Fairy Flag / 165

17. The View from Duart Castle / 177

18. I Discover Iona / 189

19. Kamikaze Crows on Dun Bhuirg / 201

20. The Tipper Compound / 208

21. The Scone Convergence / 216

22. Castle Mor and the Lochbuie Stone Circle / 226

23. Settlers' Watch / 236

24. Macro-Fishing with Wally / 250

25. Ancient Mysteries of Argyll / 264

26. Salty Kippers and Blotting Paper / 276

27. Carnliath / 286

28. Subterranean Moons / 293

29. An Innocent Flirtation in Tongue / 304

30. High Road to Glasgow / 314

31. Glaswegian Atmospherics / 319

32. Friends from Falkirk / 327

33. Bigots Becoming Enlightened / 332

Epilogue: Glasgow Airport / 337

Index / 341

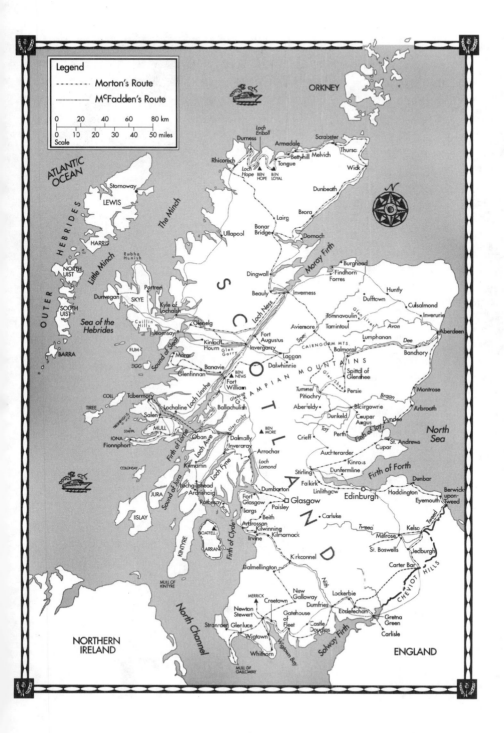

ORKNEY

ATLANTIC
OCEAN

Stornoway

LEWIS

The Minch

HARRIS

Rubha
Hunish

NORTH
UIST

Portree

Dunvegan

SKYE

Little Minch

Sea of the
Hebrides

Cuillin
Hills

SOUTH
UIST

Isleornsay

Kyle of
Lochalsh

Glenelg

BARRA

EIGG

Sound of Sleat

MUCK

Mallaig

Glenfinnan

Morar

COLL

Tobermory

Lochaline

Loch Linnhe

Salen

TIREE

MULL

STAFFA

IONA

Fionnphort

Oban

Loch Awe

Dalmally

Inveraray

Kilmartin

Loch Fyne

Arrochar

Loch
Lomond

COLONSAY

Sound of Jura

JURA

Lochgilphead

Ardrishaig

Rothesay

ISLAY

Largs

ARRAN

Fort
Glasgow

Dumbarton

Paisley

Glasgow

Beith

Ardrossan

Kilwinning

Irvine

Kilmarnock

KINTYRE

BOATFELL

Firth of Clyde

Kirkconnel

Balmellington

MULL OF
KINTYRE

NORTH
CHANNEL

North Channel

NORTHERN
IRELAND

MERRICK

MULL OF
GALLOWAY

Newton
Stewart

Stranraer

Glenluce

Wigtown

Whithorn

Creetown

Wigtown Bay

New
Galloway

Gatehouse
of Fleet

Dumfries

Castle
Douglas

Nith

Ecclefechan

Solway Firth

Lockerbie

Gretna
Green

Carlisle

ENGLAND

Durness

Loch
Eriboll

Armadale

Bettyhill

Melvich

Scrabster

Thurso

Wick

Rhiconich

Loch
Hope

BEN
HOPE

Tongue

BEN
LOYAL

Dunbeath

Brora

Lairg

Ullapool

Bonar
Bridge

Dornoch

Moray Firth

Burghead

Findhorn

Dingwall

Beauly

Inverness

Forres

Huntly

Dufftown

Culsalmond

Inverurie

Loch Ness

SCOTLAND

Tomnavoulin

Aviemore

Tomintoul

Avon

Lumphanan

Aberdeen

Fort
Augustus

Kinloch
Hourn

Glen
Garry

Invergarry

CAIRNGORM MTS.

Dee

Banchory

Laggan

Dalwhinnie

Balmoral

Spittal of
Glenshee

BEN
NEVIS

Banavie

Fort
William

GRAMPIAN MOUNTAINS

Glen Coe

Ballachulish

Tummel

Pitlochry

Persie

Braan

Montrose

Spey

Aberfeldy

Blairgowrie

Arbroath

BEN
MORE

Dunkeld

Coupar
Angus

Dundee

Crieff

Tay

Perth

Firth of Tay

St. Andrews

Auchterarder

Cupar

North
Sea

Kinross

Stirling

Dunfermline

Falkirk

Linlithgow

Edinburgh

Haddington

Firth of Forth

Dunbar

Berwick-
upon-Tweed

Eyemouth

Carluke

Tweed

Melrose

Kelso

St. Boswells

Jedburgh

Carter Bar

CHEVIOT HILLS

GREY SNEAKERS

Port Glasgow • *Greenock* • *Gurock* • *Largs* • *Kilwinning* • *Irvine*

Wednesday, May 29. In his book, *Six Action Shoes,* excerpted in today's *Glasgow Herald,* pop philosopher Edward de Bono claims grey sneakers should be worn for investigation and the collection of information. Fortunately, I happen to be wearing grey sneakers. Along the south shore of the Firth of Clyde, the leaves are out but they haven't reached the dark rich green of summer; everything looks freshly washed. Across the grey waters, strangely shaped and perilous rock formations, some capped with stately homes, appear on the north shore. My long-dead travel guide, H. V. Morton, refers to these as "romantic rocks." In a rest stop a funny little lorry has MCCLENAGHAN OF SLAMANNAN, PHONE 851060 painted on its door. As the driver gets out to relieve himself he glances my way. The look on his face says check me out all you want, my conscience is clear. So is mine, but I'm a bit confused: it's my first day in Scotland, I've just now left the airport in my little rental car, and I'm still not sure if it would be best to follow Morton's clockwise route, the one he took in his book *In Search of Scotland* (1929), or the counter-clockwise route he took in his book *In Scotland Again* (1933). But an ominously cold wind blowing along the firth makes me realize with a shiver it might be best to linger in the southern part of the country for a few more days before heading north. I'll follow the counter-clockwise route for now, but not slavishly. After all, I'm a big boy, and I don't really need Morton, although he is a fascinating character, a pioneer automotive tourist whose numerous books, stacked as they were with clichéd sentimentalities and ethnic generalities, were great crowd-pleasers in their day. I'd like my book to be at least a bit more sophisticated, and I'm definitely not going to tour any bagpipe factories.

On display in a little parkette surrounded by a steel fence sits an old paddleboat steamer known as *The Comet*. It probably served its time ferrying people across the Firth of Clyde. It may be the very boat Morton hired for a little cruise up the Clyde to Glasgow. He could have stood on those decks.

When I asked if Greenock was pronounced *Green-ock* or *Grinn-ick*, a woman running a tea wagon off the main road said, "It's pronounced *Green-ick*." I laughed. "That's all right," she said. "I mean a lot of people say *Green-ock*. But this is Port Glasgow. Greenock's the next town." Her name was the name of the month that was ending, and she presented me with a steaming bowl of Arbroath stovies. I put a plastic forkful in my mouth and looked thoughtful.

"Weel, is it the ingredients ye'd like to know?" May points to my little paper bowl. "It's jis' potatoes and beef – corned beef. What does yez call it over there, hash?"

"We call it something else, I don't know what. Let's see now, this is Arbroath stovies, and Arbroath's a town, right?"

"Yup, up in the east coast. Right, Alec?" Alec, who has joined us, confirms the statement.

"And this is the way they make them up there?"

"Yup. And here they make 'em with yer sliced sausages – that's yer sausage meat, potatoes, and onion. But that there is made with corned beef, potatoes, and onion."

"I see. And what do you call the ones made with sausages?"

"Jis' stovies. The meat's different, that's the only thing that's different."

"Put a drop of salt on 'em," said Alec. "Salt, man, salt. Put salt on 'em."

"What else? Pepper maybe?"

"Aye, put the pepper and salt on 'em."

"Aye, pepper and salt on yer stovies," said May. "How long have you got?"

"Thirty-three days."

"Oh, my! And where are ye stayin'?" She was wearing a full apron with vertical red and white stripes. She had a gold chain around her neck with a clown on it.

"I'm not staying anywhere yet. I just got here."

"Weel fer God's sakes! Yer not stayin' anywheres ther. You should go up the north – it's loovly up there, or the east. Isn't it, Alec?"

"Aye," said Alec. "It's a lovely country, Scotland."

"Och, it's loovly up north or the east. He's jis' travelling around staying at bed-and-breakfasts. He jis' got here yisterday."

"Today."

"Oh Good Lord, jis' today."

When I finished my Arbroath stovies, May looked pleased. "How was it?" she said.

"It was exactly what I needed for the hole in me tummy." She laughed. "I've only been in Scotland two hours and already I've bought a cap" – I tipped it at her – "and have eaten an entire bowlful of Arbroath stovies. And now I'd like a Bovril as well." Bovril was new to me. It was a hot drink that looked like coffee but smelled and tasted like roast beef in a cup. "Do people put milk in Bovril?"

"Noo," May replied in a tone of great solemnity. "Noo. Did people ever put milk in Bovril, Alec?"

"Noo," said Alec, in a similar tone.

"Some people maybe used to?" said May.

"Never, noo, never," said Alec.

"Do people put *sugar* in the Bovril?" I wanted to start out on a proper footing, clear on the basics. Imagine if, at a fashionable resort somewhere, the smart set caught me putting sugar in my Bovril. I'd be disgraced and humiliated.

"Noo, noo, noo," said May. "Jis' the salt and the pepper."

"Jis' the pepper and the salt," added Alec. "It gives you a wee fire. You feel the heat goin' into yer body with the pepper."

Greenock, a tough industrial town, is famed for its boxers, mostly flyweight and bantamweight, for the ships it used to build before Japan took over the shipbuilding industry, and for the terrible bombing it took from the Luftwaffe in the spring of 1941, shortly after the Germans found out that all those British warships were being made along the Firth of Clyde: the Greenock Blitz is what it's known as locally. On May 6 of that year, shortly after midnight, a squadron of fifty German planes scattered bombs haphazardly around the town, hitting mostly residential areas, including a direct hit on a tenement building. The next night, after midnight, a much larger squadron of almost three hundred planes appeared, dropping heavy high explosives, incendiary bombs, and parachute land mines, which caused widespread damage to the distillery, both sugar refineries, both churches, and the power station. The entire town was left in flames, with 280 people killed. Some were machine-gunned by German planes as they ran for safety.

One woman returned to her house after the raid and found all the windows smashed, the roof demolished, but her canary still chirping merrily away in its cage and not one of a dozen eggs sitting in a carton on the kitchen table broken. She hunted high and low for the butter, however. A week or so later she found it in the bottom of a vase of tulips.

One church had all its windows blown out except for its World War I "Victory" window, which was an excellent omen. Numerous horrendous photos of the damage were featured in a little book called *The Greenock Blitz*, put out by the Inverclyde Public Libraries in 1991. "I was terrified but I had to be brave in front of the children," said one woman. "My husband was permanently on nights at the torpedo factory so it was just a case of doing the best I could. The raid went on for some time. I sang songs to the children and read story books just to keep their minds off it." Survivors later seemed amazed at how cheerful people had been even at the height of the bombing. Tea was served in the shelter and there was a communal singsong.

Damage to the shipyards was minimal: one incendiary bomb had burned a lifeboat in one of the destroyers. Another destroyer was knocked off its berth, but with no damage worth mentioning. This was because the positioning of the anti-aircraft emplacements was fairly shrewd as far as protecting the shipyards was concerned, but not so shrewd as far as protecting the town was concerned. The pilots couldn't get close to the shipyards, and they couldn't return home with a full load of bombs, so they dropped them on the town.

The new shopping mall in Greenock features a large painting of the town as it would have appeared before the war – if viewed from the window in front of which the painting was conveniently hanging. A red-eyed old fellow was standing there looking at the painting and comparing it with the current view.

"That brings back memories, does it?"

"Och, aye, it does," he said.

He said in the early seventeenth century Greenock was nothing but a row of fishing huts, but three hundred years later it had grown to be the world's biggest shipbuilding area.

Newark Castle sits on the south shore of the Firth of Clyde next to Ferguson Ship Builders Ltd. Something strange was being built inside the latter, as I could see by peeking through a crack in the door. It wasn't a ship, but what it was would require a wiser fellow than I to say. (Editor's note: oil rig perhaps.) The castle was once the greatest fortress for miles around, but it has been reduced to being the limp centrepiece of Inverclyde Newark Castle Park, which in spite of its small size boasts a Woodland Walk, a Fishing Jetty, a Riverside Walkway, a Boat Compound, a Picnic Site, a Car Park, and of course Newark Castle. Over the fifteenth-century gatehouse of the latter is carved: THE BLESSINGS OF GOD BE HEREIN. The castle has been badly wrecked but it's still solid – an intricate pattern of great blocks of stone, mortared so nicely into place five centuries ago. It bears the signs of having been a comfortable castle in winter, for the latrines on each floor are adjacent to the fireplaces. The topmost floor and the roof have been smashed away.

Around 1580 Patrick Maxwell built a "Renaissance mansion" between the old tower and the gatehouse, and the mansion became the main part of the castle. His tombstone is on display: I PATRICK MAXWELL BUILDER G'FIST HELO. They're playing tapes of medieval Scottish music, but then the music stops and a canned voice says: "Newark once graced a smiling Clydeside that was ignorant alike of shipbuilding and social deprivation. It may be so again. James IV stayed here in the 1490s." By the nineteenth century it had become "so derelict as to be suitable only for working men's families." Now, that's derelict!

Being the only visitor, I had a guide all to myself, so I pointed to the tombstone and asked her what G'FIST HELO meant.

"I dinna know what that means." She laughed. "That's noo a gravestone, is it?"

"I thought it was, but what would it be?"

"Och, I have jis' started last month," she said.

"In ten years you'll know everything about this castle."

"I learn it all off of the tourists."

This was nothing more than a job for this young woman. She didn't have the virus of history in her bloodstream, nor was she well-informed. Perhaps I became prejudiced against her right off when she wanted to know if I was sixty-five so she could give me a discount. The nerve!

On the motorway there's a deep-green grassy highway median smothered in tulips. No signs say KEEP OFF THE MEDIAN, for people are civilized here and would not drive on the median unless there was absolutely no other way out. Sitting square on the horizon ahead is a range of interestingly shaped pale-blue mountains, probably belonging to Kintyre, Argyll, or the Isles of Bute or Arran.

West of Greenock is Gourock, full of great rows of stately seafront hotels, villas, guest homes. Gourock is the northern terminus of a holiday belt that runs down the shore of the Firth of Clyde to Stranraer, with numerous nostalgic old tourist towns that have been nicely maintained, like Llandudno in Wales, rather than modernized into a digital nightmare like Blackpool in England. Working-class families from Glasgow come to Gourock for the summer break, and take a ferry across the Clyde to Dunoon or down to Rothesay on the Isle of Bute.

From Gourock one looks north across the firth to the coastal town of Kilcreggan, and west across the firth to a little fiord-like indentation called Holy Loch, which is bordered on the north by the Benmore Forest and on the south by the holiday town of Dunoon and the villages of Sandbank and Ardnadam. To the south one can see the relatively flat Isle of Bute and, behind it, the hills of Kintyre (largest one Cnoc Na Meine at 1,612 feet), and the great pyramid-shaped mountain of Goatfell (2,868 feet) on the Isle of Arran. This is a spectacular and all-inclusive view, wide-angled but highly detailed. It's interesting to have such a view of the fairly large town of Dunoon, in its entirety, and still have room for a great vista of coastal indentations, sky, sea, hills, mountains, surrounding communities, and islands rising up behind islands far off in the distance.

Further along, in the large Brightonesque town of Largs, we enter an area of deep superficiality, with the locals playing the role of rapacious wolves and the tourists (mostly from the north of England) rolling in on monster buses to be sheared and shorn in vast rows of souvenir shops and tourist casinos. The more well-heeled and energetic will take the little ferry across the Fairlie Roads to Great Cumbrae Island, which is encircled by a good coastal road and is twice as expensive as Largs – or so the shrewd Largs merchants maintain. There's a golf course and a Buddhist monastery on the island. And there's a Little Cumbrae Island, but nobody goes there except adventurous birdwatchers, who row across the Tan from Great Cumbrae Island to add to their bird lists. In Scotland one doesn't actually have to see a bird to add it to one's list: it's enough to hear it singing its little song. Nighttime bird-watching is said to be big in certain parts of the country.

Although Largs does not have the air of a serious town at all, there was a battle fought here in the thirteenth century – a rather slapstick battle but one that marked the end of an era. Alexander III, who had been crowned on the Stone of Scone at age eight, had now reached the age of twenty-two and was beginning to take an interest in continuing his late father's attempts to kick the Norse out of the Western Isles. Accordingly, the peaceful young king sent an emissary to Norway to offer to purchase the Hebrides. Unfortunately for Alexander, King Haakon of Norway had more money than islands and wasn't interested in selling any of the latter. Yet reports had been reaching him that his lieutenants on the various islands were becoming more Gaelic than Norse. Now that it was obvious that Alexander's interest in the islands was increasing, Haakon began to sense trouble. He was also receiving reports that Scottish raiding parties were attacking settlements on Skye with barbaric gusto. The newly demonized Scots were even reputedly running around with Norse babies on the ends of their spears – always a good line to use when you want to wage war.

So, in July 1263, King Haakon left Kirkwall in the Orkneys with his fleet and sailed to Skye, where he was met by King Magnus of the Isle of Man and some miscellaneous Celtic and Norse chiefs. The combined fleet entered the Firth of Clyde, but severe storms came up. On the last day of September, Haakon's ship was torn from its moorings and, along with ten provision ships, driven out to sea. All eleven ships eventually were cast ashore at Largs, where they were fired upon by bands of Scottish archers, who had been following their progress. The next day Haakon got his warriors organized and they found themselves facing the entire army of Alexander III, drawn up on the ridge overlooking the sea. Confusion prevailed, the gods guffawed, and the Norwegians waded back to their ships and sailed away.

Yet the battle was decisive. A dispirited Haakon returned to Kirkwall and died that winter. Three years later, the Isle of Man and the Western Isles were relinquished to Scotland for four thousand silver marks. The Norse threat was over, but this did not mean that Scotland was now united, for the clans of the Western Isles were intent on carrying out their bloody dynastic disputes no matter who claimed ultimate power over their homelands.

Poor John Muir, whoever he might be. Up into the hills and winding roads back from the coast is the pretty town of Kilwinning, with newer houses carefully built to blend in nicely with the older ones. Someone has done a superb job of painting in sober yellow block letters two feet high along a tall stone wall at the edge of town: JOHN MUIR IS HAVING AN AFFAIR.

In Irvine, at Mr. and Mrs. Boyd's tourist home, I found a nice large clean room with a wondrous view out over the tidal flats of Irvine Bay and across the sparkling sea to the Isle of Arran and the Kintyre peninsula behind it. The sun was setting behind both, and Goatfell looked splendid in silhouette. The eye ran along the dark-blue horizon with its mysteriously distant peaks and valleys like a hand along a piece of rare silk.

STEPPING ON SNAILS

Irvine • Kilmarnock • towards Dumfries

Thursday, May 30. When I said I needed an adapter for my laptop computer, Mr. and Mrs. Boyd directed me last night to the late-closing Tesco department store in Irvine, where I was treated like a visiting Martian: all work stopped and staff members from every department gathered around to discuss various aspects of electronic theory and which adapter would work for me. They finally decided none of them would, but I insisted on taking the one that said FOR SHAVERS ONLY – even though the consensus was that I should expect dire consequences if I used it with a computer.

Tesco was the only store open late in a shopping mall that had been built in part along an ancient bridge that was put up to span a loch, but the loch was drained a century ago or so, and now the bridge merely spans the narrow River Annick, meandering its way down to join the Irvine River and then to run into the Garnock estuary and the sea. On my way back to my room I popped into a pub for a pint. There were about ten old boys in there, for the most part in their mid-sixties or so. They didn't get strangers in there often. It was an unpretentious hole in the wall, with the same faces every night. Unfortunately, I couldn't understand their accents.

They were tolerant of my incomprehension, but I felt like a right idiot: if only I could find an adapter for my ear. It didn't help that it was a noisy little pub, with everyone trying to talk to me and to everyone else at the same time, and the television was blaring out a festival of old *Coronation Street* episodes. Somebody would say something and I would look blank, while someone else would say, "Well said!"

One fellow wanted to know how long my holiday would be. I had to ask him to repeat his question about four times: I thought he wanted to know why I looked so salty. One fellow said he had an older brother who worked at the steel mills in Hamilton, Ontario (my home town). "That's a wonderful mountain ye've got there," he said, then proceeded to tell me about the Russell brothers of Hamilton, who both got "poisoned by mustard gas" in France during World War I and died. "Another uncle of mine, he would be a cousin of the Russell brothers, he was a lumberjack, Willie Russell was his name, and he was over in France and a British officer came by and said 'You must salute me,' and Willie Russell said in his great deep rumble, 'No way, we're not here to salute English officers, we're here to kill Germans.' Och, I tell you they were wild men when they were in France. There wasn't a German who popped his head up that didn't get it blown right off. Och, and the Canadians, I tell ye, they got the worst of that mustard gas in that war, they got the brunt of it."

At one point someone asked if I was a Burns man and I said yes, I imagined he would be much loved in these parts. "Och, aye, yeah. He was jis' an ole saixual pairvert that could write poetry." This fellow insisted on buying my drinks and popping cigarettes in my mouth. As soon as I'd butt one he'd insist I take another. And I hadn't smoked in years.

At breakfast I told Mrs. Boyd how at Tesco everybody took my little two-pound purchase so seriously. And in spite of their warnings I tried the adapter when I got back to my room and it worked fine. "You took a chance and it worked," she warbled.

Mr. Boyd came into the breakfast room. He was preparing to get away for some brown-trout fishing in the lochs up in Sutherland. "He's going with two other gentlemen," said Mrs. Boyd. "No ladies allowed."

He'd be staying in a fishing lodge. "The crofters took over their own estate about five years ago," he said. "And they've developed these lochs and stocked them. They've set up these walking parties and fishing parties . . ."

"The crofters bought out the laird?"

"Yes."

"Refresh my memory. What exactly is a crofter?"

"He's a fellow who's got historical rights to farm a very small bit – about five acres, ten acres at the most. He'll fish and he'll work his acreage on the laird's land instead of paying rent to the laird. His family's been there probably a thousand years. And they all work together . . ."

"And the crofters would be native and the lairds English, right?"

"Or Dutch or German. Certainly not local. If he was local, the way his tongue is changed you wouldn't recognize him as local. Because he's been anglicized, he's been to public school in England, and he's gone away from his clansmen."

"So when little things like this happen, like the crofters buying out the laird, it makes the Scottish heart feel a little proud, does it?"

"Yes, and they make us feel welcome, they do."

"And you drink a bit of Scotch on these fishing holidays, do you?"

"You have to, it's the only thing that keeps the midges away."

"Them midges don't know what's good for them."

"Aye, but when you're into that sort of country up there it's a different philosophy of life, that's what it is. No rush." His voice was passionate and full of character, with an unusual range of musical intonations: each word was set at a different pitch, up and down the scales. Mrs. Boyd's voice was extremely high-pitched, but with similar qualities. The various North American intonations seemed predictable, tired, tuneless, and a bit irritating by contrast.

He went into a description of the history of the various bridges where the shopping mall is now. "There've been four bridges there. At first there was a ferry there, but somebody built a bridge and charged them money for crossing it. Also there was a loch north of here and it was all flooded south of here. So if you wanted to go from here northwards you had to come through this neck of land: if you control that neck of land you can make some silver out of it, and you can also keep the enemy sitting down there. And Edward I, he sat down there, and the Scottish army sat up here" – he was pointing out the window with its panoramic view – "and they looked at each other and growled at each other and made rude remarks about each other for about a month. But Edward had more money and he also reminded the Scots there was land for them down in England if they wanted it, and if they'd just join him he'd be giving them a wee payout. So gradually the Scots drifted over, and they disbanded without even a fight, and left Wallace sitting up there high and dry."

This account was consistent with the history books, which said it was William "Braveheart" Wallace's titled friends who abandoned him and went over to the English side, forcing Wallace to retreat northwards to Aberdeen.

"Besides that, what's Irvine most famous for? Besides this tourist home of course." Not a good joke but they broke into great peals of laughter and tears started running down their faces.

"Historically, you mean?" said Mr. Boyd, upon recovering his composure. "The most famous thing along this coast is this is where the Industrial Revolution started way back in 1680. It started here because of coal. They used the coal to heat sea water to make salt. And then they found themselves with sulphuric acid, and from sulphuric acid all the other chemicals came. So now we have the Imperial Chemical Industries plant, the biggest chemical plant in Europe."

Rain was pelting the windowpanes, and soggy songbirds had been whistling grumpily for hours in the branches of backyard trees. Mrs. Boyd assured me it would clear up by noon.

"It was Alfred Nobel," said Mr. Boyd. "He couldn't find a place to make nitroglycerine. He tried to do it in Sweden, but they said, We're no having that here, and he went to Germany, and they said, We're no having that here, so he came here and we said, Oh, well, aye, there's a bit of land over there that's doing nothing, why don't you use that? This was the thing that was going to stop all war. There's nobody could possibly fight a war with something as horrible as that. And that's where your Nobel Peace Prize came from — with the money he made over there." He pointed out the window. "But it's a Swedish prize now, because he was a Swede."

I gave him the name of the bar I was in last night and asked him about it. He laughed and said, "You went in there wearing that shirt?" I said yes. "Well, be very careful. It's amazing you went in with a green shirt and came out alive. This is a dangerous country. But your accent will save you."

"Yes, they knew I was ignorant. But they don't like the Irish there?"

"Och, well, they're staunch, blue, ultra-right-wing Protestants — fanatics — the UFV, Irish Free Fighters, and such stuff."

"I didn't realize that."

"Well, you wouldn't realize it, but that's one of their pubs."

"They were friendly enough."

"Oh, of course they are. Of course, the Irish are always friendly. That's not Irish, that's Irish–Scots, but don't go in there wearing the green."

Mrs. Boyd went into a fit of giggling. "They were just pulling your leg a bit," she said when I told them about the difficulty I had understanding the accents.

At one point I said something about being one of those people who are interested in everything and therefore know nothing.

"That . . . shouldn't . . . stop . . . you . . . from . . . speaking . . . about . . . it," said Mr. Boyd, his voice rising in pitch with each syllable so that the remark started at a low basso and ended up soprano. Then in a sober medium tone: "Look at the politicians!"

It may have stopped raining in Irvine by noon, but I was in Kilmarnock and it was still pouring. Kilmarnock – famous for Johnnie Walker Scotch, although my grandmother who was born there, preferred cognac for her medicinal purposes – is one of those little towns nevertheless complex enough to get lost in. In the cobblestone town square I queried a fellow about the absence of street signs. He said, "I think they all get pinched." Two little boys went by hand-in-hand chatting merrily away and both wearing red parkas. One appeared to be East Indian, the other ethnic Scots, if there is such a thing any more. They were about four years old, and it was startling to see children so young walking along without adult supervision – but they seemed happy to be with each other and without their parents. Nobody else seemed to be noticing them at all. Without a word they made an abrupt left turn and walked straight into the pet store to check out the kittens and puppies.

The square has an ancient shape but a sparkling new demeanour. There is a towering statue of Robert Burns, side by side with one of the local printer who, in 1786, had the foresight to bring everlasting glory to Kilmarnock by publishing Burns's first book. Actually it was the only book of Burns's that appeared during his lifetime. An attractive young woman came over as I stood gawking up at the statues, and started chatting me up in the rain, her nose an inch from mine and her warm dark eyes dancing merrily. She told me I looked exactly like Robert Burns. She said many women in town don't like the statue, because they resent Burns for his philandering and drinking. I told her I find such behaviour rather disgusting myself. She looked disappointed and wandered away.

In the Dick Institute, Kilmarnock's all-in-one cultural centre, I told the man who ran the little library next to the little art gallery that I was having a problem finding the gent's. "Well, we all are these days," he said, mournfully, "for the simple reason there aren't any."

"What do you do? Do you have to go down to the train station?"

"No, just a minute and I'll call somebody." A tall young man, badly in need of a shave on his face but with a close shave on the top of his head, showed up. Sweating profusely and complaining about the heat, he took me down a long hallway, unlocked a staff elevator, took me up to the top floor and showed me the staff washroom. I asked if he had a lot of such requests. "Oh yes, these days we do while all the public toilets are being repaired."

I popped into a "bar" for a pint and the place looked exactly like a "pub." What's the difference between the two? I asked a bright-looking young fellow sitting next to me.

"I think the bar-versus-pub type thing was applicable perhaps ten years ago, but drinking habits have changed quite radically in Scotland and in the U.K. We have a more liberal licensing law today. Ten years ago you used to have the pubs not open all day. People would go home at five o'clock and you would get yourself washed up, cleaned up, and back out for seven o'clock – and then by ten o'clock they were shutting the place again. So, in those three hours you found the people were trying to cram in quite an awful lot of serious drinking."

It was a good answer, but had little to do with my question. This fellow had spent four years working in the Sudan, had visited Alberta and camped in the Rocky Mountains, and was currently working as a supervisor in a paper mill on the coast near Irvine, but he, like me, didn't know the difference between a pub and a bar, although, unlike me, he didn't want to admit it. When I asked again about the pub-bar difference, he started talking politics: "We've seen a dilution down of the National Health Service, schools, hospitals –

things that are fairly critical to the people. Now, maybe in today's day and age it is difficult to keep these things at the standard that they were at in the past. But now we're actually seeing schools and hospitals closed, and nothing really appearing in their places, and that tends to worry the normal man in the street."

I asked once again about the pub-bar split and this time he began talking about last summer's heat wave – the worst in a hundred years. I said I'd heard that by Canadian standards it was just a bit warm last summer. He laughed and said, "That's the Scots for you, we moan when we don't get it, and we complain when we do get it, so really we're pretty hard to please."

In the archives of the Kilmarnock registry office I spent an hour tracking down ancestors. Soon I was back in the eighteenth century and, without going into details, I left with a sense of being descended matrilineally from an offspring of one of Burns's many little romantic flings in the area.

The road south and east from Kilmarnock enters a rolling landscape of countless narrow streams winding their way between tall and brilliantly green hills, patches of old hardwood forest, and the River Nith (which also flows through the poems of Robert Burns), widening gradually as it makes its way south to the Solway Firth. This is the Dumfries and Galloway Region, an area of low population density, low tourism, high unemployment, and soulful scenery wherever one cares to look. I'm becoming something like a character in Colette's novel *Claudine Married* – "Drunk with landscapes, dazed with movement and new skies and unknown towns, more impressed by a landscape than by a painting, more excited by a tree than by a museum, or by a river than a jewel." To be suddenly airlifted into these landscapes of green hills, forests, and winding rivers has given me a pleasant shock. Although I've visited Scotland twice previously, I've somehow missed the natural beauty of this country. Soon I've abandoned the car and am wandering along woodland trails and listening intently to the unfamiliar music of a great variety of Scottish songbirds. You look up and see all these hills fading off in the distance and then it's all green pastureland with the mist making the green even more intense. Then you step on a giant slimy jet-black snail about three inches long. There are dozens of them – like slow-motion World War II torpedoes with little tail fins.

At one point I stood looking down from a height of about twenty feet at the juncture of two shining burns, one bouncing from rock to rock down a hill and the other just swirling along. In the half-light of early evening the plunging burn was shining silver, and there were silver patches, sparkling away like minnows, in the slower burn as well. The streams meet like a pair of predestined lovers and flow together till they plunge into the River Nith further down. The trees in this forest are culled, for you see sawed-off stumps surrounded by the giants that would have been here when Burns was a lad. There are oaks, beeches, sycamores, yews, and the occasional redwood and gingko transplants – and the burn widens considerably and slithers under an old stone bridge before plunging over a sheer cliff into a deep pool below. The forest floor is covered with green grass and cascades of bluebells.

Here's a stump graced by a whole flotilla of those great black snails and other kinds of snails as well, some carrying their shells and others not. If it weren't for their shells you could step on a snail and never know about it. But when you hear the crunch of the shell you know what you've done. The birds are going: "*Too too too, too-wee too-wee too-wee*," "*Pip poo-ey, pip poo-ey, pip poo-ey*," "*Come-hear, come-hear, come-hear.*"

It's amazing how we filter out the song of birds. I walked through this forest for some time before suddenly becoming conscious of the wraparound arboreal concertos. City-dwellers are forced to filter out so much ugly sound, and when we find ourselves in an ancient forest full of warbling birds the filters don't become unplugged immediately. Also, when one drives one can't be listening all the time to the engine snarling away, the tires whistling, the horns honking. In order to protect the entire brain one must close down the part that quietly listens.

The road crosses the River Nith, which is widening mile by mile and is now about a hundred feet across. Two fellows in their sixties are standing in an alcove in the middle of an eighteenth-century stone bridge – an alcove designed for standing in and leaning over. They're watching another fellow in hip waders casting flies, and are probably enjoying themselves as much if not more than the fisherman, principally because they don't have to do as much work and they won't be as disappointed if the fish aren't biting.

I'm lying in bed watching the blue sky out the west window of a room above a pub on the main street of a town on the road to Dumfries. It's 10:07 p.m., and there are a few high puffy pink clouds floating southward, but as I watch, a large bank of dark clouds sweeps in from the south, and then a strong wind comes up, and the temperature drops almost instantly, with dogs barking and garbage pails rolling down the lane behind the pub.

I close the window and flick on the television. Prince Philip is being interviewed about conservation: "Don't blame me if the message isn't getting out," he says. He's a bit testy with the interviewer. He says conservation of hedgerows and wetlands, and so on, is mostly of concern to older people, because they have a long memory and can remember what things used to be like, but the "average commuter" doesn't notice that things are going downhill fast. The interviewer doesn't appreciate Prince Philip's testiness, so he retaliates by asking him why people should take him seriously as a conservationist when it's well known that he shoots tigers. So Philip becomes even testier and says that he only went tiger hunting once in his life, and that was a long time ago. He only shot one tiger, and it so happens the tiger was sick and lame.

MAJOR BILL AND
MR. TINGLE

The road to Dumfries • bypassing Dumfries • Gretna Green
Ecclefechan • Lockerbie • Ruthwell Church • Dumfries

Friday, May 31. Scottish weather is so unpredictable. The sound of someone shovelling snow wakes me up. It's cold in the room – but a snowstorm on the last day in May? I rush to the window and it's not snow the fellow in a yellow sweater and a pink scarf is shovelling, it's cherry blossoms. A high wind overnight blew every blossom off every cherry tree in town. A great high drift of pink has formed in this fellow's driveway and he can't get his car out – at least he doesn't think he can. The trees look ragged, and smoke is coming out of pretty well every chimney in town.

In the dining room I compliment my waiter on the kippers. He appears to own this handsome pub, and is wearing a T-shirt with a giant *T* on it. I mumble something about kippers being no longer popular in England. "Och," he bellows, "those bloody Pommies, they don't know what good food is."

One of those rare and amusing examples of instant karma presents itself. A German couple were complaining that they couldn't get the shower to work. Mr. T. thundered at them, in tones that suggested the Germans were a stupid race of people and always had been, and that any intelligent race of people would know that you have to pull the string before turning on the hot water. He was rude, and the Germans were embarrassed.

With otherworldly timing, a man pops in wearing a grey suit, white shirt, grey tie, and carrying a clipboard. He's from the oil company – and he has an English accent. Mr. T. has lodged a complaint that their new furnace hasn't been working properly. So now the turns are tabled, and Mr. T. has to endure a lecture about how he has been told time and again that he has to read the instruction manual and learn how to operate the furnace, for it is in perfect working order, but he's not operating it correctly . . .

The Germans and I exchange amused glances. They quietly tell me that "what comes around goes around." They get it backwards, but at least they get it. I laugh a little too loudly and Mr. T. disappears, down into the furnace room presumably, with his place being taken by Mrs. T.

It was raining, the car was running so well, and the views were so enchanting, that I unintentionally bypassed Dumfries and found myself heading east and around the Solway Firth. My Scots-Canadian friend Ian McConnell had been insisting my book wouldn't be complete without a visit to Hadrian's Wall. But that's in England, I whimpered. "No matter," he ordered. "Go there and stand on the wall and look north and experience what those Roman soldiers would have felt when they looked north, never knowing when a combined army of bloodthirsty tribes of Picts was going to come charging over the hill with their great shields, spears, and two-handed swords." And full-body tattoos? "Yes, that too, and screaming their bloody lungs out."

So here I am in England, a snitch over the border from Gretna Green, where runaway lovers from England used to go to get married in a hurry, and the green in England doesn't seem as green as the green in Galloway, and the grey clouds which are splitting up and showing the blue sky, well, the blue isn't quite as blue as it is in Scotland. All in all, I'd say England is an inferior place entirely.

There's the Famous Old Blacksmith's Shop Marriage Room Visitor's Centre, which H. V. Morton visited. There's the Lover's Leap Lodges, the Anvil Bar, the Woollen Mill, the WELCOME TO SCOTLAND sign, Scottish Souvenirs, the Tea Room and Crafts Centre, and the GRETNA GREEN THE ROMANTIC HEART OF THE WORLD sign. Wherever Mr. Morton went in his old jazz-age roadster that was forever getting stuck in the mud, there are now parking lots full of great air-conditioned tourist buses playing Glenn Miller music and full of mild-mannered retired couples from Cleethorpes. Also, there were scores of wedding parties in hired limousines, the men proud in their hired kilts, and the women romantic as all get-out in their orchid-bedecked pastel gowns.

Gretna Green caused me to become so disoriented I forgot I was heading down to Hadrian's Wall, and found myself back in Scotland, and taking another run at Dumfries from the opposite direction. The eclectic but unpleasant Scottish essayist Thomas Carlyle (1795–1881) is no longer read, but he was revered as a sage by the Victorian reading public. He was a courageous man with a tragic view of life, and when the only copy of his ambitious manuscript on the French Revolution was accidentally destroyed in a fire, he sat down and rewrote it from scratch. He also wrote on Dante, Shakespeare, the early kings of Norway, Oliver Cromwell, Frederick the Great, John Knox, and Robert Burns. At his death, although burial in Westminster Abbey was offered, according to his wish he was buried beside his parents in his home town of Ecclefechan, a few miles north of the midway point between Gretna Green and Dumfries.

On a hill overlooking Ecclefechan, a powerful wind has blown up, and is causing Carlyle's statue to moan, whistle, and roar. The great man is portrayed sitting cross-legged on a hard-backed chair atop a high cairn, and thoughtfully looking down the main street to the end of the town. I'm craning my neck to see his gaunt, bearded face, and begin to feel the soft but rapid breathing of an elderly gentleman standing beside me. He has a fresh smudge of chocolate on the side of his mouth, though as soon as I glance at him he begins telling me he's a diabetic.

"Me maither died twenty-three year ago, an' it was right after she died I took it. An' tonight at half past five me faither will have died fifty year ago. Aye, an' he was seventy-four when he died, it makes him 124."

"And how old would you be?"

"I would be seventeen an' a half."

"No, how old are you now?"

"Comin' sixty-eight in November. I din look my age, do I?"

"Heh-heh, no. Do you think you'll outlive your father, even though you've got diabetes?"

"Me faither never had diabetes. But he used to tell us o' the times when they used t'take the teeth oot away back. He used t'go wit' a half-bottle of whisky and hit ye over yer head wit' it, and then when ye'd wake up, all yer teeth would be oot. There was naiver a dentist when ye needed one. Nae dentists then. He came doon into this area 110 year ago. And see this eye? It's a glass un. I have a struggle readin' and writin' like. I've jis' this eye. You canna see wit' a glass eye, I mean even if it's a good 'un like this 'un is."

"Which one's the glass eye?"

He shows me. "That's a glass eye. I got it two, three year ago. An' where d'ye come from? I'm pleased t'meet you." He shakes my hand. "I've met Canadas, I've met New Zealands, an' I've met Australias, an' Taiwans."

"Do they all come to see this statue of Thomas Carlyle?"

"Och, yes, yes, aye. Och, he's a famous man, aye."

"You're sixty-eight. Did there used to be a stream running down the middle of the main street of this town?"

"Yes, yes, there is photos somewhere, I'm not very sure . . . The old lady had 'em. I think they might be in there, but me wife has all the details. I naiver bither wit' 'em. There be some photos in the village somewhere an' there was a stream right through."

I introduce myself and he says his name is David Manson. "Manson? That's not a Scottish name, is it?"

"'Tis. If you go up the country a bit, 'tis."

"You don't mind the English though?"

"No. Aye, I have t'git on wit' the English, cuz my wife's Scotch and her sister's England, and she lives doon there. They come up here about seventy year ago. But I'm gittin' a bit shaky, so I better go and git somethin' t'eat."

The statue of Carlyle was erected in 1929; Mr. Morton came through a shade too early to have seen it. But he made it in time to see the stream running down the middle of the main street. A little whitewashed two-storey eighteenth-century house is signposted as the birthplace of Thomas Carlyle, but it's locked up. Mr. Morton speaks of the polite disapproval he felt from behind closed windows as he walked around this town. That hasn't changed.

In Lockerbie, where hundreds of dismembered bodies fell from the sky a few years back, there's a funeral cortège going by: the people in the first two cars look terribly grieved, in the next few cars they appear somewhat sad, then in the remaining cars people are merrily chatting away – like any funeral cortège since the beginning of time.

In the town, they're doing a good job of forgetting their horrendous nightmare, and in doing so they've learned to avoid unnecessary contact with strangers. Lockerbie has some decent restaurants and bookstores, and it's a prosperous town, surrounded by green hills and trout streams.

Back on the elusive road to Dumfries, a great wind is building up and causing me to feel feverish and panicky. Complex patterns whip across the wheatfields like schools of green fish in yellow waters. I had to push with all my might to get into the Ruthwell Church, but once I did I was amazed by the sudden silence and stillness. An ancient cross has been beautifully installed: one can see down to where it starts, about six feet below the floor, and then it goes up to over twenty feet high, almost to the ceiling. The Ruthwell Cross is from Anglo-Saxon times, and it was partially destroyed during the conflicts that followed the Reformation. It lay hidden in the earthen floor of the church from 1642 to 1790, was erected in the manse garden in 1823 then sheltered indoors and declared an official monument in 1887. Carved into the stone are swans, winged snakes, a whale, an archer aiming his arrow at heaven, and Thomas and Jesus in profile, with Thomas feeling the side of Jesus for the wound. At the back of the cross, in the centre, is an interesting image of a solar God with a heavy brow: he's in a state of extreme concentration, causing the rays of the sun to extend out all around him, dispelling the satanic clouds. Also, the vertical edges of the cross contain extracts from the Anglo-Saxon poem "The Dream of the Rood," inscribed in runic characters.

It's tea time in the television room of George Clark's tourist home, the northernmost of four elegant Georgian townhouses on the west bank of the Nith, with a charming view of the river and the old town of Dumfries across the bridge. The room is furnished with well-tended antiques, and numerous saccharine paintings hang from the walls. These little narrative paintings are in a loose but skilful style, and must have been vastly popular in their time. In one, an ordinary seaman stands in the portrait gallery, worshipfully gazing up at a portrait of Admiral Nelson. He's wondering, if only fleetingly, if he too is fated to be an admiral some day.

The television says today's winds caused numerous power interruptions all over the country, a school bus was blown off a cliff in

Aberdeen, with numerous injuries – but worst of all, Scotland has been beaten by a second-rate New Zealand rugby team in Wanganui.

H. V. Morton expressed great appreciation for the poet Robert Burns, and offered penetrating insights into his life and work. Although he also expressed self-righteous contempt for Burns's habit of fathering illegitimate children all over southwestern Scotland, he rhapsodized about his visit to the little bar where Burns drank, the Globe Inn, in Dumfries. Now I'm in the same bar, chatting with Major Bill and Mr. Tingle, and the place has changed little since Burns's time, never mind Mr. Morton's. The latter was occasionally guilty of bad jokes, cultural insensitivity, and a certain kind of kneejerk sentimental dishonesty. But there's something lovable about him, and it's terrific to be here where he stood seven decades ago, and where Burns stood two centuries ago. I get taken upstairs to visit the bedroom frequented by Burns on occasion, when he wasn't in shape to go home – even though he lived just around the corner, with Mrs. Burns and the bairns.

Major Bill, the retired army man, is saying Burns was in this room only once. It was some military thing, he had to get out of one uniform and into another in a hurry, so the owner said for him to come in here and change. The major seems to have forgotten that Burns composed poetry on the windowpanes with his diamond ring – not exactly the sort of thing you do when you're in and out in a rush.

"This is probably original," I say, referring to the furnishings and layout. "I bet not much has been changed in the past two hundred years." Major Bill and Mr. Tingle enthusiastically agree.

"Yeah, this is all original," says Mr. Tingle, who returned to his birthplace of Dumfries and opened a garage after serving in the Royal Navy and seeing the world. "It has hardly been touched in well over two hundred years. Fireplace the same. Sure it's not the same mattress." He pulls back the cover and sheet and recoils. "Well, it might just be, it looks very old. He was a great philanderer. Wonder who was in this bed with him. He was only thirty-three when he died. He had a hard life. Serious drinking and serious womanizer. Och, he was a terrible philanderer. Sent the same poem to different women, just changed the name. Serious farming too, he did, but he wasn't particularly good at it. This whole building is settling so badly it's bulging, but there's really not a lot you can do with it. It's amazing the glass has stayed in there like that so long, it's amazing someone hasn't accidentally put their fist through it. Look here, he wrote that with his diamond ring":

> *O lovely Polly Stewart!*
> * O charming Polly Stewart!*
> *There's ne'er a flower that blooms in May*
> * That's half so fair as thou art.*

And then he signed it. Later I learned this was the first verse of one of his last poems, written less than a year before his death. And here, much fainter and easier to miss, is another one, an often-expurgated verse of another of his last works, "Comin' Thro' the Rye":

> *Gin a body meet a body*
> * Comin' thro' the grain;*
> *Gin a body kiss a body*
> * The thing's a body's ain.*

"He was probably stuck in here one night without a pen and paper, so he took his ring and started writing on the glass," said Mr. Tingle.

"Waiting for the lassies, no doubt," said Major Bill.

I asked how Burns scholars – which neither Major Bill nor Mr. Tingle were, unfortunately – sleep nights knowing these panes of glass are sitting here so vulnerable. Mr. Tingle suggested that, since they've been there two hundred years, the Burns Society would feel foolish if it took charge of them, paid for them, and accidentally smashed them while conducting them to a safe place. He also spoke of the sewage system at the time: "There was no hygiene or anything. To draw your water, they'd send the girls down into the river with the buckets, and that was your water, that was what you put in your Scotch, or your tea, or what you'd use to make your porridge or whatever. And the sewer would just run openly down to the river and that would be it. No hygiene or anything. The next morning the girls would be down there again filling their buckets with water."

Back down at the bar folks were arguing about what Burns drank.

"This is the beer that Burns drank," said one. "It's called Bard's Ale."

"That's just for the tourists, ye nit," said another. "I don't think he drank anything."

"He didn't? That's not what I heard. He was the biggest drunk and philanderer the world had ever known."

"Well, this was one of the biggest ports in them days for French imports, right?" said Major Bill. "So he would drink French wine, red. Very sweet."

"Oh no, not sweet, never sweet. Dry, he'd drink dry. He'd drink something they called in them days 'biddy,' a kind of claret."

"I was tryin' to tell Dave here," said Mr. Tingle, "that Dumfries had some of the worst slums in them days in the 1800s in all of the U.K. Absolutely poverty-stricken."

Major Bill seemed to be fixated on Burns changing uniforms. Because of the Napoleonic wars, he said, Burns in the last part of his life was associated with the military, but actually worked as an excise officer. So he sometimes had to get out of one uniform and into another in a big rush. And when he died he was given a military funeral. He didn't want one, but he was given one. "He was a famous poet, you see, but there's not much money in that, and he was not at all well off right up to the very end."

A somewhat drunken local Labour Party council member rudely

interrupted: "Burns was a son of the soil if there ever was one. And he was always trying to transcend the social mores —"

"If I can just finish this military thing, please," said Major Bill, a born Conservative. "Ahem! And when he died he hadn't paid for his uniform, 'cause he was broke. And on his deathbed he was worried about this. And his brother officers clubbed together and paid the tailor's bill for him. It wouldna happen now."

The council member, Tom McAughtrie by name, was sobering up: "And his use of words, I don't think there was ever anybody with such a lexicon, and that's why he was taken up to Edinburgh and paraded. Again, you take gutter humour, nothing classy, and ally it with a good lexicon, that was it. Nae time for pretendin' like, nae time for fear: if it was bad enough it was good enough. Oh, he was an honest fuckin' guy, and he had the gift of the gab and a bit of charisma."

What was Tom's take on the Scottish Nationalists? "They're very idealistic, but they preach divisions that are not necessary, and they tend to be a wee bit xenophobic. They don't like it when the non-Scots come to live here, because it weakens their vote. You're not going to get the non-Scots voting for Scottish independence. And I own a kilt, and I can trace my family back a millennium. But if I'm going to be in politics, my main aim is to give the poor people opportunities, and that's why I don't have time for any party but Labour. I have been a socialist all my life, and I will die a socialist."

"What would be the part of Scotland that is most SN?" I queried.

"That would be the east coast: Aberdeen, Dundee, and Inverness areas."

"What about those islands? Skye, Mull, Harris, Lewis, and all that."

"That's Labour."

As for Bill, everyone calls him Major Bill, because he's a bit of a hero for his anti-government stance. He'd been on television, forcing the government to reverse its attempts to close down his regiment. He was, in fact, the chief spokesman for the beleaguered

old regiment. With a little help from Major Bill, the regiment survived their biggest battle in history. But it was late: he put his hat on.

"You're going home to say hello to the missus, are you?"

"Mother," he corrected. "I'm a bachelor. Mother is not very well.
She's broken her hip, and I look after her. She's great, she's eighty-
seven, and tough as old boots. Tremendously strong woman. And it's
jolly hard for her, too. And it's sad to watch her. But she's still at
home, that's the important thing. Mother was fine till she fell over
and broke her hip when I wasn't there . . ."

Stewart Tingle looks so fit and youthful it's hard to imagine he's
spent twenty-five years in the Royal Navy. What about the name
Tingle? "My mother was a McLennan. There's still a lot of Tingles in
Yorkshire, but they don't travel much. My father came from
Yorkshire, he joined the army before the war in 1938, and he came
up to Dumfries and met my mother. Then he went to Italy and
fought all the way up Italy, and when the war finished, he ended up
in Trieste. He came back three days overland by truck to Dumfries.
And they're still alive; they're in their seventies and live just outside
of town here. It's a true love story."

There wasn't much in the way of true love for Mr. Tingle; though
he's an attractive man, he lives alone in a wee house. Any romance
in his life these days? Sometimes, he says. He mentions that some of
the barmaids here are pretty cute. About four of them at that
moment happened to be looking at us, and he was right: they were
cute as buttons.

He was stationed at Key West for several years, in the late seventies and early eighties, and every night they'd take the Royal Navy
destroyer out. "We'd leave at eight o'clock at night and it was sixty
miles to Cuba and we'd be there in two hours. We'd lie off the coast
and pick up all the refugees that were coming off Cuba on all sorts
of boats and rafts and God knows what. Then we'd wait for first light;
any boats we couldn't tow back with us we used to sink them with
gunfire. Then we'd rush the refugees off to Key West, off-load them
for resettlement, and then do the same the next night. This is what

we did. We sank a lot of boats and rafts, otherwise they'd be a hazard
to shipping. So anybody aboard could go up and have a shot at them
– even the junior stoker of the whole lot."

Princess Diana was still alive and Stewart was horrified about
some scoundrel who had had an affair with her and was now publishing his story. "Selling stories to the newspapers! So he had an
affair with Princess Diana. So, big deal! Would you go and tell the
Sun about that? Bloody sure I wouldn't; I'd keep it under my hat and
just smile. I wouldn't care if somebody offered me three million
pounds, if I was the lucky one to have been in bed with Princess
Diana and somebody found out about it. They could get me as pissed
as a priest and I still wouldn't bloody tell them. Past loves you never
divulge."

"And dear was she, I dare na name," I said, quoting Burns.

"But I will ay remember," said Stewart with a sad smile. It was a
favourite of his.

He had seen the same interview with Prince Philip the night
before, and his reactions were deadly. "Imagine shooting a lame
tiger. As if the tiger being lame was an excuse. It's like admitting
you shot a sitting duck. Some sportsman. Because the tiger's lame,
he figures it's okay to shoot it. I mean, I've met the guy and I've met
the Queen, too. I actually stayed out of the Queen's way, because I
had a terrible flu."

"Someone was saying you met Prince Charles."

"Yeah, on the HMS *Brunington*, a minesweeper. Chug Wilson had
had a few beers too many, and he said, I'm not getting off this boat
till I've met Prince Charlie. Prince Charlie must have overheard
from his cabin, 'cause it was a very small boat. So the prince leans
out from his cabin and says, 'Okay, you've met me, get yerself off my
fuckin' ship.' The guy was so well thought of in the navy."

"Why would that be?"

"Well, he was safe when he was at sea, he was on his own domain
on the sea, he didn't have any bodyguards looking after him, just the
ship's crew, whether it was hand-picked or what, I don't think so,

and he could come in off his sea duties and go into a little place like Stornoway or Tobermory. I mean, the press didn't have a clue where the hell he was."

"But the locals did."

"Not until he got there, they didn't. His ship could come sliding up at eight o'clock on a summer's night into Tobermory, anchor, Charlie could get ashore into the local pub, not a soul knew he was comin'. He would go in the local pub with a few of his shipmates, buy a round of drinks, have a good night, a couple hours, a few drinks, and go back to his boat, not a soul to bother about it. By the time the press get the news that he's in Tobermory, he's long gone. The locals, they just acted as you or I would if Charlie walked in. He'd just stand his round the same as you or I would. The engineer would say, 'It's my round, Charlie, I'll get the beers in here.' He's a very well-educated chap, you know. He's very . . . I don't know how to describe it."

TATTOOS FROM
TIP TO TAIL

Dumfries • Castle Douglas • Gatehouse of Fleet

Saturday, June 1. The River Nith is murmuring by, with the medieval spires of Dumfries in the background. On the dining-room window table are four Victorian gas lamps, each a different model, two vases of imitation roses, and a pair of 8x30 binoculars, which I pick up to look across the river at a woman in a purple coat who seems tired this morning. She stops and sighs, then resumes walking on rubbery legs. She looks as if she's been up all night calling bingo. George Clark, an athletic-looking, slender, self-deprecating, soft-spoken septuagenarian, comes into the room. "Help yourself to the cereal."

"Oh yes, just checking the binoculars." I felt embarrassed to be caught spying on his townsfolk.

"That's all right," he says. He's wearing a sweatshirt and jogging pants. I have a couple of Walker's Highland Oatcakes with my first cup of tea, and from a large assortment of marmalades I select Scott's

Orange Marmalade Medium Cut with Glenfarcas Pure Malt Whisky (whisky content 2 per cent).

After breakfast a small, red-haired woman with bright lips and a shy smile appears at my open door. She announces she's from Newcastle and is up with her husband for a holiday. I caught a glimpse of her husband earlier. He looked about seventy-five, she a youthful fifty. Her blue eyes have a degree of child-like purity that shouldn't be there somehow. Her attention is one-pointed and powerful.

"From the north of England to the south of Scotland."

"Aye, and it's very clean up here, it is."

"Dirty down in Newcastle?"

"Aye." She stands there looking at me in silence, as if silence is something she's used to.

"Do you come up here a lot?"

"No, it's the first time I been here."

"First time in Scotland?"

"Aye."

She seems to dislike the smoke from my cigarette, but she isn't making any motion to leave.

"It's a very dirty habit I have here."

"The same with my man, yech! The stink!"

"It must be awful for a non-smoker to be married to a smoker."

"Maybe that's what's made me bad, the smoke."

"You'll notice I have the window open."

"I should open up my window too, aye. He even smokes in bed, and I don't believe in that. And he coughs and spits in the cotton sheets and that."

Then she starts whispering.

"Pardon?"

"He's . . . like . . . a . . . bairn" (pronounced "ben").

"Oh, but all of us men are like bairns, wouldn't you say?"

"They try to get their own way, eh?"

"It's the job of the women to help us grow up, right?"

"Yeah-ess, ah." She seems to like that notion. She looks at me with her blue eyes and smiles sweetly.

"Do you have any little ones yourself?"

"Oh, aye. I've got three grown-ups. An' I've got five grand-bairns – daughters."

"Five granddaughters! Heavens!"

"Och, this is me fifth marriage, this one."

"Five husbands! Good heavens! And did they all smoke?"

"No, my second and third husband didn't." She whispers again: "But he's the worst one. All he does is sleep."

"How long have you been with him?"

"Just over a year."

"He seems a pleasant enough fellow."

"Oh, he's pleasant enough, but he likes his smokes. And he has a filthy tongue, and everything – even when he's bein' nice t' me. An' he's got tattoos all over him. An' all his lot's the same."

"All his lot. Where's he from?"

"From here – Dumfries." She peeks around the corner to make sure he's not lurking.

"So! Five husbands – and you haven't liked any of them."

That hit her funny bone. "Mmmph-kkk, heh heh heh haw haw." She laughed with great musical verve. "No, me last one died of cancer."

Husband Five stuck his ancient, grizzly, smelly, pockmarked head in the door. "D'ye want some he'p wi' yer baggage, dear?"

The rain is coming straight down in torrents as I put my bag in the car then come back in to the dining room.

"This weather makes you want to hang around here all morning, doesn't it?"

"Aye," says Number Five, as he digs into his bacon and eggs. "An' no pollution from motorcars runnin' up and down here. An' no factories or smokestacks and that. An' have you been to New Abbey, Sweetheart Abbey, yet?"

"No, do you recommend it?"

Mr. Clark brings in another pot of tea, then vanishes again.

"Oh, it's lovely scenery, all along the coast there, y'know, the southern coast. Up over the bridge there, take to the vurry end, turn left, it's a straight road right through, in fact you can even go to Dalbeattie, Southerness, Sandyhills, New Abbey, it's all good scenery anyhow, beautiful scenery. There's rocks and everything there." All the time he's talking his missus is whispering bitterly sarcastic comments in the background, judging that I'll be able to hear her but he won't, owing to his partial deafness.

"Do you ever get up to the Highlands?"

"Oh, I go up there many a time. I've travelled from the north of Scotland to the south of Scotland, as well as from the east of Scotland to the west of Scotland – with two fishing trawlers on the Solway here we had. A little business here up to about twelve year ago – and the old fellow, me dad, I lost him last March, he was ninety-six, and we never bothered about the trawlers after that, like y'know. An' well I been in nearly every fishing port in Scotland, selling fish."

"So you're a retired fisherman." He had STUART tattooed on the back of his hand, and his name was, coincidentally, James Stuart.

"Oh, I'm a retired fisherman, aye. Seventy-two and I'm not doing too bad yet." It's true he was a bit hard of hearing, but that didn't stop him from becoming impatient when I asked him to repeat something I'd missed. Most people tend to be flattered that you're interested enough.

"You've got twenty-four years to go – if you live as long as your dad."

"He was ninety-six when he snuffed it, aye."

"Did he smoke the cigarettes?"

"He didnae. He smoked the pipe. An' he drank a bottle of the whisky a day. An' he had a better head of hair than I had. I'm telling you, he had a beautiful head of hair when he died. He had more hair on his head what I had anyhow."

"And did he have all his wits about him?"

"Oh, aye. Oh, he knew what he was sayin' and doin', like, right up to the end."

I had to say something about his tattoos. His arms were covered in them.

"Me tattoos? Ah hell, I got them from tip t' tail. They were done in the war camp. I was a prisoner of war in Germany. Four year and ten month and you had nothing else t'do but think about decorating yerself."

"Were you mistreated at all?"

"Oh no, I wasn't mistreated, no. I was in the salt mines in Poland. On my shoulder, on my chest, my legs, my arms. Didnae do them all meself like. Other lads in the camp, we'd do each other."

"Jesus," whispered the missus.

"Jesus," said I.

He stands up, backs off, and whips up his pant legs. He has a battleship on his right leg, and a dancing girl on his left.

"Aye, an' Jock the Boxer on me chest, an' Scotland the Brave."

"And Brenda, I see. Is that you?" I said to his missus.

"No, I'm Patricia."

"Also known as Geordie," says he. "A Scotchwoman wi' her brains battered in. Isn't that right, Pet?"

"Yeow." She snarled like a cat that's had its tail stepped on. He seemed not to notice.

"We had a nice day out yesterday. We were way up to Locharbriggs, and we had dinner with our niece. They were glad to see me." Me? What about Patricia? She tucked her chin in and blinked. "And then we went up to the garage. My nephew's got a big garage, sells cars and that. We nearly bought a car off him. But we had no that kind of money with us." Patricia starts humming what sounds suspiciously like the Scherzo from Schubert's String Quintet in C Major. "But he's goin' t'have a talk t' me afore I go back. And he said, 'It's about time you moved back up here.'" He poured himself a cup of tea and we all had a bit of a stretch then sat down again. Mr. Clark stuck his head in and asked if we wanted more tea, then went back to the kitchen.

"What a gentleman he is," said Mr. Stuart. "A proper gentleman. I used to sell him fish from out here years ago. I was a poacher, aye."

"What do you mean by that?"

"Fishin' illegally. We used to go out at nighttime, about one o'clock in the mornin', wi' a net, an' net th' river for salmon and sea trout. And about half past five in the mornin', or six o'clock, we used to take it to him – he worked in the hotel, the big hotel in the centre of Dumfries – an' sell it, around t' the back door."

"So you're old friends."

"It doesn't matter," whispered Patricia, in a cautionary tone.

"Oh, I knew him all right but, eh, as I say, thirty-odd years since I last saw him, like. But eh, me nephew and niece, they knocked about wi' his daughter, and they recommended to come here, an' I was glad I came, oh I was."

Mr. Clark brings in fresh tea. "There we are," he says, then leaves us to chat.

"So you want to put that in the book?"

"Oh, shut up," says Patricia, with amazing venom.

"Thank *yoooo*. That's the way I get spoken to."

He wanted to know if I had a wife. I looked as if about to cry and said I was an incorrigible loner, unlucky in love, afraid to take a chance, and set in my ways.

"Best way t'be, son," he said, consolingly, "best way t'be. Mind ye, I'd a' never married this one here" (Patricia looks out the window with her chin at a haughty angle) "on'y she was as different to the one I lost as chalk be to cheese, and I says right, I'll make a last go o' it, and I have, and I've made a vurry good job of it – up to now."

The opportunity arrived for the question I'd been dying to ask, especially with the memory of yesterday's gale so strong in my mind. "Did you ever run into any big storms when you were a fisherman?"

"Oh hell. I'll tell you something you'll never believe."

"Oh, I'll believe anything."

"I'd to tie the old man to the mast, once, when we were in a gale force 13. I was engineer, netter, and skipper on the boat, an' I had t'do the cookin' in the bargain, and we went out one day from Kirkcudbright, and we were headin' our way for the Isle of Man. I be quite honest wi' ye, it were a beautiful sunny morning, and the sea were like a plate-glass winder. Beautiful smooth. Soon as we gets out we gets a radio call, 'It's comin' over fast – gale force 11 to 13.' And by Christ, when it came it did come, it came like a hurricane. Now it was on'y a thirty-seven-foot-long boat, and it tossed it about like a cork, an' my dad was slippin' and almost fallin' overboard, so I sez, I tell you what I'm goin' t'do wi' ye, Dad, I sez, so ye don't slip again, like. It's either you go down the hold, or I tie ye t' the mast. Well, what d'ye want? 'Tie me t' the bloody mast,' he said. So I tied 'im t' the mast now, turned around, an' I met the sea, I met the storm, and I was up an' down like that, and d'ye know, he loved me for that. 'For you,' he said, 'I can give you my life. I can put my life in yer hand.'"

"A good story and well told," I said.

"An' eh, I went overboard once. That was there, the anchor chain" – he pulls up his trouser leg again and shows a dim scar around his tattooed ankle.

"Ah, the anchor chain," I said. "The anchor chain around your ankle sent you overboard."

"Right over. An' lucky enough I had me knife on me. An' I cut the rope an' I came back up. I was never so close to death in all me life."

"Was it a chain or a rope?"

"There's a chain, and then a rope. Yer chain's about maybe eight metre, what they call a spey chain, and ye throw yer chain down, and when you pull the chain t'tighten the rope, it opens up an' it digs into the sand an' it can't move. Well, I threw it, and the ol' man kicked the rope, an' it wrapped aroun' me ankle, an' o'er the top I went."

Patricia is quietly giggling with a distinctly malicious tone.

"Anyway, I got airlifted from Auchencairn on a Monday night, out on a Tuesday morning, and I was back on the trawler on Tuesday afternoon."

"What were you treated for, the cut on the ankle?"

"Oh, I had stitches, they thought I'd broken my ankle like. And when I got back on Tuesday afternoon the ol' man was paintin' the boat and cryin' his eyes out. 'What's wrong wi' you?' I says, and he says, 'I thought I'd lost ye, son,' he says. I says, 'It'll take a harder man than you to lose me, Dad.'"

"That gale you were in, would that have been worse than the one yesterday we had around here?"

"Oh, yesterday was nothin'. Oh no, when you're out in the open sea, it toss you about like a corkscrew, aye. And me brother-in-law, he what married me late sister like, he won't even look at the river, he goes ill when he sees water, aye. We were up seein' him last night, visitin' like, an' he's not married like, he's courtin' again, but I don't think he'll ever get married like. He thought too much o' his wife. He's courtin' a bingo-caller, and he wanted me to go up and meet her last night. So we went up and we were two and a half hours watchin' television."

"So you didn't get much chance to chat with the bingo-caller."

"Oh," said Patricia, "they were both chattin' away all through the film we were watchin' wi' Harrison Ford."

"And what did you think of the bingo-caller?"

"Oh," said Mr. Stuart, "I didna think much of her, t'be quite honest wi' ye. His son, what owns the garage like, he doesna want to meet her."

Mr. Clark comes back in because we seem to be done. "I hear this man used to sell you fish years ago," I incautiously comment.

"Oh, aye. But that's a long, long time ago, that."

I've embarrassed him. He's all respectable now and prefers not to be reminded that he used to run a hotel that bought fish from poachers in the middle of the night.

But the magic of the rainswept road was calling me, and I had to say farewell. A few hours later, twenty miles west of Dumfries, on a dark, miserable Saturday afternoon, I pulled up in the town of Castle

Douglas, hoping for a bite to eat. But the Indian restaurant was closed, the Chinese restaurant was closed, the fish-and-chip store was closed, and the big old Douglas Arms Hotel, which Morton wrote about so enthusiastically, refused to serve me, because everybody was getting ready for a large party of Danish veterinarians who had booked the place for their evening meal, several hours from now. They had no time to waste on a scruffy-looking lout like me. I told them I understood perfectly. The bastards of the world always hate it when you say that.

In the Touch of Class, the only eating place not closed, I felt sorry for the young lady who was waiting on tables, for she seemed to be wilting under the stern and disapproving gaze of the woman who ran the place and was sitting at the back, smoking cigarettes and following her every move with a nasty eye. The waitress was extremely awkward and, like the customers, had a horrible fear of being overheard. She looked about fourteen, and when she asked, nervously, if I would like sauce with my locally caught smoked salmon, instead of just saying yes, I foolishly asked what kind of sauce it was. She grimaced and replied that she had only been working here three days and would I please not ask difficult questions. She definitely did not want to have to go and ask the owner what kind of sauce it was. She was shaking in her shoes with stage fright, and I could see the grouchy owner glaring at her from behind bushy dark eyebrows, so I told the waitress any old sauce would do; I thought she was doing a terrific job considering she'd just started, and I told her I was going to leave her a huge tip. But it didn't work out that way. A car pulled up outside the door. The driver gestured to the waitress. He looked as if he might be her dad. She took her apron off, handed it to the owner, and said she had to leave and she didn't know when she'd be back. The look on the owner's face was one of dark resentful astonishment and anger, but the waitress didn't know it because she was gaily tripping towards the door, happy to be free.

What a strange town Castle Douglas was, or at least it was in the grip of a strange mood at the hour of my visit. Even the guy in the health-food store, from whom I bought vitamin C, tried to sell me some zinc tablets, because "less vitamin C is wasted when you take zinc with it." I told him I didn't feel any overwhelming compulsion to buy five pounds worth of zinc to help me retain five pence worth of vitamin C. When I'd asked him for vitamin C crystals, he looked at me as if I'd just escaped from the funny farm. It only comes in tablet form, he declared. I told him I understood perfectly.

A perfect rainbow is curved over the lovely village of Gatehouse of Fleet. That rainbow is God telling me to spend the night here. But at the first bed-and-breakfast establishment I try, an unsmiling woman comes to the door and, without even pretending to be sorry, gives me one of those "I know I have a bed-and-breakfast sign in the window but that doesn't give you the right to knock on my door" sort of looks, and grumpily avers that she doesn't have any singles. "I understand perfectly," I say. At the second place an unsmiling woman (this time an artist with a palette and brush in hand) gives me a "what kind of insect do we have here?" look and, with a quiver in her sneer, says she doesn't have any singles. "I understand per-fectly," I say. At the hotel, where two unsmiling guys are drinking beer and watching *Casper the Friendly Ghost* on television, I'm told they're all booked up. When I say how could you be all booked up when the town's so quiet, they say it's not as quiet as it seems. There's a big wedding in town, as if it's any of my business. "I understand per-fectly," I say. A couple of little kids come running out of a house screaming, "Mommy, look! A rainbow!" And Mommy, unsmiling, and without even glancing skywards, rushes out onto the street and scream-whisper-snarls at them, "Keep quiet!"

So God didn't mean me to spend the night in Gatehouse of Fleet after all. She meant me to suffer three rebuffs with saintly patience for the benefit of my eternal soul. I felt as if the entire population of the town was aware that a single man, a stranger, was among them, and they didn't like that one little bit, even if there was a rainbow celebrating his arrival. One would have to be an idiot not to understand.

Later, it seemed in retrospect that the two bed-and-breakfast ladies, the two hotel men, and the Rainbow Lady, all spoke in English accents. Earlier I'd been warned to watch out for small towns in Scotland with quaint names such as Gatehouse of Fleet. I was assured they're full of snobbish English people who have moved in because they want the cachet of a quaint mailing address. And as for their unsmilingness, I am certainly not criticizing them for that. Maybe they thought I was smiling enough for both of them. Maybe they thought I found them amusing. And the bastards of the world seldom like to be found amusing.

CHAPTER 5

DEEP PEACE OF THE
SHINING STARS

Creetown • Newton Stewart • Minnigaff • Wigtown • Whithorn
The Isle of Whithorn • Saint Ninian's Cave

Sunday, June 2. Cherrytrees is a small whitewashed two-storey house on the high street of Creetown, overlooking Wigtown Bay on the Solway Firth. My host, Kenny McElcheran (I'll soon begin to think of him as Clear-Cut Kenny), is a handsome heartbreaker, a big bruiser, with a heart as sweet as a day in June. When I arrived last night he showed me to my room, since his wife was at a meeting. In dozing off I was treated to numerous bitter and nasty lamplit arguments and silly shouting matches from disaffected youth on the street under my window, and finally I went into my emergency sleeping-pill supply and took one. Then I didn't hear a thing until eight-thirty, when someone pounded on the door.

When I tiptoed downstairs, I caught Kenny and his wife sitting at a table in the large kitchen, smiling dreamily at each other. They both stood up and Kenny announced that this was his wife, Linda, and she was from Canada too. They were both solid, youthful types, and they looked as if they were still much in love. In fact Kenny had a little lipstick smudge on the side of his lip.

"I was born in Canada, but I left when I was about eighteen months old, so it's about my only claim to fame," said Linda, in her aura of bright beauty, "because I grew up in Essex, you see, and I don't know if you know, but in England there are a lot of Essex-girl jokes" – she laughed to think of them – "about them being stupid. So whenever I hear one of those jokes I say I was born in Canada, so the joke doesn't apply to me, and they can't call me stupid." She spoke with clarity and simple ironic shrewdness. There was nothing stupid about her.

She announced we were having haggis for breakfast, fresh from the Creetown family butcher, who sold it to her last night before flying off to Greece for a holiday. "Some haggises are spicier than others," she said. "Some are quite hot on the tongue."

Kenny was wearing a Red Rock Cider T-shirt. He left the room then returned with two cute little well-behaved kids and an armful of teddy bears. He started talking about his job. He was a logger, boyishly enthusiastic about the newfangled "harvester" he was working on to clear-cut forests at a phenomenal rate.

"We clear-fell all the time now," he said, with effervescent pride.

"That must be what's called clear-cut in Canada. Environmentalists don't like that. They like to see the forests thinned out and replanted."

"There's no thinning at all any more. There's no money in it. Forest Commission's gotta make a profit now. That's why they give us these machines." He spreads out a catalogue on the counter, with unsuppressed glee, like a kid at show-and-tell. "This is the same harvester I'm working. Exactly the same as that."

"What kind of trees?"

"Norway spruce, sitka, pine. It's usually sitka spruce we cut. It's a better tree anyway, they seem to be better grain."

"No hardwood?"

"No, we don't cut hardwood. The commission actually plants a lot of hardwoods now. If you go along the roads and you see the wee plastic squares stickin' in the ground in a patch of forest, they're all hardwoods in there." He shows me another picture from the catalogue. "That's the harvester I'm workin' on in the clear-fell there. You see, he's cuttin' it up and cleanin' up the rows. Then I come along an' – well, there's two of us. I'll work on it the one day and the partner who works wi' me, he'll work that" – he points to a picture of some gleaming bright-yellow monstrosity – "that's the forwarder. Same machine as that, brand new, same as that. Lifts the timber."

"Fun to operate?"

"Ah, it's okay, aye." He pauses significantly. "We had a bigger machine than that an' it was quite fairly stabilized. This one tends to rock away a bit. You know forestry, you know there's some rough grounds you go over. If the trailer tips over it takes the cab with it."

"Did you ever tip over?"

"Oh, I have, aye. Once."

"Hurt yourself?"

"Nah. Happens so quick next thing ye know ye're jis' lyin' lookin' out the window. They're safe machines like. I've on'y tipped the small one."

Linda has been listening all along. "You've had a tree fall on top of you," she says, remindingly, "and nearly killed yourself."

"I've had a few trees over the top of the machine like," he admits.

"So how fast is this clear-felling going on?"

"Whooh! That machine can get three a minute."

"And are there a lot of companies around clear-felling?"

"Aye, there's a lot. Aye, that can do about three a minute easy, an' about 140 ton a day o' finished timber."

Linda broke in again. "There is an organization, and they've had a lot to do with planting. There used to be a lot of planting done at the tops of hills. So now sometimes they'll clear-fell behind and leave a bit at the front, so everybody that's going along the roads, or walking along, thinks it looks like a forest, but behind it it's open clear-felled and replanted. The only trouble with that is, once they start taking trees out like that, the ones that are left are unprotected, and they end up with the strong winds blowing them away."

"So this must make you sad, because you're ripping the heart out of your country."

"I don't think of it," he said. "Honestly, it's jis' a piece o' job t' me. I jis' keep cuttin'. There is a lot o' forest round about here."

"But at three a minute there soon won't be."

"But it's like a farm, it's like a tree farm," said Linda. "No, there will be, because as fast as they're cutting they're replanting."

"Y'see, we don't exactly go in an' decimate a forest."

"But that's what I understand by the term clear-felling: you go in and decimate the forest."

"Yeah, but the Forest Commission, they tell you, they decimate a patch, a few acre, a hectare maybe, a few thousand ton, but they leave the rest, but it doesn't pay to thin the timber now, for the simple reason nobody wants that timber, an' it's too expensive to get out. But I like trees, and I'll put it this way: I've never cut a hardwood down and I've been with the Forest Commission since 1971. An' I won't even cut a rowan tree down – you know, wi' the berries on it an' that."

"That's your superstition, that is," said Linda.

"In olden days they were planted to keep witches away or somethin'. That's superstition. I wouldna cut one of them doon. I never would cut a rowan tree doon, 'cause I'm superstitious that way."

"You wouldn't want to have witches around."

"I know it's a daft stupid thing, but I wouldnae dee it."

"There was one out there," said Linda, "and we had to widen the drive, so we got somebody else to cut it down, 'cause he wouldn't cut it down."

The haggis was spicy and not at all pleasant to my taste – though I can imagine others loving it. "This haggis looks like sausage," I observed.

"He didn't have any proper haggises," said Linda, "because a proper haggis is actually put in a sheep stomach. It's all washed and cleaned and everything. And they tie the ends, so it's like a bowl shape. He didn't have any of those left in his fridge, so unfortunately we had to get the slicing haggis, like a big salami, or like the big German sausages. But it's all the same recipe, he makes them all the same."

"It's a bit too strong for me."

"I don't think it's as strong as some of them."

I told them it wasn't as strong as a blood pudding – a "black pudding" – I'd had a couple of days ago up in Kilmarnock. "That was a big challenge to get down. I had to blank my mind. I kept wondering where the blood comes from. Do they get it out of the gulleys in the floor of the slaughterhouse?"

"Oh, yuck! You won't put me off a bit, 'cause I like black pudding. I have it every Friday."

"I believe you, but millions of Scots have emigrated to Canada, and the first thing they do when they get there is stop eating haggis and black pudding or blood pudding or whatever it's called."

"Maybe there are no butchers over there that make it."

"They go out of business fast. Every little neighbourhood of every community in Canada has at least one Scots butcher, and you can get anything you want, but no haggis or black pudding. Sorry, no call for it."

"Now there, you see, there's a little niche there for somebody to go and slide into." Linda, lovely as they come, was also wickedly witty. And, like all good people, she's had some disappointments in her life. Her father still lives in Stroud, Ontario, but she's only seen him on two occasions. "Once when I was eleven and again when I was thirty-one. I don't know when I'll see him again. My mother came back over here. 'Cause they were originally from Essex, both of them. They emigrated over to Canada and then she came back with us three oldest girls."

"How did you and Kenny meet?"

"Uhhh, well! That is a real, real story! Because, I mean, I am not normally the sort of person that takes risks. I moved up here seven years ago with my ex-husband and my three children – and his parents. My ex was going through a bad state of depression. He got involved in things that he shouldn't have really got involved in, and one thing led to the other until he couldn't take any more." They split up shortly after moving to the Creetown area. She was about to head back to England when she got invited to a local wedding. "And that's where I met Kenny. And a fortnight later, when I was supposed to be moving down to Cheshire, I moved in with him." By this time she was whispering so softly I had to strain to hear her.

"Well, you're a smashing couple. Five years and anyone can see the romance is still going strong."

"But fancy that! It had to be fate, didn't it?"

"What, did he come up and ask for a dance?"

"Yep. Well, I mean he kept on giving me the eye, y'see. I told him to stop looking at me like that, so he said, Do you want me to dance with a box on my head then? I said, You can if you want. So away he went and got a cardboard box. And there we are in the middle of this dance floor, and everyone's looking at us 'cause he's dancing with a cardboard box on his head. Imagine! The least neurotic person imaginable, and he's got a box on his head."

"He was smitten. You too?"

"No, not really. I mean I had so much going on when I was back there, but straightaway, immediately, I felt so safe and secure with him. And this is a total change from what it had been like, 'cause I had always had to be the strong one, but it's all evened out now." The little girl comes in. "You've done a lovely job of getting yourself dressed, apart from your shoes are on the wrong feet, darling."

"Hi, little gal," I said, tickling her tenderly under the chin with my knuckle.

"Ayeeee," she squealed. "Don't do that, don't ever do that."

"I'm sorry."

Mother smiled sweetly. "We have decided that she has been here lots of times before. She's a strong-willed, determined young lady, and has been since the day she was born."

"Wouldn't you say you and Kenny are a bit like that, too?"

"You can tickle my chin all you want, and Kenny's too, for that matter."

Linda gave me a book on Creetown. She also gave me a chunk of haggis. I still have the book, but no idea what happened to the haggis. She asked me to write something in the guest book. I flipped through the pages. One guy said it was the best food he'd had since he was in jail. Another said thanks for the vodka. When I complained that I didn't get any vodka, they said there was a flu epidemic at the time.

"Next time there's a flu epidemic, I'll know where to come."

"Tell us when you're coming, and we'll have the vodka ready."

Morton was right when he spoke of the "charming" stone bridge that spans the broad River Cree at Newton Stewart, a few miles north of Creetown. The river swirls by at a fairly good speed, pouring over a small waterfall, then there are floating swans, paddling ducks, gluttonous geese. I'm standing in the middle of the bridge looking north, exactly where Morton stood, and I think his description was a little off. To the often hyperbolic Morton, it was like Venice the way the houses dropped straight down to the river – but there's nothing like that here now. Of course maybe those old houses weren't properly maintained and fell apart. But now what we have are houses with gardens that sweep gradually down to the river in a pleasing fashion on both sides of the river, the houses being forty or fifty feet up from the bank of the river. Some people are sitting blissfully on benches in a little riverside park, watching the river run. It's a good 150 feet across, and in a few miles it will widen and deepen into a tidal estuary, and empty into Wigtown Bay on the Solway Firth.

Two young ladies are walking across the bridge. As they squeeze by me, one says to the other: "You don't like spaghetti, do you, Nora?"

The Old Edinburgh Road is a mere footpath. An enormously fat lady in her fifties is sweating her way up a sharp incline and smoking a cigarette. And here's a war memorial in honour of the gallant men of the parish of Minnigaff who fell in the Great War, sixteen of them, including the Ion brothers, Privates Adam Ion and John Ion. The churchyard is full of daisies among the rich tall green grass. And here's a dead crow, freshly killed and surrounded by a few little flies.

On the footpath back to Newton Stewart I meet a frail elderly man, eighty-six. I mentioned I'd been reading about Morton's visit to this churchyard. He got into a conversation with the old gravedigger, but now I'm disappointed, because there are no gravediggers around at all.

"Nae, nae, they dae it wi' a machine noo. The council recommended a digger machine when the old gravedigger died. The machine can dig three graves a minute." I pictured Clear-Cut Kenny at the controls.

The old fellow confesses the biggest problem in his old age: he's lived in Newton Stewart since childhood, but he can't remember anyone's name. "I know faces, but I forget names. I go doon the street there and I'm talking to some person jis' the same as I'm talkin' to you, but I donna put a name on them. I know them, but I don't know their name."

"Do you tell them? Do you ask them to remind you?"

"No."

"You wouldn't want to insult them, is that it?"

"Heh! Noo, it's I don't like to make myself to feel that stupid-lookin'."

The birds sing. No cars roar, no horns honk. Two men chat away among the blossoming trees.

Back in Newton Stewart, one fellow, with a salesman's smile, or what the Irish call a Saxon smile, called across the main street of town at an acquaintance, perhaps a potential client. "Hello, Mr. Lowry, lovely day, isn't it?"

Mr. Lowry called back, "Don't care much for it myself." And he kept on walking.

The other day in Kilmarnock, it was a blustery, rainy day, cold. Two men passed one another. One said, "Weather!" and the other replied, "Yes!"

That semi-lovable clown Morton calls Newton Stewart "one of the bonniest towns in all of Scotland." Odd the way the word *bonny* seems to have dropped out of the Scottish vocabulary, but *wee* remains.

Off the main parking lot of Newton Stewart there's a sparkling new brick building: it's a public washroom. You stick a coin in a slot and go in through a polished chrome turnstile. NO EXCEPTIONS, says the sign. There's a young lady inside the washroom. She's in a spot-less glass booth avidly watching TV. The whole place, which was probably put up by the local council member who replaced the dead gravedigger with a machine, sparkles and shines in chrome, glass, and ceramic tiles.

"Hi. I've never seen a washroom like this before. What do you do?"

"I keep it clean and make sure there's no vandalism, y'see. We have to clean it every so often, an' jis' watch the young uns comin' in an' watch they doon't destroy it."

"You ever catch them doing anything?"

"Oh, they try, yes."

"How many have you had in today?"

"You'd be the first. It's a slow day."

"At first I thought you had hidden TV cameras in the toilets and were monitoring people secretly. What are you watching?"

"It's *The Waltons.*"

"You get a lot of the American programs on TV here these days, not the English ones at all." I meant to say *British* but it came out *English.*

"Yeah. Well, really when it comes down to it the English are no good at making films and stuff are they? I can say that cuz I'm Scottish."

"Of course you can. What do you think of the English?"

"Eh, well, really I'm not prejudiced about it, but the English don't like the Scottish. They're movin' up here an' takin' over. It's because we sort of get the brunt of everything. It's all politics, y'know. Bein' English they want to own Scotland. So they make us suffer when it comes round to taxes and wha' have ye, council taxes for the houses an' stuff like that. We want to be independent, that's the thing like. But ye see, there's too many English here who are votin' for the English parliament. We want the SNP, the Scottish National Party, but there's not enough of us now."

Back in the car, I flicked on the radio and – Irony Alert. – today is British Cinema Day. All over the United Kingdom today, you can get into the theatre for one pound, and it's a celebration of the success of British cinema over the years, and particularly recent years. Unfortunately, it's a beautiful day all over this island, so nobody will be wanting to sit in a cinema.

A few miles down the peninsula known as the Machers (also known as the Machars), which dips down into the Solway Firth, is Wigtown. From Windy Hill all of Wigtown is spread out below. The two churches are the tallest buildings. Wigtown comes with some terrible history. Behind the town is Wigtown Bay, and from up on Windy Hill one can see little Creetown on the other side and Newton Stewart a few miles to the north. This is the bay where two women were tied, at low tide, to stakes, and the shore was lined with people watching as the tide rose and snuffed out their lives. These women were two of the five Wigtown Martyrs of 1685. Atop Windy Hill stands a tall monument dedicated to the memory of eighteen-year-old Margaret Wilson, a farmer's daughter, and Margaret McLochland, sixty-three, a farmer's tenant. Along with three men who were hanged in Wigtown, they died, says the stone, "because they refused to forsake the principles of the Scottish Reformation and to take the government oath abjuring the right of the people to resist the tyranny of their rulers." Like the women, the men were from this immediate area: William Johnstone, gardener, John Millroy, chapman, and Gilbert Walker, servant. Today the town is absurdly quiet, nothing is going on, there is no traffic, all you can hear is the wind sighing as it strikes the monument and whirls around it, birds sing, an occasional cow moos a mile away.

The ancient Wigtown Parish Church is surrounded by a walled graveyard, with the tombstones of the martyrs painted white and the lettering lovingly blacked in. An elderly but youthfully fit English couple stand there, and within ten seconds we're arguing about whether things in general have improved since the seventeenth century. "Why, my father was gassed in World War I," Ernie says in grievous tones, "and he died when I was three, and my wife and I served in World War II. And what have we gained? I think we're worse off in this country now than we ever were, aren't we?"

"Most of the nations," says Margaret, "that lost the war —"

"They lost the war," Ernie interrupts, "and they seem to be better off than anybody – Japan, Germany."

"If it hadn't been for your sacrifice, we might have been a lot worse off today."

"He's right, you know," says Margaret.

"Well, my wife and I met during the war." Ernie seems to have decided I'm okay. "We met in Australia. I was in the Royal Marines, I was on HMS *Indomitable*, an aircraft carrier, and my wife was a naval nurse."

"I bet that was a hot romance."

Ernie ignores Margaret's laughter: "And we found we both came from London, and I lived a penny tram-ride between my wife's house and mine, yup. Marvellous."

"We had to go to the other side of the world," recalls Margaret, "before we could meet."

"And where do you live now?"

"We live in Norfolk now," says Margaret. "We're up on holiday at the —"

"And I served with some Canadians during the war – Princess Pats," says Ernie.

"Yes," says Margaret, "a lot of people think Norfolk's flat for a —"

"No, it isn't," says Ernie. "North Norfolk is beautiful.'

"Cambridgeshire and Lincolnshire are flatter, where the fens are," says Margaret. They are pretty well both talking at once, Ernie doing more interrupting than Margaret, who is shy, with a soft voice and a sense of humour. But whenever she starts talking, Ernie jumps in and drowns her out. Her laughter particularly annoys him.

"It's an area of outstanding natural beauty," says Ernie. I glance to see if he's having me on. He isn't. "But we've been coming up to this part of Scotland for twenty-five years. And my aircraft carrier, we were off of Manila when they dropped the atomic bombs. And when the Japs surrendered we headed to Hong Kong. We took the surrender there. And unfortunately, on Kai Tak airfield I got malaria, and they sent me back to Australia and put me in Margaret's hospital."

"Unfortunately, eh?" I say.

"Yes, and that's where we met," says he.

"It must have been a romantic time," say I.

Margaret started laughing again. "He had a stiff upper lip anyway," she says, with wicked wit that wings over Ernie's wig.

This was the perfect World War II couple: they had danced to Glenn Miller and later laughed at the *Goon Show*. Now they were not all that wild about the direction civilization was heading. They were staying at a little "caravan site" near Creetown.

"The old chap, he owned it and he also owned the little village store," said the husband, "but he's retired and sold it and there's a young couple have taken it over. Only trouble is, this young couple, they keep stretching the new restrictions."

"Yes, they don't like —"

"They don't like children under five on the site —'

"And all sorts of things —"

"How do you feel about that?" I inquired.

"Well, I think it's a bit much really, um —" said she.

"Don't like it, don't like it," said he. "When we used to go many years ago there was no modern facilities: there was the caravan and a little coal fire or whatever and no running water, you used to meet on the hill in the morning, everybody took their container, and they all met up there getting their water and they were all friendly and they had a little chat. Now they got running water and showers and colour televisions."

"All in their caravans," said Margaret.

"It used to be much friendlier," said he.

"And you don't have singsongs any more," I said, sympathetically.

"No," said Margaret, laughingly. She looked into my eyes, wondering how I knew about the singsong issue.

"You don't have bonfires and wiener roasts any more," I said.

"You don't have fun, you don't have fun any more," said he, broodingly.

"You don't have euchre parties," said I.

He was sad because their daughter, married and with three children, doesn't want to come up to Scotland with them any more, though "when she was a little girl we used to fetch her up here and she thoroughly enjoyed it, didn't she? That's life, I suppose."

"I call it progress," said Margaret.

"Well, if you like that kind of progress, I don't know," said he, in a near-whisper.

In the spacious Wigtown square, the whole town's out lawn bowling, not just the elderly. Every wall is bespattered with anti-Whithorn graffiti. Whithorn is a similar-sized town further down the peninsula, and they're rivals. "The Wigtown Posse Is Going to Murder the Whithorn Scum." These amiable lawn bowlers would be descended from the wild Picts of this area, who had been plaguing their British neighbours as Roman rule crumbled in the fourth and fifth centuries. And who should show up, as if sent by God, but Saint Ninian, when he was most needed. Nobody knows where he came from, except that he was a native Briton, but by AD 450 he was busy converting the Picts of this area, and when Picts get converted they stay converted. By the time Saint Ninian died at Whithorn, and was buried among other saints of the early church, almost every Pict had been converted. And were they still attacking their southern neighbours? No way! By the seventh century the newly arrived Anglo-Saxons had established the kingdom of Northumbria, and had taken complete control of the Galloway region. A bishopric was established at Whithorn about AD 730. A shrine to Saint Ninian was built in the neighbourhood, and miraculous cures were commonplace.

I couldn't resist chatting up some bored Lolitas in the town square of Wigtown. "I guess you have a little rivalry with the people down in Whithorn, do you?"

"Weel, it's been growin' fer years, I heerd, aye," said one.

"It's the younger ones, the young kids our age and all that," said another.

"*Their* age," said the first, proudly. "I'm older."

"How old are you?"

"Fourteen."

"What do you fight about?"

"Don't know. It's been growin' since like our parents were kids. It was always Wigtown against Whithorn."

"We don't get on well," said another.

"You know them all I guess though, eh?"

"Aye, ye know them all. We all go to the same school and all that."

"And you don't associate with each other."

"Well, the girls get along all right, but the boys don't. The boys fight with each other."

"Do they actually fight with their fists and that?"

"Sometimes."

"Well, there are some bad boys down there in Whithorn," I told them. "I saw some boys in a car, and they were throwing stuff out the window at a store, because it was open Sunday."

"Aw, nah!"

"It was terrible. If I had to choose, I think I'd choose Wigtown."

"Would ye? That's nice t'know. If I had t'choose, I'd choose Canada, I think. I'm ambitious t'travel a-Merry-cuh. What's Canada like?"

"Too many people all crowded together, then nothing for thousands of miles."

"It's lovely in Florida. I been to Florida, aye."

A drunk went by with his fly undone. The girls said, "Hi, Billy!" They turned to me and said, "He's a bowler."

"Does he bowl with his fly undone?" I said.

"Was his fly undone?" They all started laughing.

My room above the pub on the Isle of Whithorn overlooks the little harbour. The Isle of Whithorn is not really an isle, just a tiny village at the southern tip of the Machers, a few miles south of the town of Whithorn. This is prime pilgrimage country. The spirit of Saint Ninian is still alive. The hotel is on the Pilgrim Way, and the signs along the way stress the unity of all religions. For instance:

> The pilgrimage is shared by every great creed – Mecca, Lhasa,
> Benares, Jerusalem, Rome, Lourdes are a few of the great pilgrim
> centres. In its own quiet and remote way Saint Ninian's Cave is
> also one of the great focus points of faith. Deep peace of the
> flowing air to you, deep peace of the running wave to you, deep
> peace of the quiet earth to you, deep peace of the shining stars
> to you, deep peace of the prince of peace be upon you.

The bartender said I shouldn't go down to the cave, it was too late for such a long walk, but it wasn't bad. The footpath was along a deep, dark glen, fringed with great currents of bluebells and cascades of what looked like hyacinths flowing among the sycamores and oaks, and a narrow burn gurgling along and occasionally spanned by an old stone footbridge. Then there was a half-mile further along the awkwardly sloping shingled beach to the cave.

The cave is remarkably like the nave of a small church. As tokens of devotion, pilgrims have laid out little crosses made with driftwood, wildflowers, and some scratched on stones from the beach, a tradition going back a thousand years. They're on the floor of the cave, in niches in the walls of the cave, and on the beach near the entrance to the cave. A larger wooden cross has been placed upright in a Multi-Service Industrial and Automotive Grease container. The entrance is a natural isosceles triangle with an apex twenty feet high. The cave narrows to an altar-like formation thirty feet in. Several crosses adorn the altar. The sea is sparkling calmly out front.

Saint Ninian regularly travelled a few miles from his church at Whithorn to be alone here with his thoughts and prayers, according to the stories. Excavations in 1884 and 1950 show the cave being in use at least from the eighth century. Pilgrims then had time to carve much more elaborate crosses than they do today: some are carved straight onto the walls of the cave, and others, much larger, are cut onto freestanding stones, which are now on display at the Whithorn Priory Museum back in town. The seven crosses on the walls of the cave are somewhat more amateurish, but pecked into the surface of the rock with skill and patience. The earliest of these probably predate the Northumbrian conquest of Galloway. Today's crosses are slapdashedly crude by contrast: hastily scratched onto stones with a penknife or a coin, or scrawled with a burnt match.

A stout red-haired woman, her dark-haired daughter, and their brown dog are coming up the beach. They see me and stop dead. But eventually they arrive on the scene. We chat, then walk back along the beach, and back along the footpath, through the woods, and along the side of the pretty little winding stream. The mother's name is Elizabeth: she lives in a four-centuries-old fortified towerhouse on the Isle of Whithorn. The area is always quiet, even in the high tourist season, but I can hardly hear her speak, because she speaks so softly, and the loose shingles screech when stepped on, as if alive.

Had I visited the dig in Whithorn? I had, and I spoke to a gentle-man with a full, dark beard, who said he lived down here. His name was Ian Sunderland. "He's the one who suggested I might take a room at the pub. But he said he didn't think he'd be able to join me for a pint, because he was over last night and he couldn't do two nights in a row any more."

She laughed in a knowing manner.

"I think I might look him up and say come on over for an hour," I said, trying to read the crystal ball of her mind.

"Ian, I'm sure, would be easily persuadable, but I'm not too sure about his wife."

"He did give me the impression that he wanted to be persuaded. He had that look in his eye."

I asked what she did. "Whatever I can really. I do craftwork. And I'm a musician. I play the harp. Mostly traditional music, some medi-eval. I have a full-size classical harp, but I usually play on the smaller ones. They're easier to carry, but they're murder on the fingers." She also has a wardrobe full of fifteenth-century costumes for when she is called upon to give concerts or attend the medieval fairs.

"I think you're the first harpist I've ever actually met. Do you get a lot of work along those lines?"

"I'm trying to build it up a bit – with weddings and things like that."

"I suppose a lot of things you get called upon to do are for benefits. No pay?"

"That's right. That's the problem exactly."

MIRACLE AT SAINT NINIAN'S CAVE

The Isle of Whithorn • Glenluce Abbey • Stranraer

Monday, June 3. Last night I phoned Ian Sunderland, the fellow who'd recommended this pub, which is run by a former reporter for the London *Daily Express* (or so I'm told) and his wife, who are greatly admired in the community for their practice of hiring local young men and women and training them to be bartenders. On the phone Ian reiterated his stand, saying he was fifty-three years old, and couldn't take two pub nights in a row any more. I thanked him for recommending the place, and said that if he later wished to change his mind about coming over, I'd be at the bar and I'd buy him a pint. But if he was later than ten minutes, he had to buy his own pint.

At exactly the ten-minute mark he showed up at the bar, with his beard combed and wearing a fresh shirt. We talked for two hours about his coming up from Yorkshire, marrying a Scottish woman, and settling here, and what it's like in the different seasons – but little about Saint Ninian and that period of the Dark Ages that is his special field of interest. As we talked we gazed out the window, watching the tide come in. Soon the flotilla of little fishing boats and pleasure craft, all freshly painted and ready to tackle the deadliest storms, were proudly bobbing up and down in the waves instead of awkwardly leaning over on the tidal flats.

Ian said the Wigtown Martyrs came immediately after the Reformation, and he went on about the Established Church, and how authorities were so paranoid about any threats to their luxurious way of life, their power. So they decided to put an end to the perceived threat from this new evangelical sect by murdering these young people. It was certainly not because the sect was a threat to their Christian principles or anything like that, just to their privileged position.

One of the bartenders, it was her first night on the job. She was eighteen, blonde, and the slight defect in her teeth emphasized her beauty. She was being trained by a somewhat older woman, equally lovely, but the young one had an air about her of such purity I found myself praying that she would have a wonderful life, she would not suffer from abuse at the hands of stupid men, and that fate would be kind to her. She was so intelligent, so pleased with herself to be learning her job so quickly and getting admiring glances from the clientele. I made an encouraging remark: she said this was a part-time job only and she was going to be going away to college to study office administration.

But a fight broke out on the other side of the pub; there was a lot of shouting, screaming, and loud banging noises. "Git outa here, you wretch," someone kept screaming. "I don't ever want to see you again, you dirty rotten son of a bitch, you fucking swine!" The older bartender started in on the man, a fisherman who had just that day sailed in from the Isle of Man, and she figured he was the perpetrator, she told him what a loathsome creature he was, then she dragged him out of the bar and up to his room. He didn't look loathsome, just a misunderstood character. Our eyes met as he passed, and he pointed at me and said in a loud voice, "It's all your fault!" He said it in such a comical way, I laughed and he laughed as he was being dragged along, as if to the gallows.

This morning, a cool, rainy breeze coming in off the sea blows my hangover right away. On the other side of the harbour is what used to be a pub, or so it looks. The faded sign can still be read – SMUGGLER'S ISLE. The seagulls swoop and soar. Out of all the little harbours on all the coasts of Europe this is the one they chose on this particular day and, since I have done the same, I feel a kinship with them. We're all scavengers.

Fishermen are standing on the pier watching the boats ride up and down at anchor. "Who fed you that line of codswallop?" said the old fellow who runs the hotel when I said I'd heard he used to be a reporter for the London *Daily Express*. He in fact recalled quite clearly that he used to be a features writer for the London *Daily Mirror* – and that was a bloody good time for such a job, London in the sixties, what could be better – and that's where he met his wife, and a bloody good wife she's been as well, and now they run this lovely hotel up in Scotland.

The older bartender, who had been giving the younger one the lessons last night and who broke up the fight, her name was Theresa. She's twenty-two, said the pub manager. She's got a little baby, and she's got a husband too, he quickly added, as if this was quite the coincidence. The younger girl was Anna – "just old enough to be in the pub, and she's working in the pub." He agreed with my Wolf Solent-like assessment of her loveliness and said he was going to try to get her into the movies. With his connections and her brains and beauty he didn't anticipate any problems. He said he'd arrange to have that tooth of hers fixed up.

"No, no," I pleaded.

He looked at me inquiringly. "You have a point there," he said.

In the breakfast room there's only one other table occupied – by an elderly couple, tourists from England. I was sitting at right angles to them, at the next table, and I could see both of them in profile by looking straight ahead over the top of my newspaper. They were painfully making their way through their huge Scottish breakfast, making sure they got their money's worth, and, when I ordered my Manx kippers, they looked at each other, as if to say, Why didn't we order that? I hate to generalize, but English tourists are often like that – they spend half their time spying on the other tourists and the other half trying to pretend they're not.

They would have been embarrassed to know what a good sense of hearing I had. The wife would ask her husband, "Did you put the fungicide drops between your toes this morning, dear?" And he would say, "I did, dear, but thanks for reminding me," and she was wondering aloud if she should have washed out the white socks last night, or if she should change her shoes. "Time enough for that later, dear." Or maybe I should leave these ones on. "I don't see why not, dear." They were exasperated that it was raining on their holidays. At one point I got up to get some toast from the serving table, and they didn't realize there was a pane of glass reflecting them, so that, even though my back was turned to them, I could see them clearly. And what did I see but them staring at me, vigorously looking me up and down, checking out my clothes, particularly my grey sneakers, of course, since footwear was so much on their mind this morning. I resisted the impulse to turn around abruptly. When I did finally turn around (with plenty of warning), they had composed themselves and were quietly looking out the window at nothing at all really, just the rain.

When they were leaving, I said, "Another cold, rainy day." He said, "Oh yes, we always come up here in June, and it's always fine. I don't know what's the matter with it this year."

"Oh, the weather's going crazy, isn't it?" I inquired.

"Yes indeed," he replied, "it seems to be. Tornadoes and floods and that all over the world."

"Somebody's going to have to do something about it," I urged.

"Well, I don't think there's anything anyone can do about the weather now, is there?"

At the tip of the Machers (a.k.a. Machars), there's the most glorious stretch of beach, one of the great beaches of the world, with great rollers rolling in, up to ten feet tall at the point of cresting. A strip of kelp, looking like a sales graph, marks the high-tide mark, and it goes on in its zigzag fashion for miles. The road is up high and looks down on this marvellous vista. There's no real traffic on the road, just the occasional tractor pulling a cart full of arcane farm equipment, plough blades and whatnot.

In the pouring rain, Glenluce Abbey on the winding Water of Luce is a tragic sight – a damp, cold, hollow shell of its former vitality and beauty. It's so sad-looking I'm glad not to know anything about its history or who wrecked it and why. In fact I'd rather sit here absorbing the gloom and listening to "Woman Sounds" (presented by Jenny Murray) on the car radio than getting out and reading the Scottish Heritage plaque. There is a magnificent row of seven ancient sycamores, and even they look terribly mournful, as if they were saying "Last Exit to Hell." Like the ruined abbey, and the magnificent trees, the cows stand motionless in the rain. There's nowhere to go and they're so depressed they can't even bend their necks for a chew of grass now and then: they appear to be absolutely wretched.

No doubt this was once a magnificent abbey, but the ruins are not at all pleasing to the eye. This whole scene is saying to me, "Vanity of vanities, all is vanity," and "Of the writing of books there is no end," and "Why carry on, why not lie down and die?" and, simply, "The entire human race and every member of it is damned for all eternity." There's an interesting article on this abbey in the *Encyclopaedia of Scottish History*, but it's too brutal, upsetting, and depressing to summarize here. Reading it made me feel my mood had been perfectly justified. The most famous ghost connected with the abbey, even he was a particularly nasty piece of business: he was known as the Devil of Glenluce, and flourished in the early seventeenth century.

Serendipitously, Jenny Murray quotes a Monty Python line: "If life seems jolly rotten / There's something you've forgotten." I feel rotten, but what have I forgotten? Oh oh! My green raincoat! The same one readers of *An Innocent in Ireland* will remember my having bought in Dingletown. I left it at Saint Ninian's Cave yesterday. After intense deliberation, I head all the way back through the driving rain, and, praise be to Saint Ninian, my raincoat is here! Someone has spread it on the ground in such a way that, with its hood, it forms the shape of a perfect green waterproof cross, and it's pointing at the altar of the cave where yesterday I took a large rock from the beach and placed it over a sickening, glistening human turd that someone had deposited there an hour earlier at the most. Perhaps the spirit of the place was pleased with my action in that regard, and made sure my raincoat was preserved for my benefit. Maybe it was the spirit of Saint Ninian drawing me back from the outskirts of Stranraer.

As I was emptying water from the coat pockets, a tiny fish flipped out, and seemed to be looking sadly at me as it expired on the stones. And man, what a storm! High tide and explosively huge waves, each coming up a little higher than the one before. The tide isn't fully in yet. I'm sitting in the cave watching the waves smash against the cliffs. The sea out further is grey, but in here, where the waves start breaking, the foam is whiter than snow and comes all the way up almost to the lip of the cave. All the way down the coast the waves are smashing against the cliffs. The spray from the crashing waves is coming right in the cave. But I've got my raincoat. The gulls are flying overhead, looking dark in silhouette against the shining grey sky. Every once in a while a wave comes roaring in with such a screaming sound I become startled and feel I'm about to get swamped, swallowed, and swept away by the savage sea. But, as have others before me, I scratch out a little cross on a little stone and find a perfect little niche for it on the wall of the cave.

Back in the pub, Elizabeth, the red-haired medieval harpist, is telling me that, although she is not an actress, she had a role in the film *The Wicker Man*, which was shot around here, though it was set on a small, remote, fictional island in the Hebrides. At first she didn't wish to divulge the name of the film, thinking it was so bad I'd never have heard of it, but when she finally did I told her it was a terrific film, I'd seen it twice, and it was popular in the video stores in Canada. She was amazed. Where exactly was it shot?

"It's the Allan Gallon pub in Creetown."

"It wasn't even shot on an island!"

"Noooo! They filmed the seaplane coming out at Plockton, which is way up the coast near Skye. The rest of it was shot at Creetown. Amazing the things they can do."

"They say the camera never lies."

"Hoooh, boy, it certainly does. But it was an awful lot of fun. There was a lot of local lads and lassies who hadn't jobs applied for work as extras, and we all got paid and got fed and they made fun of us and we made fun of them and it was great fun."

"Did you get to meet Britt Ekland?"

"Oh, yeah! She sort of stamped in and stamped out again. Diane Cilento, who is actually an actress" – a slam at Britt – "was involved in it as well. And Ingrid Pitt, they were the three blondes. And there's a scene in it where Britt Ekland is sleeping in the room next to the policeman and she's naked and she's doing a dance and she's beating on the wall – it wasn't her at all, it was a stand-in."

"Not you by any chance?"

"A different shape from me for sure. But it was filmed in late September or early October and it was freezin'. All right, darlings, they'd say to us, get your lovely coats off, you have to go and dance in your summer frocks. Summer is a-comin' in. Brrr!"

Elizabeth said that, with a name like McFadden, I'd probably be descended from Tinkers, the traditional wanderers of the British Isles. Maybe not further north, but the Ayrshire McFaddens were Tinkers.

"Well," I said, "that has the ring of truth to it. I've always been ready to clear out at a moment's notice and I have a fearsome anti-establishment streak."

"There are worse people to be descended from."

"That's for danged sure." We both laughed. "The Tinkers get a terrible bad rap in Ireland, though. What's the Tinker situation like in Scotland?"

"Tinkers and Travellers over here definitely do not go around thinking they are better than other people. And they are a wonderful repository of song and story. You hear them at the folk festivals, and when they sing an old folk song they sing it as if they mean it, they're not singing a song because they learned it from a tape recorder. They sing it because they learned it from their mother and father as children, and it sounds wonderful."

BEYOND THE
CHEVIOT HILLS

Dumfries • Lanercost Priory • Banks East Turret • Carter Bar
Redesdale Forest • Jedburgh • Kelso • Abbotsford • Melrose

Tuesday, June 4. In the Sherlock Holmes in downtown Dumfries, there was an amusing young woman behind the bar last night. Her boyfriend was sitting next to me with a pint in front of him. She kept prancing up and down singing "Anything you want, you got it" – and looking deeply into my eyes. She was trying to get her boyfriend jealous, but he was refusing to play the game. She kept saying to me, "D'ye know, he shoots birds, can ye imagine? How can I go out wit' some jerk who shoots birds?"

"That was years ago," said her boyfriend, with a wee smile on his face, being on to her sexy little tricks. "And besides, the bird was lame." Everybody's doing Prince Philip impersonations these days.

Why am I back in Dumfries? Well, it's hard to explain I might seem confused, it might seem as if I'm having a terrible time getting out of this part of Scotland, but believe me I know exactly what I'm doing: I'm gradually heading back to England, to come up through the Borders Country on the east side of Scotland, as Morton did on his first visit.

On the closed-circuit TV we got to watch people upstairs shooting pool. And, since I was a Scot returned from the colonies, even if after innumerable generations, the sexy bartender dutifully, as per her job description, got out the reprints of old Dumfries directories from the nineteenth century. I flipped through them, but quickly got bored – especially since the McFaddens were all homeless wandering folksingers and wouldn't be listed. As for the names that were listed, they were so widely represented in Canada, I couldn't find a name I hadn't heard before numerous times. All the names were Scottish!

At breakfast this morning I was chatting with a middle-aged couple from a suburb of London about last night's TV documentary on Sarah Ferguson. This was a lengthy and embarrassing film about the follies of Sarah, revolving around some allegedly perfidious Americans who secretly exploited their friendship with her and her love of charitable work to promote their own business interests. The show was sponsored by a wittily named product – "Toe-pedo, Sinks Athlete's Foot," the latter apparently a big problem in the fungus-ridden United Kingdom. This was in the TV room at George Clark's place in Dumfries, to which I'd returned last night, causing him to smile thinly with pleasure – and perhaps consider raising his rates.

"Well, you know, after all, at the end of the day, Sarah Ferguson is an ordinary woman," said the husband. Chilly silence ensued. He turned to his wife and said, "And I don't mean anything disparaging by that remark, dear."

"I should hope not," said she, always ready for a fight. She'd been complaining that they only had a week to travel around all of Scotland.

"It's actually ten days, isn't it, dear?"

"No, it's a week."

She was curious about George and wanted to know if he ran the place solo. I told her I thought so.

"No woman?" she said.

"I think he's a loner, but I'm not sure."

I had heard some children's voices in the back rooms, so I later asked George about it. He confided he did have permanent residents: his daughter and her children had recently returned to live with him after the breakup of her second marriage.

The English couple had flown to Seattle a couple of years ago, drove the west coast to San Diego, then flew home. It was a lovely holiday, but unfortunately it was a little rushed because they only had two weeks.

"It was two and a half weeks, wasn't it, dear?"

"No, it was two weeks."

It appears she likes to travel on their vacations, but he'd prefer to stay home and watch television, particularly documentaries on UFOs and crop circles.

After crossing the River Esk into England again, I didn't become disoriented and actually did what I'd set out to do. The Esk is presumably the river Sir Walter Scott was referring to in the poem in which young Lochinvar "swam the Eske River where ford there was none" – and in which Lochinvar sadly observes that "love swells like the Solway, but ebbs like its tide." I want to visit Hadrian's Wall, then come up into the Scottish Borders Country through the high border village of Carter Bar in the way H. V. Morton did in his first book. There certainly are a lot of Wall names around – Walton, Footwall, Wallfoot, Walby, Walmer, and somewhere around here is the town of Wall – we must be getting close to Hadrian's Wall. It's so pleasant driving along listening to old Bing Crosby songs on the radio. Low Crosby and High Crosby are to the right. We've passed Wallfoot, Wallflower, and now here's Wallhead – I can almost smell that Wall.

There's a football match between Wallfoot and Footwall coming up.

In the parking lot of Lanercost Priory (founded 1186, halfway between Walton and Low Row), a carful of English people are staring into space, as if they've died but their eyes haven't started to drain yet. I walk around to get my asthma inhaler from the boot, and pretend I don't notice anyone there. I give myself a puff, then suddenly, without warning, I shoot a glance towards their car, causing all four of them to look away in different directions.

"Are you real Canadians or Americans pretending to be?" I said to a retired married couple, serious hikers with backpacks stitched with Canadian flags.

"We're real Canadians. In fact we're from Ottawa, the Nation's Capital." They were touring northern England on foot. But they accepted my offer of a lift to the Wall. He's a retired army colonel, and the two of them want to spend the rest of their lives walking around the United Kingdom. They spend six months walking, then six months back in Ottawa getting organized for the next six months of walking. They have everything planned, and they always know where they're going to be on any given day. They don't spend much time reading British history, however: they thought Hadrian's Wall was built to defend against marauding Druids.

They disembarked at Banks East Turret, of which there is little left. This part of the Wall, halfway between the villages of Banks and West Hall, is built on a high escarpment. Remains of the Wall's old turrets are all around here, but the stones over the centuries have been carted away and the turrets don't come up much over the surface of the earth, brown stunted stone turrets in the green countryside. The Wall from here affords a wide-angle view of England, with rolling hills going on forever, and a great sweep of West Northumberland and East Cumbria, with dozens of dreaming villages scattered amid the winding rivers. But as for the view towards Scotland, all you can see is the backside of the next barren hill. It's not a high hill, but it's right there, and you can't see anything beyond: it's a blank. Perhaps this is some kind of military strategy that is beyond my ken.

The Scottish Borders Snack Bar sits in a spacious roadside lookout point high in the Cheviot Hills. The park is full of little English caravans, and everyone's out gazing at a prime vista of Scottish countryside: the Borders Country, rolling hills, farmers' multi-hued fields, patches of forest. What a contrast between my pale description and Morton's wild bursts of enthusiasm at the beginning of *In Search of Scotland!* Way off in the distance sits a tiny Jedburgh Abbey and beyond it are the strangely attractive Eildon Hills. The village of Carter Bar was once known as Rede Swire. The Roman legions invaded after AD 79, building Dere Street, which passes five miles east of here. Redesdale Forest, part of the Border Forest Park, is a bit further to the east.

This Borders area didn't come into its own as a perpetual battlefield until a vacuum left by the accidental death of Alexander III, the peaceful and revered King of the Scots, when he fell off his horse in 1286, led to three centuries of Scottish–English conflict, with frequent wars and invasions, continuous raiding, and general anarchy – so much so that for centuries Alexander's reign was regarded as a golden age. This was the era of the ferocious, blood-drenched border rievers, or moss troopers, familiar to readers of Sir Walter Scott, if there are any left. By the time of the union of 1707, peace had been established between the two countries, and the Scottish and English flags were joined to form the Union Jack.

Jedburgh Abbey, a mere eight miles into Scotland, was burnt and blown up in 1545 by an English army operating under Henry VIII's "Rough Wooing" policy against Scotland. The English were supported by certain famous Scottish clans, and they rolled on the ground in gleeful hysterics when they saw what a mess they'd made of the abbey. "Looks a lot better now," someone shouted, causing a fresh outburst of hilarity. Morton's inspired photograph of the west entrance to the roofless, windowless pile of stone shows it hasn't changed a sliver in seventy years, if not four and a half centuries. Even the shadows are in the same position, so he must have taken the shot at the same time of day. The only difference is a tall iron fence has been erected, which, although not intended specifically for this purpose, prevents me from getting to the exact spot where he had stood to take the picture. The spot was only a few steps away, but to get there I had to go on a hike through the centre of town, and ended up embarrassing a trombonist.

North of the abbey, in the main square of Jedburgh (it's cool to impress the locals by pronouncing it *Jeddart*), a thirty-person brass band is playing to an admiring crowd of folks with time to stop and listen. The band is dressed in kilts, and they're playing that famous traditional Scottish song, "New York, New York." The trombonist takes a solo, blows a wrong note, and I let out a great guffaw – completely involuntarily. The poor trombonist has turned rose red, and I wish I could vaporize myself. Actually I wasn't laughing because of the wrong note, it was because, when the trombonist hit the wrong note (these things have to be expected), all the other members of the band turned and shot dirty looks at him. There are about a hundred people watching and listening to the band, and I'm the only one to let out a guffaw! Geez, I should be shot like a dog.

Now they're playing "(I Did It) My Way" (in their kilts). Ten years ago they probably would have had a full repertoire of Glenn Miller songs, but tastes change and now they've evolved all the way up to Frank Sinatra. This band is from Edinburgh and, when they finished playing "(I Did It) My Way" I asked the conductor if they knew any Scottish songs. "Ye musta read my mind," he said, "cuz that's what we're gonna do next." So now they're playing a snappy marching-band arrangement of "Loch Lomond," a favourite of tourists old and young – but probably not a favourite of the musicians. They're talented, but they'll quit if all they get to play is Scottish songs. They want something jazzier, more with-it, ergo Frank Sinatra.

There's more to Jedburgh than Jedburgh Abbey and a marching band. Vast pear orchards surround the town. They also have the Robert Burns House, where the poet stayed overnight in 1787 and everybody treated him nicely, including no less a personage than the city magistrate, according to the plaque. On the other corner is the Mary Queen of Scots House. She spent a night or two here once; thousands of people have spent a much longer time in this house, but they will be forgotten. Morton talks about this sad injustice, for he has a feeling for ordinary folk. He's not a bad guy really, in spite of his sentimentality, and his hapless harlequinades of hyperbole. His *In Search of Ireland* perennially places high on the list of worst books ever written about that country, but sometimes the worst books have charms the best books know nothing of.

"One glance of Kelso, and I held my breath in amazement," notes Morton, slyly. It must have been all those years working for the country weeklies. But Morton's right when he declares that Kelso, ten miles northeast of Jedburgh, does look like a pretty French town. There's an enormous "*grande place*," paved with cobblestones. And there's the enormous old Crosskeys Hotel facing the *grande place*. The photo store by the hotel has been run by Hector Innis for decades. Hector is a distinguished-looking old fellow, tall and thin, with bushy white eyebrows. When he laughs, as he often does, usually in ironic counterpoint to something he has said, often something to do with what he sees as his own personal failings, his laughter is spontaneous. He said he'd certainly heard of *In Search of Scotland* by H. V. Morton, but had he read it? I held it out to him.

"No, I haven't. Heh heh heh!"

"Not even the Kelso section?"

"Well, let's have it, let's have it." He was a bit impatient, even though his store was empty. Later he cleaned my camera without charge.

"He keeps going on how Kelso looks like a pretty French town . . ."

"Yes, and we've had to live with that ever since. Now everybody has to say Kelso looks like France. And I suppose there is, in some way, a slight resemblance. The big town square."

"*La grande place*, as he calls it, and he says *au revoir* to the policeman as he's leaving – and he fears he hasn't been understood. But he certainly had a huge pig-out at the hotel next door. I went in, but they'd never heard of him, so they suggested I speak to you."

Hector agreed the hotel hadn't changed much in seven decades – nor had the entire central part of town. He said eight centuries ago the *grande place* would have been the monastery garden, and the houses would be clustered round about: "This part here would probably develop after the abbey was destroyed, I would expect. Fifteen-something or other, I can't remember."

"Who destroyed it?"

"Hertford the Englishman. The Earl of Hertford came up and destroyed the whole thing, all the major buildings – to subjugate the peasants. But no, as a historian I'm not really much good."

"You know a lot more than they do over in the hotel."

"Yes, but Charlie, he's only been here for twenty years."

"That Morton, he buzzed into town, spent an hour pigging out in the hotel, spent an hour walking around town, then he was gone."

"That's about all he'd need. And of course in those days this town would be stinking to high heaven."

"He did say something about holding his breath 'in amazement' upon first seeing Kelso."

"Aye, he was a sly one. But that was before we managed to get our sewage system working."

Unfortunately, Abbotsford, the home of Sir Walter Scott (1771–1832), on the outskirts of Melrose (Melrose, Jedburgh, and Kelso form an equilateral triangle, in the heart of the Borders Country, with sides of ten miles each), is closed, as most major tourist attractions are in Scotland during the tourist season, or so it seems. But I slipped inside the grounds and gazed at the mansion, which Scott built himself and which he worked furiously for the rest of his life to pay for. He moved here in 1812, the main block of Abbotsford was built between 1817 and 1819, and here Scott died in 1832. Maybe I can get back tomorrow.

The Scots regard the tourist business in large part with a cheesy, narrow little mind. There's NO ADMISSION WITHOUT A TICKET at the ruins of Melrose Abbey, and NO ADMISSION WITHIN HALF AN HOUR OF CLOSING TIME. This was Morton's favourite of the four Borders abbeys, but he came by before the erection of a stone wall eight feet high that surrounds it, so now it's impossible to get a glimpse at the ruins. In fact it's impossible to determine where Morton was standing when he took the picture in his book. The occasional gate in the wall is padlocked, of course, and even there you can't look in, unless you're standing on top of a beer truck on tiptoe. Since the hours are so limited, even in high tourist season, not even the locals get to see Melrose Abbey by moonlight, or by starlight – or even streetlight for that matter.

C H A P T E R   8

THE GREAT
COLLECTOR AND
THE GREAT EXPLORER

*The Eildon Hills • Scott's Lookout • Abbotsford
Dryburgh Abbey • Rosslyn Chapel*

Wednesday, June 5. In the great Down Under tradition, an Australian couple were taking a ten-week tour of the world: they'd taken a similar tour thirty years earlier, between graduation and embarking on their life's work, and now it was time for their second and final one. The husband, a recently retired architect, was bored: the trip was at the halfway point only, and he was dying to get home. This was too much like work. His wife, who was having a wonderful time and never wanted the trip to end, couldn't find her keys.

"Well, you had them last," said her husband. "You're the one who went up to the room before. I don't have them." Amid numerous sighs of impatience, he emptied his pockets to prove he didn't have them. After an agonizing quarter-hour of frustration, it turned out that the tall and toothy uppercrust beauty queen, Angela, who runs this palatial tourist estate somewhere between Melrose and Kelso, had inexplicably removed the keys from the breakfast table and put them in her key drawer. This was the same Uppercrust Angela who last night, when I was innocently asking her about the history of this interesting old manor, suddenly said, rudely enough to hurt my feelings terribly, "What is this? Twenty questions?" This morning she giggled when she found out we'd been looking all over for the keys.

Her husband, the laird of the estate and much older than she, was similarly afflicted with strangely rude behaviour. Very late last night, after midnight actually, when I was trying to sleep, the television downstairs was blaring mercilessly. I tiptoed down and politely tapped on the door of the television room. No answer, since the volume was up so loud. Finally I opened the door, and there was the laird watching some idiotic transvestite program. I asked if he'd turn it down. He laughed wildly, rolled his eyes, and said, 'Having a hard time getting to sleep, are we?"

Also a bit annoying was the fact that he began vacuuming the rugs this morning just as we sat down for breakfast, and didn't finish till we'd finished eating. Angela had plunked the breakfast down in front of us without asking our preferences, not even if we'd like tea or coffee, an experience previously unheard-of in my travels.

Now, as we were getting ready to leave, we could hear Angela and her husband having a serious discussion in the background. She appeared to be scolding him about something, and in response he was again laughing idiotically and rolling his eyes. The maidservant, an old lady in a wig, kept going "ooh-WHIP! . . . ooh-WHIP " as she worked, like some exotic bird call. This is a strange place. For the room, Angela charged twice what we were told in Saint Boswells it would be – and she insisted we *not* sign her guest book, presumably for tax-dodge reasons. There was no apology this morning about last night's roaring television or for the heist of the keys, not even a tiny nod of acknowledgement. Disgraceful, I thought.

In the hills somewhere north of Dryburgh Abbey (ruins) and east of Melrose Abbey (ruins) there's an extraordinarily heavenly place called Scott's Lookout: one looks across the glen of the winding

Tweed at the three volcanic Eildon Hills. "Volcances here? Absolutely not!" Uppercrust Angela had exclaimed with horror when I asked if those hills, also visible from her digs, were volcanic in origin. But here a plaque says the glorious Eildons were created through volcanic activity in the Carboniferous Period about three hundred million years ago, rising through the sediments of old red sandstone. From the same plaque is a line worthy of Vladimir Nabokov: "In the foreground, fringing a meander of the Tweed, a fragment of ancient woodland is preserved." With the three peaks of the strange and heavenly Eildons and, in the foreground, the U-shaped and forest-bracketed meander of the Tweed, the whole vista of landscape is a rolling sea, with rolling hills covered with farmland, forest, stone bridges, streams, and villages suddenly getting a burst of energy and throwing up these three immense hills.

A bus full of elderly tourists from England pulls up, with a driver, a commentator with microphone, and with a third person whose job is to shepherd the people in and out and make sure they don't lose their bags. The old people are not too interested in what they see, they'll never remember the names of those hills or the dates of those monasteries, but they laugh like the dickens when a sheep jumps up in the air.

A huge crowd at something like Abbotsford, to which I did in fact return as planned, isn't a problem, but at ruined abbeys and megalithic monuments you don't want crowds at all. The genius of certain places absorbs the crowds, at other places the crowds absorb the genius. Abbotsford is an experience of the former sort. In a little windowed alcove in a quiet corner of the Scott mansion sits Scott's death mask. He probably stood in this room many times looking out at the garden, without thinking his death mask would someday be on permanent display here. He had a rather large cranium above a small face – the look of a genius to be sure. Politically he might have had some questionable friendships, people involved in the Highland clearance atrocities for instance. But he was a great poet, a great novelist, a great historian, and one of the world's truly great collectors – collecting was a lifelong passion with him.

In another room a painting depicts a meeting between Robert Burns and Walter Scott, with Scott, a lad with blond hair, looking a little resentful of Burns's fame. Scott is being pushed forward to meet the great philanderer, who has dark hair with a pony tail tied with a blue ribbon, and is glancing down at Scott superciliously. Twenty or thirty people are looking on, and they all seem, of course, dramatically aware an historical event is taking place. Burns was twenty-seven, Scott fifteen. It was their only meeting.

One room contains Scott's amazing collection of stone gargoyles with obscene grimaces on their faces. Among the gargoyles are knives, guns, and various instruments of torture and war: a Persian battle-axe, a Turkish bell-mouthed flint blunderbuss, a magnificent crossbow, and lots of swords and knives of various sizes and styles, a breastplate dated 1550, the often-reproduced portrait of King James IV, and a gruesome painting of Mary, Queen of Scots, one day after her execution, with her head sitting by itself on the table. There is a portrait of a certain ancestor of Scott's who was sentenced to be hanged, and somebody said we'll let you off if you agree to marry my ugly daughter; the fellow held off for three days, and it wasn't until he was on the scaffold with the rope actually around his neck that he capitulated and said he would marry her if the deal was still on.

From 200 BC there's a terrific pair of metal horns and face mask, designed to be worn by a horse and found in the earth in Galloway, west of Dumfries. A whole room is dedicated to the spoils collected by Scott from Waterloo shortly after the great battle. It must have been inspiring to have all this stuff around. Perhaps that's why he had it, although it of course would have added greatly to the value of the house, so that when the bank was threatening to foreclose, as they often were, he could say, "But come and look at all the stuff I have in it." In that regard he wasn't much different from many collectors. But each little item has a great dramatic story connected with it, so everywhere you look there's an historical novel waiting to be written.

Unlike the vast majority of us, Scott also had a collection of great two-handed swords of the sixteenth century, a clock that once belonged to Marie Antoinette, a shred of a piece of a gown once worn by Mary, Queen of Scots, Lord Byron's mourning ring, which was sent to Sir Walter upon the former's death, a lock of Bonnie Prince Charlie's hair, and a toadstone amulet belonging to Scott's mother and which she frequently lent out for mothers to place around the necks of the newborn to protect them from witchcraft. There was a piece of oatcake found in the pocket of a dead Highlander on the field of Culloden, and a spent bullet from the same battle. And he had a glass tumbler with four lines of verse scratched thereon by Robert Burns with his famous diamond ring. In spite of his enormous literary output, Scott comes across as a collector who wrote on the side.

Later, at the naveless ruined shell of Dryburgh Abbey, where the great collector is buried, near Saint Boswells, a few miles southeast of Melrose, a solemn, otherworldly, well-modulated, and well-groomed curly-bearded gentleman at the ticket office takes me to see the initials RB carved on a stone wall. It's a memento of Robert Burns's visit in 1787. He admits it's badly faded, but I can't see it at all. He shows me a picture of Burns on a scaffold, chiselling his initials in the stone, so it must be there.

In the graveyard, several tombstones depict women happily reading, always in profile, dressed in gowns and bonnets, and looking youthful and proud. I asked the same gentleman about this, and to his credit he admitted he didn't know what it was about. He doubles as the official abbey photographer, and his photos of his favourite tombstones are framed and on display all around the office. Depending on the season, he rubs snow or grass on the stone to bring out the lettering. He speaks slowly and mournfully of the ladies reading: "There was snow on the ground, and so I was able to rub the snow into the lettering, and that helped bring it up. So these are all very early 1700s." He liked my suggestion that it might have been a short-lived fad, some stonecutter offering this as a new idea for tombstones, and some of the more *au courant* families went for it. "I think it's been the fashion of a local sculptor," he said. "They're all in a short time period in the early eighteenth century."

"It might have been at a time when literacy wasn't all that common," I offered, "and was intended to show, with pride, that the dead soul had been literate."

"That's right, and the sculptors wouldn't have been that learned either."

"They'd have to be able to carve the letters, though."

He spoke faster: "Not necessarily the right ones. The customer couldn't read anyway." We burst out laughing. "And there are indications that sometimes one person did the sculpting and another the lettering."

We looked at more of his photographs. It seemed odd to be looking at snapshots of tombstones when the very tombstones were all around us. "I bet a lot of people come in here looking for their ancestors," I wagered.

"Oh, they do, there's a fair number," he said. "But, you know, if we don't record it, it's so easily lost." He meant recording the tombstones photographically. "This sort of thing takes time . . ." Some customers came in and he excused himself momentarily to sell a couple of tickets.

"Some of those stones have actually become clearer over this last year," he continued. "With the very dry conditions, the mosses died off, a lot of the lichens have died off, so the printing is clearer than it was, so now is an ideal time to take photographs of the stones so as to record them."

I mentioned some stones I'd seen at Irongray Church, near Dumfries. They were lying flat and the moss was growing in the letters, improving their legibility.

"The water rests there in the letters," he said, "and fine dust particles collect, and this provides the nourishment, so that the moss grows freely. But of course there comes a stage when the moss forms a cushion and gradually begins to obliterate the letters." His lip quivered.

His name was James Stenhouse and he told me many strange things happen to people in this ruined abbey. Nothing's ever happened to him, but some people can't get into a certain cellar, they get down halfway and they can't get any further. Other sections as well. It's almost invariably women to whom this happens, because women seem to be more sensitive to this sort of thing. They become inexplicably overcome with a sense of horror and can't proceed. It's as if parts of the abbey are infested with tortured spirits.

The first of three major attacks on the twelfth-century abbey was in the fourteenth century, when Edward II, retreating to England after an unsuccessful invasion of Scotland, apparently became annoyed when he heard the abbey bells ringing. So he went over and set fire to the place. Heat-cracked stones from that attack can still be seen. Sixty-three years later, Richard II's army set the place afire again. In 1544, the notorious abbey-wrecker, the Earl of Hertford – again as part of Henry VIII's "Rough Wooing" policy – attacked with seven hundred men, including members of certain famous Scottish clans, and blew the place sky-high.

On the long winding road up to the mysterious Rosslyn Chapel I spotted a dog that looked like Sir Walter Scott! This sort of thing must be a matter of natural selection on the part of human beings who decide which pup gets drowned and which one gets saved. Any pup that looks like Sir Walter gets saved, and pretty soon the countryside is overrun by four-legged Scott lookalikes. Nevertheless, it was spooky.

"I've come to investigate the sensational secret of Rosslyn

Chapel," I told the women in the ticket office. The chapel is located in a remote area just south of Edinburgh, near the village of Roslin, where Dolly the sheep was cloned.

"Well, you tell us when you find it, and we'll be delighted," the younger of the two replied joshingly.

A choir of female saints was singing medieval plainchants over the speaker system. I pulled out a tabloid-sized paper.

"This here's the *Scottish Banner*," I said. "It came all the way to Canada from Scotland, and I've brought it back to Scotland with me."

They became engrossed in the page-one picture story of Rosslyn Chapel, with a headline saying THE SENSATIONAL SECRET OF ROSSLYN CHAPEL. It was right next to a story about Mrs. Fraser's Wee Bakeshop.

"It says in there," I said, "that Henry Sinclair from Rosslyn Chapel went to North America a hundred years before Columbus."

"That's correct, and he came back, too," said the older lady. "There are plants carved in this chapel that obviously came from the New World before Columbus. There's lots of information inside, but ask if you need anything more."

"Maybe one of you could come with me and be my guide, and I could actually pay you for it."

"Och, this'll be a freebie," said the young lady, "for that's what we're here for."

She ushered me into the chapel. The entire ceiling and walls were sculpted with bizarre botanical designs in geometric patterns. She flashed her torch on a pattern showing ears of North American maize. "There, see?"

"Now what makes you think that's corn, and not just a design?" We were whispering to avoid disturbing the other people in the chapel, all solitary men, wandering around with their guidebooks open and perplexed looks on their faces.

"Well, they had botanists look at it. And that's leaves coming out the top."

"I don't see any kernels, though." The other men were casting envious looks at me because I had a real live guide to these sacred mysteries.

"Yeah. I don't know. Anyway, that's what they reckon."

"Who do they figure it was who did all the sailing?"

"Prince Henry Sinclair," she said, "who was the founder's grandfather. He was the first prince of Orkney. And he brought back stories of the Micmac Indians. And there are these narratives which kinda narrate this voyage. And there are these cactuses that they reckon were only found in the New World. Of course there were Templars in the family as well, you see. The family were Knights Templar that built this place. Prince Henry was, and so was the founder." She was whispering in my ear, while the others, without wanting to appear obvious, strained to hear from their respective distances. "It's sort of a combination of different kinds of Christianic, paganism, Celticism, Templarism, Masonic." She shone her pen-sized torch on a row of crosses carved into the ceiling. "These are the Engrailled Crosses, the Templar crosses." She led me into a room at the back of the chapel and pointed to the top of a narrow column. "This up there, this is called the Agnus Dei, which was one of the Templar seals, and it's the Lamb of God."

"Is that an elephant up there?"

"Where? Up here? No, I think that's, uh, I don't know what that is. Some of them are quite old and worn. And there were statues in all the ledges as well. But during the Reformation some of them got destroyed and some of them we think were put in vaults which are under the pews. And the last body to go down there was 1650. So there's supposed to be twenty-odd knights in full armour laid out down there on stone shelves."

"Let's get into it and see!"

"We can't get into it, unfortunately. We don't know how to get into it. A few years ago they did quite a bit of research and did some electronic scans and stuff like that. They picked up the various vaults underneath, but they don't know how to get into the vaults, and that's the thing, you see. Anything they tried, it didn't work. The theory is it's actually all been sealed off, but where the entrances were we don't know. So there's no plans either, nothing."

"Great mysteries!"

"There certainly is. Some people say there's lost scrolls down there in the vaults – apparently the last teachings of Christ."

"Do they make a good argument for it?"

"Uhh, some of it, but then a lot of people say they don't list a lot of references. And it sounds as if a lot of this stuff was dreamt up."

The typewritten guidebook claims that Prince Henry Sinclair, First Prince of Orkney, was born in the Robin Hood Tower of nearby Rosslyn Castle, in 1305, which apparently is a misprint, it'd be more like 1350. He's also interred in the chapel. He became known as the "Holy Sinclair." With the aid of Templar funding, Henry commissioned twelve ships to be built for a voyage of exploration to the New World. With Antonio Zeno, a member of a prominent Venetian family, as navigator, Henry sailed to Nova Scotia in 1398, lived among the Micmacs, and taught them how to fish with nets, to sow crops, and so on. (The Micmacs probably pretended they didn't know these things, just to make the Europeans feel better.) He then sailed down the eastern seaboard to what is now Massachusetts, and there his great friend Sir James Gunn died. Henry had Sir James's effigy carved on a nearby rockface, and that effigy can be seen to this day, although the precise location is not revealed. Henry was murdered shortly after his return to the Orkneys, and his grandson William had his body brought back to Rosslyn for burial. William commemorated Henry's trip to the New World by carving into these stones some of the strange plants that Henry brought back with him. All these ears of corn, as well as cactus plants and other flora, are carved into interesting, child-like geometrical patterns.

Above the altar are several panels. In one, forty daisies (for innocence) have been carved in a geometrical pattern, in the next, the same number of lilies (for purity), then we have roses (for love), and lastly we have stars – and among the stars can be seen four guardian angels as well as the sun, the moon, and a dove. There are about forty five-pointed stars up there. There are also some spectacular stone depictions of the seven deadly sins, and facing them the seven matching good deeds – including feeding the poor and hungry, visiting those in prison, and so on. All these figures are surrounded by complex botanical motifs. Also carved up there is this Latin inscription: "Wine is strong, a king is stronger, a woman is even stronger – but truth conquers all."

When Morton was here seventy years ago they tried to get him to buy Rosslyn Castle, which sits far behind the chapel on a much lower hill. A smooth-talking salesman showed him through. He was amazed by how low the price was and he went on about how vividly the castle stirred his imagination, but he didn't buy it. A yew tree he raved about is now surrounded by unkempt bush and is a terrible mess. Morton had been told it was 750 years old, so it would be 820 now. And it's still standing tall, but I doubt if anybody is sending clippings all around the world, as they used to, because it is now completely surrounded by new growth.

A BRITRAIL PASS
FOR LIFE

Edinburgh

Thursday, June 6. When I arrived in Edinburgh last night someone recommended a Royal Mile tour offered by a fellow named Dracula, an excellent local historian, a sensitive and interesting guy. But I managed to take the wrong tour, one being led by an insensitive and uninteresting young woman. After collecting our money, she started raving about the most horrendous tortures that took place at Market Square, but made a point of showing no sense of compassion for the people who suffered such horrors, or for the stupidity of the brutes who devised the tortures. In fact she seemed to take ghoulish pleasure in the stories, and had no sense of historical context. One tale involved two English fellows, who, upon arriving in Edinburgh in 1658, during the reign of Parliament, went into a pub for a drink, then daringly got up and toasted the King of England. They were promptly put to death in a particularly monstrous manner, which she described in full, with great relish. Not wishing to hurt her feelings,

I told her she was doing a "tremendous job," but I remembered I had an appointment.

Ian King and the poet Sally Evans run an antiquarian bookstore, Old Grindles, in Old Spittal Lane, which runs from Bread Street to King's Stables under Castle Rock. They tend to talk at the same time, apparently a conscious time-saving technique, for they never miss a thing the other says. I'd visited them on a trip to Edinburgh ten years ago, but I was dying to see them again, because I had been reading about what has become the biggest event of their lives: the discovery of a previously unknown novel by Charlotte Brontë (1816–1855), author of *Jane Eyre*. There'd been a front-page article in *Scotland on Sunday*, but the response to the article from other papers was a bit deflating. Ian was complaining about what he saw as resentment, in the London papers, of the discovery, and much down-playing of it. I wondered if this was a case of "ethnic" rivalry, if the resentment was at all because a Scot had discovered the book.

"Oh, in England, yes, subconsciously," said Sally. "Definitely so. But not in America."

"Problem is, it's a tiny country this," said Ian, "but it's a huge one in journalistic terms. The Scots papers don't go south of the border – and we canna get our hands on the *Yorkshire Post* to correct their mistakes. It's a tiny little island, but it splits right down the middle."

Random House was about to publish the Brontë book, but they were having second thoughts, apparently, because of the low-key reaction the discovery had been receiving in the British press. "With this whole idiotic campaign going on," said Ian, "they've already delayed the British edition coming out."

"The manuscript," I asked. "Does it actually belong to you now?"

"No, it isn't a manuscript," said Ian. "That's the whole thing. It's a book, a lost book." Apparently, for reasons unknown, the book had been withdrawn by the publisher shortly after it came out. "But the publisher made his deposits to the National Libraries, and sent one

to Congress – just as a sort of literary time capsule, so this thing
wouldn't be lost entirely – and it's taken an entire century for us to
notice it existed."

"So, are the English saying we knew it was there all along?"

"They're saying it can't possibly be true, but they don't want to
look at the evidence. In British journalism, one paper gets the scoop,
so its three rivals have got to knock it within twelve hours, then
everything else is based on the knocking pieces. And it gets more
and more garbled each time. The editor of *The Times* said he'd eat his
column if it was true."

"Who had the scoop?"

"*Scotland on Sunday*. But it'll all be sorted out by Christmas, I
should imagine."

Had they got an advance? "Not very much and not very soon
either," said Sally.

"We didn't do it for the money," said Ian. "I mean, we did it for
the sake of Charlotte."

Sally said, "People are going around saying we're going to be mil-
lionaires. That's rubbish."

"These advances, they're totally Mickey Mouse," said Ian. "It's
games publishers play to impress each other. It's all broken up into
little bits, each conditional on this happening and that happening.
If it was a book by Dickens, so what? There's twenty-seven of them
already. Another one wouldn't make much difference. But Charlotte
Brontë, she wrote so little, this is a huge discovery. It's like finding
seven or eight new novels by Dickens."

Also, it was business as usual, mail-order business today, with
Sally bringing in boxes full of books, emptying out the books, putting
other books into the boxes, wrapping them up, taping them,
addressing them. She would ask Ian for a postal code and he would
give it to her by memory, and occasionally Ian would say, "Oh, you
did a good one that time, Sally" – even though Sally was making a
terrible mess with the Scotch Tape. Ian was chainsmoking, occasionally reaching up through his huge thick blond beard to give his

neck a good scratch, and then going downstairs to make another pot of coffee.

As for H. V. Morton, Ian said Morton didn't have to be in print, because every second-hand bookstore in the world has a full set of Morton on the shelf and boxes full of his books downstairs in storage. Sally said every time they get a new Morton in here there's always an old train-ticket stub or bus-ticket stub that falls out of it which has been used as a bookmark. People have been reading it as they travel and then abandon it when they arrive. Apparently, Morton's publisher did so well with the books and they were so good for the tourist trade that they got BritRail to give him a free pass for life.

The National Gallery of Scotland sits on a hill called the Mound, which offers nifty views in several directions. Spring has come, birds are singing, and people are having picnics in the parks, sunning themselves, playing guitars and board games.

The gallery has a monster painting, fifteen feet high by twenty feet long called *Alexander III of Scotland Rescued from the Fury of a Stag by the Intrepidity of Colin Fitzgerald.*" Fitzgerald, having fled from Ireland, had taken refuge at Alexander's court, and is shown busy saving the king's life on a hunting expedition by spearing an enraged stag in the forehead as it was about to attack. Fitzgerald was granted the lands of Kintail as a reward and became the founder of the Clan Mackenzie. All the Mackenzies are descended from a brave Irishman named Colin Fitzgerald. Maybe all the Fitzgeralds are, too.

Rembrandt's famous *Self Portrait* (1657) is on display, Rubens's *Feast of Herod* (1638), and just now an exhibition called "The Great American Watercolourists," from the Museum of Fine Arts in Boston – Homers, Sargents, O'Keeffes, DeMuths, Hoppers – is being featured. The show has attracted numerous American tourists, homesick for native culture. "Oh," exclaims one elderly American lady, disappointedly, "these watercolours are all modern!"

In the vast, dizzying Scottish collection are works by many painters who are seldom seen and seldom heard of outside Scotland, including numerous heroic landscapes with people in them doing interesting things with moral implications, as in a work by David Allen (1744–1796) showing a man standing beneath an old oak tree contentedly watching his numerous children dancing and playing mandolins and castanets, with gleeful and alert dogs all over the place, but with a terribly mournful landscape in the background, to represent the joys of family life keeping the sadness of life at bay. The note says the painting depicts John Halkett, with his second wife, Mary, his daughter by his first wife, and his thirteen younger children.

A guard gleefully admits to having lived in Edinburgh all his life, and until he got this job at age forty he'd never once stepped inside the gallery. "And it's all free, too," he said. Now, like most gallery guards, he spends all his spare time looking at paintings and has developed a good eye, and a good knowledge of the holdings. He was amused that, although the show of U.S. watercolourists was full of U.S. tourists, there were hardly any tourists at all looking at the Scottish paintings. He was a bit of a politician, too, for he was soliciting opinions about the numerous terrific paintings that are perpetually hidden away in storage, in order to save space: would it be better to double up on the wall space so more paintings could be on display at one time? I told him his question was both serious and timely, and that I'd make that bargain: more paintings but not as well displayed. One nineteenth-century painting on display actually depicted an artist sitting and making a copy of a painting on the wall of this very gallery: the entire wall is shown, and some of the paintings are familiar from today's visit. But in the painting they are all doubled up, with one painting above the other, and all the paintings close to one another. The guard says they don't do that these days, because scientists have determined there is an optimal level at which paintings should be viewed. On the other hand, it would be nice to have more of them filling the walls, and fewer of them stashed away in the deep freeze.

At the Museum of Science, just off the Royal Mile, all the antiquities are locked away owing to extensive ongoing renovations. So I sought consolation in a modest exploration of the various chapels in Saint Giles' Cathedral, the great and imposing "High Kirk of Edinburgh," with its peculiarly Scottish "crown spire" visible from all over town. The gender-conditioning of boys and girls is well illustrated in a pair of complementary plaques here. One is from the Edinburgh and East of Scotland Girls' Club Union, and it bears a picture of a tree with two birds in it. "Friendship is a sheltering tree," it proclaims, and under the tree are three bunnies. The one for the Edinburgh Union of Boys' Clubs, however, shows a naked young man with an eternal flame in one hand and an olive branch in the other, and he is running along the surface of the earth with the sun in the grasp of one hand and the moon in the grasp of the other: "Ever Upward to the Light / Ever True to God and Right / Up and On."

The people of Edinburgh, often accompanied by their dogs, are constantly climbing Calton Hill (328 feet) and strolling up to Arthur's Seat (823 feet), both to the east of the Royal Mile but very much part of the Old Town. Even from the lower summit, you can see people miles away, walking up and down along the various paths, and you can see the islands out in the Firth of Forth and the Ochil and Lomond Hills over on the north side, and steeples all over Edinburgh. I hadn't realized how small Edinburgh is. It seems from here like a quiet medieval town; there's dead silence in the air.

CHAPTER 10

MORTON TAKES OVER

Edinburgh • Linlithgow • Dunfermline • Stirling
Auchterarder • Crieff • Muthill • Braco • Ardoch
Amulree • Glen of Strathbraan

Friday, June 7. I've been up for an hour, listening to the birds and thinking about my dream, in which Morton told me to get out of Edinburgh toot sweet, I'd be better off in fishing villages and boozy little islands in the Hebrides. He asked if he could join me from the spirit world and monitor the trip. I said I'd be honoured, why didn't he get some of the others to come along as well, like Sir Walter Scott and Neil Gunn for instance, or even Blind Harry. Nabokov would be nice, Durrell would be dandy, I could even handle Hemingway.

At breakfast, in this huge rooming house on Inverleith Terrace, by the Royal Botanical Garden, a German couple in their fifties came in dressed like stiff, self-conscious urban cowboys, in shiny, new brown leather. They were desperately keeping their eyes averted from the many other people in the large breakfast room, none of whom were dressed like cowboys. A similar discomfort was afflicting some young American couples, who were all sitting together at a big table and yet painfully shy, whispering to each other, awkward, nervous. One, wearing a T-shirt saying AIR FORCE – AIM HIGH, accidentally knocked a plate off a table and pretended he hadn't.

Under such otherworldly orders from Morton, I hopped in the car and headed straightaway for the western city limits. But I couldn't resist stopping ten miles out at the old town of Linlithgow, which was having a burst of energy: it made Edinburgh look positively pre-apocalyptic. They're tearing things apart, putting them back together again, widening roads, narrowing roads. The tower of the fifteenth-century Saint Michael's Church next to the Royal Palace is undergoing major reconstruction: from the roof they're tossing great sheets of metal, which smash onto the pavement below with a cymbal-like explosion, and a pair of howling Royal Air Force fighter jets are skimming the steeples back and forth in amusing examples of neighbourly regard. Besides, they have to get down low to be heard around here. The birds might be singing in Edinburgh, but they're not in Linlithgow.

From the Royal Palace, birthplace in 1542 of Mary, Queen of Scots, and gutted by an English army two centuries later, there's a spectacular view out over the green fields leading down to a shallow loch, with woodsy hills in the background. Once inside the palace, we're treated to the screaming of little kids crawling up the towers and running up and down the stairs, with each scream echoing off the stone walls nine or ten times before fading. In the courtyard is a spectacular rococo fountain which has been dated precisely to 1538, because they found that year stamped on a lead pipe bringing water from a spring at the far end of town. The fountain would have been gushing water in all directions. It's early Renaissance/Gothic in style, with numerous early medieval figures on it – but strangely there is not one bearing arms of any kind. The fountain, now bone-dry, was troublesome to maintain, and the palace accounts record frequent repairs. Perhaps it gurgled and kept everyone awake nights.

It sits in the centre of the large open court, which is surrounded on four sides by four storeys with a tower on each corner.

This was the residence of King James IV and Queen Margaret, daughter of Henry VII. Margaret's suite of rooms is located a floor above her husband's. She received the palace as a dower house in 1503. It was built during the reign of James IV, who was born in 1473 and killed at Flodden in 1513. The octagonal cap-house above the stairhead was where Queen Margaret waited in vain for his return. After the kids leave, a large batch of tourists arrives, hollering at each other in German, and the fighter jets flying over the roofless palace continue to contribute their ear-crushing sound effects. The town is strangling with terrible traffic jams, but with a remarkable absence of honking, as always in this recently civilized land.

Hours later, after perilously negotiating my way through heavy traffic around the ancient towns of Dunfermline and Stirling, and not being at all tempted to stop, owing to the crowds of tourists (particularly in Stirling), I found myself driving slowly north of Auchterarder along the quiet, winding road to Crieff. The road, an old one to be sure, was lined with moss-covered stone walls, and with wee old ladies in wool caps, wool sweaters, long woollen dresses, full-body woollen underwear, army boots, and thick socks: they're determined to keep warm as they prune their hedges, tend their flower gardens, and generally try to make their houses as pretty as can be. Everything's sparkling, everything's clean. No jackhammers, no traffic jams.

The ancient village of Muthill boasts its own folk museum, a small house converted to display old stuff from the area, stuff the Royal Museum in Edinburgh didn't want, presumably, folksy stuff, the best kind of museum. I seem to be all alone, but then an elderly lady dressed in a wool cap and wool sweater comes in.

"Hello?" she says, with an air of suspicion, wondering what I'm doing there. Then she remembers this is a museum and politely says, "How are you?"

"Fine, thank you. So this is the Muthill Museum."

At that point a workman comes in with a big box of tools, goes into the kitchen area, and starts dismantling the taps.

"Yes, 'tis. Just a very wee one. It's a folk museum."

I pronounced Muthill as *Mutt Hill*. She corrects me, pronouncing it *Moot Hill*. "Pardon the correction, but it comes from an old Gaelic word meaning the wet place. Or the soft place."

"Moot does have that sound to it, doesn't it? Soft, wet."

"Yes, and there is the word Moot Hill, two words, where the chief sat and had a gathering. It would sound just the same but it would be quite different. But you weren't to know, were you? Well, do have a look around, and this is a hands-on museum. You can touch anything you like. Is there anything you want to talk about?"

"To be perfectly truthful with you, I'm only here because the motorway was so busy. And as lovely as this area is, I don't know anything about it, finding myself here only by accident – except it's my impression that this is an ancient road. A Roman road perhaps?"

"That's right, it is. The Romans were all over Scotland, and there's a big encampment here, not very far away. There's also . . . let me digress." She paused. We exchanged names. Hers was Mrs. Wilcox. She looked worried. "Now, how can I tell you this? I've got it! I'm only here because the plumber's putting in a bit of threading."

"You're usually closed on Friday?"

"Yes, but that doesn't matter. The door's open and you're welcome."

I should have politely taken the hint and left, but I was frozen to the spot. The plumber's tools were back in his box, and he was standing there looking at us, waiting for the polite moment to speak. "I'm just about to go," he said.

"Well, that's all right. We have a visitor."

"Yes. That's your water full. Do you want me to leave it on just now? Then I'll just go away now and I'll come back in just ten minutes."

We resumed talking, and she gave no more hints that it might be better if I went my way. She smiled sweetly and said, "Would you like me to tell you what my prized possession is here? There are several: these are very important, they're very old and they're of great value to the collector." She was holding a set of small leather-bound books. "You know every country has its wars and its different things. Well, the ground of Drummond Castle Estate was taken from the people because they were against the government. They happened to be on the losing side."

"Which side was that?"

"They were Royalists. No, they weren't, they were Jacobites, followers of Bonnie Prince Charlie. And the land was taken, and after the war the land was offered to different soldiers who had been in the war. And there tell you who the men were – they were local people – and the plots of land allocated to them."

Mrs. Wilcox was born Flora Elder in Crieff, a few miles north of Muthill. She'd married a Wilcox from London, and lived in England for many years before returning to Scotland. "Now, what should I tell you? You know about the early radio? The cat's whisker? It's a beautiful cat's whisker we have. One visitor told me that he and his brother used to listen to German broadcasts during the war on such a radio —"

Her train of thought was interrupted by the return of the plumber, who eyed me with suspicion as if to say, "Are you still here? Can't you take a hint?" But apparently my exact time of arrival in Muthill was crucial to getting in here, and somehow Morton wanted me to stay: the spirits can be bullheaded. The plumber left, and when Mrs. Wilcox turned to me I was ever so innocently holding the Oxo-cube tin, circa 1928. "Isn't this interesting? Six Oxo cubes."

"Yes, some hubbies, you know, for a joke, used to send these to prospective bridegrooms, to ensure, as they would say, that he would get at least six square meals, after he got back, in case his bride couldn't cook."

"And what's a brose bowl?" I almost asked if she could cook, but she might have thought I was dropping a hint.

"You know about porridge? Well, brose is similar to porridge, only it's made with ground peas." She screwed up her face and whispered conspiratorially. "Och, no, no. They're horrible – well, to my mind. But when the youngsters left home, when they were about ten or twelve, to go and work out in the fields, their father would make a bowl for them, from a piece of wood, and they say this must have been quite a clever man, because he made this thing to go around it." She fingered the lovingly crafted rim around the top of the bowl, a rim which must have served no purpose really, except to make the child seem a bit special among the other indentured labourers. "It's not usual in ordinary work," said Mrs. Wilcox. She held up a spoon. "And this is from cow horn. He gave this to his son when he was twelve as well. And this cow-horn spoon and this brose bowl would be just about all he carried with him to go to his employment, apart from a few things tied up in a bit of cloth. And what they did was they had soup in that, as well as brose, and their tea. And when they went out in the fields, they would take a chunk of grass, clean the bowl out with it, then dry the bowl off on their filthy trousers."

"They probably ate well," I suggested, meaning compared with a wandering monk in the hills of Burma.

"Yes," she said. "Twice a day."

"They had that filled twice a day?"

"Pretty near."

She told me all this material had been collected by her over the years. She had been open for business about twelve years. If I was interested at all in old cemeteries, I might wish to go upstairs and look at the books. "And I'll leave you to do it while I go and deliver a letter."

Upstairs I discovered that tiny Muthill till recently had had its own train station. There was the actual station sign, looking as if alive. Another sign, originally installed by the Royal Automobile Club, London SW1, reads MUTHILL STATION 1½. And here's a large, dramatic oil painting by Donald Gibson, M.A., of Pitkeallanay

Street, Muthill, depicting a shining black train approaching Muthill Station from Tullabardine in the rain.

Mrs. Wilcox climbs the stairs. "Did you see the collar here?" she says, after sharing a quiet moment of grief with me about the collapse of the railroad age, and picking up a round wooden object that looked like a small toilet seat.

"Ah, the collar of doom! Now, a man would have to wear this for the rest of his life?"

"Yes, in fact he would be in bondage, wouldn't he? But look, he must have been quite a small person."

She closed her eyes. I looked at the collar. "This would be Alexander Stuart's collar, or a copy of it."

She acknowledged it was a copy. "Alex Stuart was sentenced to death in 1701, for housebreaking. Then he would have had his appeal, and the sentence was commuted to life bondage, so he had to wear this collar, and he was assigned to work for local farmers and the like. These sentences were known as acts of doom. I'm sure many a time he would have wished the sentence had been carried out, because life could be pretty grim, especially in those circumstances, as a farm worker. But I don't really know anything about the conditions of life in bondage. I hadn't heard of bondage before just recently."

She pulled out a big old book, *The Surnames of Scotland: Their Origin, Meaning and History*, by George Fraser Black, which offered histories of the various Scottish clans, including many of the minor ones. It said that the McFaddens had their stronghold at Lochbuie on the Isle of Mull until the MacLeans dispossessed them of it in the twelfth century, after which the McFaddens became "a race of wandering artificers" – goldsmiths, in fact – for many centuries on Mull. Also it would appear that the MacLeans dispossessed the McFaddens of their tartan, for when one looks up the name McFadden in a tartan book it says, "See MacLean," and when one looks up MacLean one finds that the lucky McFaddens are even allowed to wear the MacLean tartan on special occasions. Mrs. Wilcox said the Scots were like that all through history, "pillaging and robbing and settling down and breaking up again."

"Someone told me McFadden was originally a Tinker name," I said, "but a goldsmith sounds a cut above a Tinker, no?"

"Not entirely," she conceded, with a laugh. "The Tinkers mended pots and pans, originally. That was the Tinker's trade. But a goldsmith isn't necessarily better than a Tinker."

In another book, *Clan Traditions and Popular Tales*, the earliest record of the name was in 1304, when Malcolm MacPadene appears as a charter witness in a criminal case in Kintyre. Conghan MacPaden is listed as runner-up for the archdeaconry of Argyll in 1390. The book hints he spent the rest of his life in extreme bitterness at having been passed over: sounds like my family all right.

At Mrs. Wilcox's suggestion I headed a few miles south to the village of Braco, near which is located the old Roman fort of Ardoch. It's a complex set of ancient earthworks, indicating that something of tremendous colonial importance was here at one time, a series of forts and whatnot bigger than the present-day village of Braco and Muthill combined. It's like looking down through the depths of a loch and thinking you see the shadow of a monster. Did it move?

Rabbits are leaping into the air then vanishing down their rabbit holes, sheep are grazing all over the place, and I'm walking along the top of seven Roman forts built at various stages during the occupation of Britain. The leaflet says the watchtower is partially obscured by woodland, at the northeast corner of the largest of the forts, number 7. I'm going to have to locate northeast intuitively since I am without a compass. Here's a pine forest, there's a giant chestnut tree, here's a little loch with a liftbridge and a perfectly circular wooded island, but I'm searching for the "watchtower," with no idea what it would look like. It might be of stone or it might be a mere mound by now. This leaflet isn't much help, I don't understand the map, I can't get the aerial views to match up with what I can see from here. *Bacaaach-yeh!* The sheep is giving me one of those Presbyterian stares, having noticed me climbing a fence.

Ah, this would be it: the remains of the watchtower, partially obscured by woodland. Hewn stones are arranged in a perfectly circular pillar that comes up to my navel, and the stones are carefully cut to give them the right curve. A stone wall reaches to the watchtower, with a gap of a few inches between them: just before the wee gap the wall takes a lovely decorative curve, to match the curve of the watchtower. It was a nice touch on the part of the Roman legions to show such class when so far from home. The Romans put their flat slab stones down and along the top they put their vertical slab stones. It would have been a job to scale the wall with that clever row of flat vertical stones along the top.

An arched and unusually narrow stone bridge crosses the fast-moving River Knaik. It must have been of Roman construction, though the Picts also built well (maybe better, since their forts and walls are still standing all over Scotland), and it would only be wide enough for one horse to get across, or a single file of humans. It was in a terribly ruinous state, but it had been recently repaired. A plaque states that it's called the Packhorse Bridge, and it's also known as Ardoch Old Bridge. It was repaired in 1740, and in 1989 it was "refurbished." Now it's all filled in with soil, sprouting with bright green grass.

A motorist has his bonnet up and is scratching his head. His radiator has boiled over, and his girlfriend is about to do the same. He isn't bothered by her petulance. He has a long ponytail and a black suit, and when he sees me looking he says, "Wee bit of overheating here," in a friendly manner. His girlfriend lets out a great sigh of boredom.

"You should get a new one," I said, slyly, meaning the girlfriend, who bore a superficial resemblance to Uppercrust Angela, but he took it to mean a new car, as he was intended to, and so did she. It turned out he still had lots of water in there, so I said that if he wanted he could walk over to check out the Roman camp and by the time he got back the radiator would have cooled down sufficiently for him to proceed, slowly, to the next garage. His girlfriend immediately became angry at the mention of the Roman camp, and she said, "Well, you can go without me," snarlingly, a tall, elegant-looking woman, with a heartful of ugliness. The guy sighed sadly.

In the Highlands birds are soaring for the joy of it. It's late but it's light, for this is June, and in June it looks like noon at nine. At a comfortable farm on the way to Aberfeldy, a comfortable couple said they didn't have a single room. I asked about the hotel I'd passed a few miles south around Amulree. They phoned and reserved a room for me there. These happy, loving people, Mr. and Mrs. McLush, they had thick woollen sweaters on in the chill evening air and they showed me their Highland cattle, with shaggy orange hair and the long curving horns. They had fifty head on one side of the house and on the other side they had fifty sheep. The McLushes preferred the cattle to the sheep, because the latter are stupid while the former have character, you can tell them apart, each has a different look and a different personality. Are they fierce? They did have a prehistoric menace about them.

"Oh no," she said, with her husband nodding enthusiastically, "they're the softest, sweetest, gentlest animals imaginable. People should be so nice."

And then the boy stuck his head out the door and said, "You were talking so loud you woke me up!" – the whiny tone in his voice being redeemed by his cute ironical smile. It was the family smile, the parents had it too. Mr. McLush was a big, fat, sweet-looking guy with a soft voice. And the missus was delighted to be alive and with Mr. McLush. But it was my voice that woke up the kid, so I'll do penance by spending the night in a sedate old hotel at the side of the River Braan, deeply nestled in the Glen of Strathbraan.

After a glass of Laphroaig in the pub to chase away the driving jitters, I go walking upstream along the left bank of the Braan. Thousands of birds start chirping, for their little minds sense the approach of an appreciative ear. We're in the Highlands north of Perth and west of Dunkeld. The Amulree Hotel, "open to non-residents," and with a cornerstone dated 1711, is nine hundred feet above sea level, "where winter comes early and spring is usually late." The dinner menu featured freshly shot venison, locally caught salmon and trout, and various kinds of Angus and Argyll roast beef. It was after ten, but the kitchen was still open for orders. At one point the proprietor said in a loud voice, "I don't like anything that's trendy," and everyone in the pub laughed. I told him that was a good way to be, and it showed independence of spirit.

"It's all part of my conspiracy theory," he said. "I think all the large corporations are trying to manipulate us so that we'll buy, buy, buy. They tease us with trends. I've been fashionably unfashionable all my life, and I try to get my wife to be as well."

"Well, what are you doing, Mr. McFadden?" said his wife, who was working the bar. "Tracing your roots through Scotland?"

No, I said over my ham sandwich and pint of Guinness, but I was finding out about them without trying. I told her about Lochbuie and the MacLean takeover. She thought that was funny, but she wanted me to know that this sort of thing happened all the time, and it wasn't a terrible thing really, when you look back on it. The Scots have in this century done an admirable job of forgetting their bitter differences.

Also in the pub was a middle-aged man and his teenaged son, who was happy to be on a fishing trip with his dad in the Highlands. They were after salmon and sea trout, and they wanted to know if the river "held" any. The dad was enthralling his son with stories about Australian dingoes and giant hibernating toads. Morton's spirit seemed pleased that I noticed this little scene, and pleased that I was at the Amulree. I thought I heard him whisper that, if he were alive today, he'd be just like me.

A TRIP AROUND
LOCH FROACHIE

Amulree • Aberfeldy • Dunkeld • Birnam
Dunsinane • Coupar Angus

Saturday, June 8. The giant spruce trees, black against the turquoise sky last night, are now green against the turquoise sky. The Amulree Hotel sits in a favoured spot, and cloud shadows, interspersed with giant globs of sunlight, are moving up and over the summits of great hills. It's always a turquoise sky over the Highlands at this time of year. Those spruce trees were so gloomy last night, as if listening for the sounds of hostile clans sneaking along the river, and so cheerful this morning, as if glad they made it through another night without having someone strung up in their branches.

In the foyer a bearded young postman is delivering the mail. He lets out a big "Good morning!" I ask him what it's like in the winter around here.

"No mail delivery in the winter around here," he said. Then he laughed. "Och, don't listen to me, I'm dreaming. We have to do it in the winter, too. And it's miserable, and it jis' goes on from November right on to March and it jis' seems as if it'll never stop. It's true, we haven't had a lot of snow the past few years, but it's the black ice, you really need to watch out for that black ice. I guess you don't have black ice where you come from, do you?"

"Are you kidding? I'm from Canada, birthplace of black ice."

"Och, aye," he retaliated, "but ye'll have the dry cold there, and we have the wet cold here."

We were standing by a framed engraving of the hotel as it was in the eighteenth century, all grey stone before it was given a facelift. A group of gloomy, dour Presbyterians stand in front, glaring at the artist. But the shape of the hotel hasn't changed. The posty said that, in the early part of the last century, the mail was delivered four times a week by a runner. By the end of the century it was brought by horse-drawn vehicle every day, and then was delivered to outlying areas such as Glenalmond and Glenquaitch by men on bicycles, while the driver relaxed at the Amulree Hotel and waited for the cyclists to return with the outgoing mail. He also carried passengers. In the twenties a large black motor van brought the mail. In the fifties the post office took over mail delivery with the speedy red minivans still in use.

"Cheerio," he said, and off he went – no need to wait for incoming cyclists with outgoing mail.

They have tourists in the winter, too, says the proprietress, Kate. She shows me a photo of the four-man Dutch shooting party that comes over every winter. They shoot mostly rabbits, bring them back to the hotel to be frozen, and take them back to Holland and sell them to pay for their trip. "They'll take about four hundred back with them to Holland," she says. "It keeps the numbers down, and it's better than mixie, and it's better than us being completely overrun by them. And it's to their favour, too, for it's not nice for them to be overrun."

"Mixie?"

"Mixmetosis. It's sort of a man-made disease that's aimed at killing off the rabbits, but it's terrible to see them. For one thing you can't eat the meat of a rabbit that's had mixmetosis. And it takes them a long time to die. You see them on the side of the road, sitting there looking miserable, with their eyes all bulging out and their ears drooping dreadfully. It's pathetic to see. It takes them over a week to die after they get it. So shooting them is vastly preferable." She also said the bunnies have to kick the little ones out of the nest so that they can give birth to the new ones, that's how often they breed.

Everything in this glen is based on the philosophy that "if the laird makes a profit, everyone makes a profit." That's what the hunting is all about, says Kate. We're having a quiet conversation: she doesn't want to cause any problems or be critical. We're sitting at a small table, with our noses pointed at each other from a short distance, and whispering like a pair of golf announcers.

"Everything this side of the river and the loch belongs to Lord Chelsea," she says. "This is one of his summer residences. They're up here six weeks of the year. Everyone's dependent on the laird. And there are good and bad, the lairds, you know. There are the ones who will put money into the place and who will look after their game-keepers and look after their shepherds. And there are those where it's kind of been redundancy after redundancy, and they don't really care about the people or the place. They're different people. This is more so up north. If you travel further north you'll find all sorts of trouble, foreigners who have come across and bought the estate and have completely changed its way of life and caused so much bad feeling. It's been the Saudis particularly, and we're talking a lot of money. You'll have to go and explore."

Except for the hotel, everyone in the area works for the laird. The shepherds work for him, the gamekeepers, the cattlemen, and their wives go to the laird's house to do housework, make the beds, help with the meals. There's a farm manager, or "factor," who over-sees the shepherds and the gamekeepers, and he's in charge of the whole estate.

A short walk from the hotel is the Amulree Church, built in 1743 to serve a crofting community which declined and disappeared after the Jacobite rebellions. "The glen just emptied," as someone said. The timber used in the construction of the church had been previously used as scaffolding during the construction of a bridge over the River Tay at Aberfeldy. Bolts held the scaffolding together, and the boltholes can still be seen in the pillars and beams supporting the gallery. Services are still conducted here, but the church seems to do double duty as a museum, with numerous artifacts having to do with the old way of life, and with emigration to the New World, principally to southern Ontario. In the church nave, three heavy-duty electric heaters are bolted to the sloping ceilings and pointed directly at the pews. They look like they mean business.

Further back from Amulree, in the remote Glenquaitch area, is Loch Froachie (also spelled Freuchie), which is mentioned by Burns, and out of which flows the River Braan, which gradually becomes more turbulent through several rocky thundering gorges until it enters the River Tay at Inver. Near the southwest shore lies an island on which a dragon used to live, and on the same island at the same time was a rowan tree. The ill-fated Froach, at the request of the Lady Maidh, went to the island to get the dreaded rowan-berries. He successfully eluded the dragon, who was having a nap, and brought the berries back, only to be told that she would now like him to return to the island, pull up the entire tree by the roots, and bring the whole thing back to her. He went back, pulled up the tree with an enormous grunt, which unfortunately alerted the dragon, who woke up and attacked him. Froach's arms and legs were torn off, but he managed somehow with his dying breath to slay the dragon. Lady Maidh found them side by side, dead on the shore. It's always a thrill to visit the actual places where mythological events took place. The island in question, a quick swim from shore, is tiny and heavily wooded, yet, strangely, the area surrounding the lake isn't wooded at all.

The cathedral bells are tolling seven as I ride into the ancient town of Dunkeld after a long, scenic, but uneventful tour of the Tayside region. They are quiet bells, even though close by. The birds are chirping and carolling in Saint Ninian's Gardens. I sit on a bench for a minute, then look up to behold the twelfth-century cathedral with its wonderful old clock tower, and another tower in front of it undergoing repairs and surrounded by scaffolding, and some butchered small ornamental trees, about ten of them, all along the front.

Dunkeld's history goes back to the seventh century, when the extraordinarily enlightened Saint Adamnan, author of *The Life of Saint Columba* and an account of Arculf's pilgrimage to the Holy Land (both Columba and Arculf were Adamnan's contemporaries and friends), established a monastery here to house the ancient relics from the monastic community on the Isle of Iona, which was being threatened by Vikings. The first king of Scotland, Kenneth MacAlpine, had his capital here in the ninth century. Vicious battles have been fought in the streets. Tourists today point their videocams in any direction and shoot. Morton never mentions Dunkeld, but it pops up in most other books about Scotland.

At the entrance to the cathedral, which dates from 1107, there's an ambiguous sign: GUIDE DOGS ONLY, as if hordes of people had been taking their mutts in to chew the pews. Above it is a sign saying NO PICNICS; there's that unpleasant side of the Scottish character, the thing to do when you get a bit of power is prohibit picnics. No sign saying PICNICKERS PLEASE DEPOSIT YOUR JUNK IN THE BASKETS PROVIDED, but just NO PICNICS (signed Mayor Sourpuss McKilljoy).

We can't go in that cathedral, dear, it's only for guide dogs.

Next to Dunkeld is the equally medieval town of Birnam. There used to be a wood here, but it moved to Dunsinane, causing Macbeth to "begin to be aweary of the sun." Birnam is now the site of the Beatrix Potter Garden.

My pink room tonight (walls, bedspreads, sheets, pillowcases, and a Spanish dancing doll, all in pink) overlooks the main street of Coupar Angus, a few miles north of Perth, so for scenery we have two grungy trees and the A94 heading down to Perth. Lorries are going to be thundering by all night long. I go searching for the local pub, as a pint might help me sleep.

At the Cathkin Inn, which is not one of your more pretentious pubs, there's one door to the bar on the left and another to the lounge on the right. In the lounge two guys are playing pool. So I squeeze into the bar, crowded with fast-drinking locals standing ramrod straight and nose to nose, then grab a pint and go back into the lounge, only to find the two pool players are now leaning on their cues and looking up at the television, which is bolted to the upper wall like those heaters at Amulree Church. It was a boxing match for the featherweight championship of the world between an Englishman, Prince Naseem Hamad (a.k.a. Humid Hamad), and a Cuban, Daniel Alicea (a.k.a. Pupino). The fight was at the Newcastle Arena. It was Hamad's second defence of his World Boxing Organization title.

Both boxers were the same age, they had both fought the same number of fights, neither had been defeated, and they both had the same percentage of knockouts. So this looked interesting. The showy Englishman came in on an ornate litter, being held aloft by four black heavyweight Ethiopian tax accountants naked to the waist, while the more modest Cuban shadowboxed quietly in the ring and ignored the show biz. In the second round, Humid Hamad gave the Cuban a roundhouse right to the side of the face as he was getting free of the ropes. One of the pool players shouted out: "That's 'im oot!"

This was a working-class bar for unemployed youth rather than a tourist spot. One fellow was saying he'd never want to box, but they sure make a lot of money at it. The other said it sure ain't worth it, I'm no Einstein, I can't afford to lose any marbles up here. At one point I was in the lounge by myself when a tough-looking young lout came in on his way to the toilet. He brushed against the pool table and knocked a cue stick to the floor. It landed at my feet with a crash. He turned and glared at me, as if I had knocked the cue to the floor myself, and said, sternly, "Pick that up!" I laughed good-naturedly and picked it up. It felt like the best possible thing to do in the circumstances.

When I finished my pint about fifty voices called out, "Bye-bye now, bye man, take care man." A fellow with no pants on followed me out. He was staggering all over the sidewalk. Another fellow staggered out of a car, and they began screaming at each other. Also in front of the pub a woman was quietly trying to remove a bumper sticker from her car. She had a little knife and a bowl of soapy water. The sticker said, I LOVE BATS. So I thought maybe she'd turned against them. Later, I heard on the radio that two Scottish women had been bitten by a bat that day and were being examined for rabies.

REGICIDE AT
LUMPHANAN

*Coupar Argus • Perth • Scone Palace • Blairgowrie
Pitlochry • Spittal of Glenshee • Dunsinane
Lumphanan • Aberdeen • Inverurie*

Sunday, June 9. After my soft-boiled egg, the thoughtful Shonaidh Beattie, recently returned from a disastrous holiday in Majorca (I'll spare you the details), addressed my problem with abbeys and castles closing early: "At the moment they claim they don't have the resources, and there's cutbacks all round. But a lot of these things are of course awful top-heavy with top management. I think if that was cut in half it would be a lot better for tourism."

Speaking of top management, I cheekily asked if her husband helped with the bed-and-breakfast work.

"Well, no, actually he doesn't. Well, a little. But he works full-time with the Environmental Health in Perth."

"Important job?'

"It is, yeah. It's quite an important one, and it's for the whole of Perthshire."

"Is he a scientist?"

"No, he's an assistant manager. In charge of all the contracts and such like. Waste bins, et cetera."

"Important work, keeping Perthshire clean. And he must be doing a good job, because this is an extremely clean county."

"Yes it is. And he works hard to make sure it is."

At the town filling station a talkative woman with jet-black hair pumps petrol for me. It all started out with me saying, "So what did you do last night? It was Saturday night, you know."

"Oh, don't tell me about it," she said. "I stayed home, my kids had all their friends over for a sleep-out, and I had to sit minding all these nine children in the back garden. And then about two o'clock in the morning they heard a noise, and they all wanted to come in and sleep with me. I let them come in, but I didn't let them sleep with me."

"What was the noise?"

"I think it was a sheep or something."

I mentioned my adventures last night in the Cathkin Inn.

"Oh," she said, "this is a hard-drinking town, there's no doubt about that."

"More so than other Scottish towns this size?"

"Probably, because of all the poverty and ignorance we have here. Half the people in this town haven't had a job since the Falklands War, and if you asked them they wouldn't be able to point on the map to the Falkland Islands. Or even tell you what the war was about – if indeed they managed to remember that there was a war by that name. They wouldn't be able to tell you the name of the prime minister if you offered them ten bob."

"Surely you exaggerate."

"Not at all. All they do in this town, I tell you, is drink, get confused, and fall down or get knocked down. There's a nice library in town, but nobody has borrowed a book in twenty-five years. As for television, all they watch is sports, and then they have trouble

al sign
 FAMED
. And then
orley's side, for
ave been written
o is quoted, shame-
, with an imitative tau-
ING ROLLS ARE THE BEST
HE BEST. Not one of the best,
orley. And, tsk, even the fish-
e window saying WE FRY IN VEG-
ust have been playing hooky the day
ntransitive verbs. Even the galleries and

l footpaths and nature trails signposted right
orical walks, cultural walks, nature walks, walks
, walks along the river, and it's a glorious town for
ound, even for people who use Perth as a starting point
mbitious cross-country walks. What better criterion is
r a city or a town or any place you want to live than that it
e seen as a good place for walking, and will probably continue
be long after you can't walk any more?

On entering the vast regal gardens surrounding Scone Palace, two
miles north of Perth, back on the road to Couper Angus, there's a
sign saying MIND THE JACOB'S LAMBS – but there don't seem to be
any lambs at all, though there are plenty of cows grazing away among
the giant oak trees and serene peacocks. Scone Palace is a vast
ictorian country home, very pleasing to the eye, and it's adjacent

following it or remembering the score. You hear them saying, 'What's
the score again?'"

She mentioned that she likes to talk, and her husband does too.
He was a fisherman, but when he got out of that and moved back to
town he developed "sensitive 'earing." He couldn't stand the sound
of the traffic going by after being out on the quiet sea all the time,
and spending all that time in the quiet fishing ports where the only
sounds are the gulls, the waves, and beer barrels running down the
gangplank from the truck to the pub.

So they sold the house and moved out of town to some place
by the river where, aside from the occasional bleating of a sheep, it's
dead quiet. Also, her husband is obsessed with hitchhikers: wherever
they go, if they see a hitchhiker, they stop. And when they pick up a
hitchhiker, such is her husband's kindly nature that they quite often
end up at the place where the hitchhiker wants to go rather than
where they had intended going.

"We even had a gentleman of the road once." She was speaking
about an old Tinker they spotted sitting on a bench in town looking
woebegone, homeless, with a big bag. So they, of course, invited him
home to tea. And he turned out to be the most well-spoken man you
ever did see. He'd never been to Oxford or Cambridge but he was
very heavily educated nevertheless. He was a man of the road, constantly on the move all over Britain. So he had the tea, he said he
had to go now, they said where are you going to sleep, and he said
he was going to sleep in the bus shelter, for he always slept in bus
shelters here and there around the great world.

They said he could sleep over at their place, but he said no,
because if he did, it would get him used to it, and it would spoil him,
it would make it hard for him to sleep anywhere but in a bed any time
in the future, and he would have to go through the ordeal again of
learning to sleep comfortably in bus shelters, garbage dumps, under
bridges, and the like. So they told him he didn't have to sleep in the
bed if he stayed over, they would be pleased and honoured to have
him sleep on the floor. So he finally caved in and slept on the floor

in the guest bedroom right next to a soft, fresh, inviting b
morning they could tell at a glance that the bed ha
touched. It was November, getting close to the coldest
year, he was heading right up to the stormy frozen nor
Scotland, and he had no idea what he was going to l
there, with the possible exception of sleeping in bus she

Rows of English oaks line the road and their tend
branches meet in the middle, causing a sudden delic
with shafts of light beaming through, and at the en
another blinding blast of daylight, with everything a l
trees, the grass.

The proud city of Perth (often pronounced *Pairth*)
for the Isle of Skye Hotel, but there it is. It's a hand
ture too, and one would suppose they might have a
the remote Isle of Skye itself. The Iona Hotel, 1
course, is also here. One might surmise that Perth
been a stopping-off place for English tourists r
Western Isles, except of course for the fact that
route. But one could not imagine a lovelier town
old ladies are ravishingly dressed as they sashay t!
on this warm and sunny Sunday morn, their husb
with Sunday-morning flu.

The Inner Ring is the oldest part of the city, a
seem to be Greek temples all over the place. The
House looks like a Greek temple, as does the City Water works,
which was built in 1832 and has been transformed into the Ferguson
Gallery, with an ugly sculpture of a naked geometric woman out front.
The sculpture has no curves, just angles. There's a lot of that around
Scotland – as if curves were of the devil, and angles of the angels.

There were great tragedies in this town in the storied past, for
sure. A lot of people were burned to death here for such things as
sorcery, dancing on Sundays, and playing cards one minute after

---

a Sunday morning, too. He also seems to be probing her ear with the
tip of his twitching tongue. Maybe the Reformed Baptists looked so
miserable because their eyes had offended them as they passed b
these horny devils.

I'd like to pop into this little bakery with a rather unus
out front, reading MCSORLEY'S MORNING ROLLS AF
MORNING ROLLS. But the store's closed for the da
there's Mrs. McIntyre, obviously a thorn in Mr. Mc
her morning rolls are not only famed but also
about by top authors such as Peter Irving, wl
lessly, right in the window, as having writte
tology perhaps: MRS. MCINTYRE'S MORN
ROLLS IN SCOTLAND, IN SCOTLAND
but the actual best. Take that, M
and-chip shop, with a sign in tl
ETABLE OIL, is closed. They
they studied transitive an
museums are closed.

Perth has wonde
through town, his
along the cana
walking all a
for more
there

can

them for the

A small yellow bus goes by, take
BAPTIST CHURCH, a miserable face in each window. They
they're suffering from too much moral superiority. As the Scots
themselves say (but not these Scots), "One can die of too little
whisky." Right in front of a bakery shop on High Street there's a man
cheekily putting his hand all the way up his girlfriend's skirt, and

following it or remembering the score. You hear them saying, 'What's the score again?'"

She mentioned that she likes to talk, and her husband does too. He was a fisherman, but when he got out of that and moved back to town he developed "sensitive 'earing." He couldn't stand the sound of the traffic going by after being out on the quiet sea all the time, and spending all that time in the quiet fishing ports where the only sounds are the gulls, the waves, and beer barrels running down the gangplank from the truck to the pub.

So they sold the house and moved out of town to some place by the river where, aside from the occasional bleating of a sheep, it's dead quiet. Also, her husband is obsessed with hitchhikers: wherever they go, if they see a hitchhiker, they stop. And when they pick up a hitchhiker, such is her husband's kindly nature that they quite often end up at the place where the hitchhiker wants to go rather than where they had intended going.

"We even had a gentleman of the road once." She was speaking about an old Tinker they spotted sitting on a bench in town looking woebegone, homeless, with a big bag. So they, of course, invited him home to tea. And he turned out to be the most well-spoken man you ever did see. He'd never been to Oxford or Cambridge but he was very heavily educated nevertheless. He was a man of the road, constantly on the move all over Britain. So he had the tea, he said he had to go now, they said where are you going to sleep, and he said he was going to sleep in the bus shelter, for he always slept in bus shelters here and there around the great world.

They said he could sleep over at their place, but he said no, because if he did, it would get him used to it, and it would spoil him, it would make it hard for him to sleep anywhere but in a bed any time in the future, and he would have to go through the ordeal again of learning to sleep comfortably in bus shelters, garbage dumps, under bridges, and the like. So they told him he didn't have to sleep in the bed if he stayed over, they would be pleased and honoured to have him sleep on the floor. So he finally caved in and slept on the floor in the guest bedroom right next to a soft, fresh, inviting bed. In the morning they could tell at a glance that the bed hadn't been touched. It was November, getting close to the coldest part of the year, he was heading right up to the stormy frozen northern tip of Scotland, and he had no idea what he was going to be doing up there, with the possible exception of sleeping in bus shelters.

Rows of English oaks line the road and their tender tangle of branches meet in the middle, causing a sudden delicious darkness, with shafts of light beaming through, and at the end of it there's another blinding blast of daylight, with everything a light green, the trees, the grass.

The proud city of Perth (often pronounced *Pairth*) is an odd place for the Isle of Skye Hotel, but there it is. It's a handsome big structure too, and one would suppose they might have a Perth Hotel on the remote Isle of Skye itself. The Iona Hotel, much smaller of course, is also here. One might surmise that Perth has traditionally been a stopping-off place for English tourists rushing up to the Western Isles, except of course for the fact that it's not really en route. But one could not imagine a lovelier town, and all the little old ladies are ravishingly dressed as they sashay their way to church on this warm and sunny Sunday morn, their husbands being at home with Sunday-morning flu.

The Inner Ring is the oldest part of the city, and at a glance there seem to be Greek temples all over the place. The Perth Sheriff Court House looks like a Greek temple, as does the City Water Works, which was built in 1832 and has been transformed into the Ferguson Gallery, with an ugly sculpture of a naked geometric woman out front. The sculpture has no curves, just angles. There's a lot of that around Scotland – as if curves were of the devil, and angles of the angels.

There were great tragedies in this town in the storied past, for sure. A lot of people were burned to death here for such things as sorcery, dancing on Sundays, and playing cards one minute after midnight Saturday night. As I think these ugly thoughts, a stiff, hot wind comes up from the southwest and almost blows me away. "When you're here," says Mr. Morton, "never for one minute can you feel unconscious of the wildness which lies beyond the gates of Perth . . . you walk through greystone streets, modern; but still, in their skyline and their grim bulk they recall a more ancient Perth, and you smell a wind that comes sweet over miles of desolate heather."

I don't know about that, but two ducks and a tennis ball are floating by on the River Tay, spanned by an old bridge with its seven round arches, any one of which is large enough to coast through on a beer barge. I feel a terrible stranger in Perth. People glance at me, then glance away quickly, wondering if there's anything they could do to hasten me on my way.

Mr. Morton, there are some interesting-looking people around this town, but the hordes of "small, pretty girls" you raved about ("Perth, like Gloucester, where matches are made – this is no pun – is full of small, pretty girls") seem to have lived their lives out and died. You described Perth as being "as Scottish as a plate of cockaleekie or a warm bannock," and that's pretty darned Scottish if you ask me. Also you climbed that hill over there, and came back with a terrific line for your book: "I climbed Kinnoul Hill before breakfast." You mention Bob Andrews, a famed golfer from Perth "who could drive a ball off the face of a gold watch without damaging it." And you have a refreshing comment on a young fellow who wants to be a farmer when he grows up: "What a refreshing lad! No engines in his soul!" When I was a kid there were scads of old-timers with Mortonesque senses of humour. Reading Morton resurrects them for me.

A small yellow bus goes by, taking people to the REFORMED BAPTIST CHURCH, a miserable face in each window. They look as if they're suffering from too much moral superiority. As the Scots themselves say (but not these Scots), "One can die of too little whisky." Right in front of a bakery shop on High Street there's a man cheekily putting his hand all the way up his girlfriend's skirt, and on a Sunday morning, too. He also seems to be probing her ear with the tip of his twitching tongue. Maybe the Reformed Baptists looked so miserable because their eyes had offended them as they passed by these horny devils.

I'd like to pop into this little bakery with a rather unusual sign out front, reading MCSORLEY'S MORNING ROLLS ARE FAMED MORNING ROLLS. But the store's closed for the day. And then there's Mrs. McIntyre, obviously a thorn in Mr. McSorley's side, for her morning rolls are not only famed but also have been written about by top authors such as Peter Irving, who is quoted, shamelessly, right in the window, as having written, with an imitative tautology perhaps: MRS. MCINTYRE'S MORNING ROLLS ARE THE BEST ROLLS IN SCOTLAND, IN SCOTLAND THE BEST. Not one of the best, but the actual best. Take that, McSorley. And, tsk, even the fish-and-chip shop, with a sign in the window saying WE FRY IN VEGETABLE OIL, is closed. They must have been playing hooky the day they studied transitive and intransitive verbs. Even the galleries and museums are closed.

Perth has wonderful footpaths and nature trails signposted right through town, historical walks, cultural walks, nature walks, walks along the canal, walks along the river, and it's a glorious town for walking all around, even for people who use Perth as a starting point for more ambitious cross-country walks. What better criterion is there for a city or a town or any place you want to live than that it can be seen as a good place for walking, and will probably continue to be long after you can't walk any more?

On entering the vast regal gardens surrounding Scone Palace, two miles north of Perth, back on the road to Coupar Angus, there's a sign saying MIND THE JACOB'S LAMBS – but there don't seem to be any lambs at all, though there are plenty of cows grazing away among the giant oak trees and serene peacocks. Scone Palace is a vast Victorian country home, very pleasing to the eye, and it's adjacent to the sacred site of Scone Abbey, in which kings from Kenneth II to James VI were crowned. You don't have to be Morton to feel in the air, and in the prickling of your skin, that numerous wondrous and legendary things happened around here in days of yore.

Elspeth, the gap-toothed seductress at the ticket gate, doesn't mind stating unequivocally that she doesn't know the difference between a palace and a castle, but as for bars and pubs, she thought bars might be a tad more expensive. (Why couldn't that fellow in the "bar" in Kilmarnock have told me that?) We're surrounded by peacocks, but they don't seem to be of the familiar yappy, screeching variety: perhaps they've been trained with royal jolts of electricity only to wail when they absolutely must, so as not to deter tourists from buying tickets.

The occasional tourist bus features a driver behind the wheel reading a golf magazine, taking a break while merry holidayers elbow their way through the palace. Elspeth has a dangerous look in her eye.

"And the palace is actually open on Sundays?" I say, amazed.

"Oh yes," she says, "we're heathens around here."

"I'm not surprised. You have that look about you."

"Oh yes, when I was young I told the minister I didn't think one had to go to church to believe in God, and he told me I was a heathen." She pouted appealingly.

"If the minister said that, you must be, because they oughta know."

"And I've never been to church since."

"Naturally you haven't."

"And the funny thing is, the minister still comes to tea every Sunday."

"That is strange. Probably a tribute to your excellent tea."

"Yes, in this country if you make good tea it doesn't matter if you're Presbyterian or heathen." She smiled broadly, then added that, coincidentally, she was named Elspeth after a famous witch from Dundee.

"And you yourself, would you be a witch?"

The eye contact was like a stick of dynamite.

"You'll have to find out yourself, won't you?"

In the palace, ropes guide the tourists along and discourage them from touching things. Tall, aristocratic-looking ladies, semi-literate but well-versed, dressed splendidly in the tartan of the family, but without the vulgar name tags of the lower classes, chat amiably with the tourists, though not without a whiff of condescension. One can imagine that, as the tourist load increases, the amiability will decrease.

One such woman tells me the eighth Earl of Mansfield lives here. Good guy? Yes, he's just retired. He was a barrister by profession, in London, but when he was made earl, he came back to live in the family home. "He's at the moment sitting in the garden."

"I thought I saw some lazy bastard out there."

"He's no bastard, but he is a bit lazy these days, because we haven't got barristers in Scotland, so he couldn't carry on with his accustomed rigour in his profession. He would have to become an advocate, which is the equivalent of a barrister." I told her I understood perfectly.

The tourists move on, and we continue chatting. "I hear they're having trouble with the lairds up there in Sutherland."

"That all depends who you've met. I know the one they're having trouble with, and he's really a nice guy. You can't help what your forefathers did, can you? He is really a good laird, if you mean the one from Dunrobin Castle. Is that the one?"

"Yes, Lord, Lord . . ."

"Lord Melancholy," she seemed to say, but that can't be right. "Could not be a nicer guy – and he's done everything possible. But he's hated all the time. This chap was in the Metropolitan Police, you know, and he's an aristocrat. He's absolutely switched on to everything that's going on today and everything else too, he's not old, he's in his early forties, and absolutely the most capable person you could meet, and doing the best for everybody. There's always a few wild cards who cause lots of trouble."

She says the problem is simply that the lairds insist people get working harder. And they want to open their castles to the public.

"You can't fund an estate unless you open it for the public."

"Mind you, they also complain about the Saudi Arabian lairds —"

"Oh, the Saudi Arabians are different. Somebody like Lord Melancholy" – that's what it sounded like – "is on every committee for keeping Scotland green, he's on every conservation program known to mankind, he is the most up-to-the-minute chap you could ever meet, and I've met him personally very often and I can tell you he doesn't deserve any of the bad publicity he gets every now and then. And the Saudis, I mean, who wants them anyway? Who wants that sort of money? It's very tainted. Oh, good afternoon, I mean good morning . . ."

Saved by a new bunch of tourists.

Back at the gatehouse, Elspeth is now revealing her political convictions. When I ask if Perth is a bit of a stronghold for Scottish Nationalism, she says: "Everywhere, it's everywhere in Scotland; everybody resents England. We hate the BBC, for instance, because it's always 'we' when they mean England and England only, instead of 'we' when they mean the U.K., like when they're talking about the English football team it's always 'we,' but when they're talking about the Scottish team it's always 'they.' This is infuriating and it gets everybody all riled up." She is speaking calmly, but is giving the impression she is the sort who gets infuriated easily, and would come after you with a poleaxe if, for example, your puppy peed on her petunias. It sounds as if she wouldn't take kindly to any Scot who wasn't annoyed by such ethnic slurs on the part of the BBC.

Now for a nice, long, lonesome Sunday drive, up to Blairgowrie and Pitlochry, following Morton's route into the Highlands, through mountain passes so high that snowdrifts still line the road. In

Blairgowrie, a town of small, unpretentious, but beautiful old stone residences, and nursing homes, and a Centre for Disabled People, I asked a taxi driver, who was sitting behind the wheel reading a Catherine Cookson novel, if she would point me in the direction of the nearest public toilet. "Gent's or lady's?" she said.

North of Blairgowrie it's skiing country, with Mount Mayar at 3,044 feet, Glas Maol at 3,504, Broad Cairn at 3,274, and a bit further north, to the south of Balmoral Castle, surrounded by Balmoral Forest, Mount Lochnagar at close to 4,000 feet. Shee is the name of the glen we're passing through, and a village called the Spittal of Glenshee is home for numerous ski-outfitting stores.

Once into Aberdeenshire a certain sub-alpine atmosphere takes over: roadside cafés with roughly hewn and brightly painted timbers used as rustic columns supporting the roof of the porch. This is a heavily forested area of tall pines, and on a huge rock is engraved YOU ARE IN THE HIGHLANDS. The lilacs are out, and a large variety of fruit trees are all beautifully in bloom.

Macbeth didn't die at Dunsinane as Shakespeare, who had to get it all in five acts, tells us. He died in Lumphanan, a remote village at an obscure road-crossing twenty-two miles west of Aberdeen. Loch Ness has its monster, and Lumphanan has Macbeth. In a pub at Lumphanan the locals talk about their attempts to get Lumphanan on the tourist map as the place where Macbeth is known to have met his much-foretold and much-imagined doom. Generally speaking, the inhabitants of Lumphanan are not highly educated folks, but they have a lot of common sense: they hate the Bard and revere Macbeth, who was only doing his job, and in fact was a very good king.

From under the bar, proprietor Allen Kier whips out his little library of newspaper clippings about "Lumphanan's Curious Claim." Everyone who has written about it seems to be firmly on the side of the village: Macbeth died here. The whole thing is taken much more seriously than Loch Ness's claim to a monster.

After his defeat at Dunsinane, Macbeth, not dead yet, fled northwards. He crossed the Cairn o' Mounth, then forded the River Dee at Kincardine O'Neil. Malcolm and Macduff, hot on his trail, spent the night of August 14, 1057, at Kincardine O'Neil, where Malcolm remained the next day, while Macduff continued on in pursuit. Macduff caught up with Macbeth at the Water of Tarland, near Queen's Hill, and a running battle took the forces towards Lumphanan, Macduff finally capturing and killing Macbeth on a nearby hill. Macduff triumphantly bore the severed head of Macbeth on a golden platter back to Malcolm, who'd spent all day and long into the evening wading in the Dee with several local ladies.

Macbeth was killed atop the Peel of Glenfarnon, a circular mound surrounded by a ditch. To the east, across a farmer's field beside an old railway, sits Macbeth's Stone, where, after his death, his body was taken and his head cut off. At the side of a lane, a hundred yards from Saint Vernon's Church, the half-hidden Macbeth's well still gives forth cold, clear water. This is where his head was washed. There are other stories that seem contradictory at first glance, but on closer inspection they all ring true. This is also an area with a rich history of witchcraft, superstition, and public burnings of alleged witches. For instance, the names of several members of a coven active during Shakespeare's early years are known: Helen Rogie of Findrach was tried on charges of witchcraft and then, still protesting her innocence, she was strangled, burned, and buried in 1597 on the Heading Hill on Aberdeen's Castlegate. The strangler received 13 shillings, 4 pence, for his work.

In Morton's day, Aberdeen was famed, jokingly, as the place where all the jokes got invented. Morton has an outlandishly unfunny and boring fantasy about an Aberdeen factory that produces jokes for global consumption. Then he offers a peculiar description of the fish market there. "Seeing a man with a basket of fish," he writes, "what man could not look inside to see what is in there?"

A place may seem interesting, but after I've stayed two or three hours I'm overcome with restlessness. Such a place is the Sunset Boulevard Family Entertainment Centre, which skirts the Aberdeen seafront. It's a vast amusement park sitting on a broad beach that runs the five miles between the mouth of the River Don and the mouth of the River Dee. In fact, in old documents Aberdeen was known as Aberdon – the mouth of the Don – which annoyed the people who preferred the Dee over the Don. So persistent and loud became the resentment of the Dee-ites, that the name of the town was changed to Aberdee, the Mouth of the Dee. But then the Don-ites started up their caterwauling, and the name was changed once again, in a brilliant Dark Age compromise, with wisdom rivalling King Solomon's, to its present spelling.

Sunset Boulevard boasts a yellow neon sign against a gold-painted background, and the sign is about half a mile long and fifty feet wide – in other words about the same size as the ancient fish market this huge funhouse replaced. One walks in to the sound of a canned voice calling out, over and over, "Ridge Racer, Ridge Racer." At the entrance are two full-size plastic statues of generic Afro-Scottish jazz musicians, one with a saxophone and the other with a trumpet. The place is bigger than a communal Norwegian barn at milking time: there's hardly anyone in here, but the noise is deafening. Everywhere there are high-tech slot machines and digital devices into which whole pocketsful of pound coins must be inserted for entertainment purposes. Each mechanical device has its own canned voice, pleading for passersby to play. The Ridge Racer turns out to be a full-scale Formula One car. One gets in, and there's a screen in front of it, and that's about all I can say about it, because nobody is playing it and I've driven enough today.

There are bumper rides, photo rides, and virtual-reality boxing matches, where you get to spar with your favourite boxer of all time, if he's on the list: you can hurt him all you want, but he can't hurt you, except in the pocket. On-screen interactive experiences, in which the human being gets to push an assortment of buttons and the electronic being gets to come alive, can be costly and probably lead to leukemia or brain tumours, impotence, drug addiction, chronic ennui, cataracts, and teenage suicide.

Fifteen bowling lanes will soon be joined by twelve new ones, owing to "public demand." "It's my party and I'll cry if I want to" is playing over the bowling-alley loudspeakers, along with the canned sound of balls going down the lane and scattering the pins. But nobody's playing. Also there's nobody in the Wobbly Pins Lounge Bar, where you can get real pints of Guinness. BOWL INTO THE NIGHT, suggests a sign. Another says, WHY NOT GRAB A FEW FRIENDS FOR A FUN-TASTIC BOWLING PARTY — STAFF PARTIES, BIRTHDAY PARTIES, ETC. — NO PARTY TOO BIG OR TOO SMALL — FOOD SERVED ALL DAY — WHY NOT SAMPLE OUR EXTENSIVE RESTAURANT MENU AFTER YOU FINISH BOWLING — WHY NOT EAT WHILST YOU BOWL. But at twenty pounds a lane, the prices seem prohibitive. Kris Kristofferson is playing the Capital Theatre in Aberdeen this week, and word is that they're trying to get him out to Sunset Boulevard for a few free frames of bowling. By the time you read this, I suspect the place will be bankrupt.

It's eleven o'clock at night and a grey salmon three miles long slowly swims across the pink western sky from south to north. My room is on the second floor of a remote old farmhouse, halfway between Inverurie and Huntly, twenty-six miles northwest of Aberdeen. Mrs. Blair, the proprietor, is a short, fat lady of about sixty, with beautiful skin and a friendly smile. I complimented her on the spacious bed in my room and made some stupidly impertinent joke about picking up a couple of floozies at the local pub.

"This is a Christian bed and breakfast," she said, with a terribly alarmed look on her face. "This is not allowed."

I apologized profusely, her face went back to normal, and she flashed her lovely smile again.

"God bless you," she said. "I had ye pegged for a good Christian man right from the start, and I'm never wrong about such things." She seemed to be using the term Christian in its broadest sense, to include Jews, Arabs, Hindus, Buddhists, Animists, Pedophiles, anything, as long as they behaved themselves.

I also complimented her on the big lily in the sunny porch, with great white blossoms. "Oh, we had the hot sun a couple of days ago and it dried them out. You should have seen it before. And they're called arum lilies." And she said the plant belonged to her grandmother. "It's about to celebrate its fortieth birthday." She'd been repotting it and replanting it all these years, ever since she was first married. No wonder she was pleased to hear people say nice things about it.

CHAPTER 13

SOMEWHERE A DUCK
IS QUACKING

*Kirkston of Culsalmond • Glenfiddich • Findhorn
Dufftown • Balvenie Castle • Glenlivet • Tomintoul
Tomnavoulin • Ballandalloch Castle*

Monday, June 10. Behind the house stands an old, black, sway-back, hammerhead horse with its snout down around its front hooves. It's standing there sunk in mystical contemplations, with a dozen free-range chickens scurrying around its dangerously bowed legs. This is a horse that has the sort of legs a cowboy gets from riding horses all day. Also, there's a collection of old blacksmith anvils, and there are two curling stones, one on each side of the back door, and each with a whitewashed cement bunny sitting on top. I didn't hear any roosters this morning, but they might have been drowned out by the numerous chickens all clucking away at top volume.

A bowlful of unusual-looking morning rolls sat on the dining-room table. "We call 'em butteries," said Mrs. Blair. "And you can eat them like that, or you kin poot them in the toaster and heat them if you want. They're fairly good, or we think so." Did she make them herself? "I cawn make them, but I didn't make them ones, I didn't have time yesterday. So jis' help yourself. Made from flour and butter they are – but you poot them in there and they'll soften." She points to the great wide-mouthed toaster. "In fact they are better warrum than they are cold. We like them better warrum anyway, so we poot them in the toaster."

She got out a map and marked with little crosses a whole series of castles and old "Pictish stowens" within an hour of Kirkston of Culsalmond. She told me if I were to consider returning tonight, after my exploration of the area, she'd give me a big reduction, "because then we wouldn't have to wash the sheets but the once, and we like to pass the savings on to the customer."

An hour's downpour left broad puddles all around reflecting the black and white clouds sailing across the upside-down sea of the sky. The Department of Highways sign says NO ROAD MARKINGS FOR ONE MILE, and some smartypants has crossed out MARKINGS. Glenfiddich Distillery is over to the right. Findhorn, the world-famous New Age meditation centre, is a bit north of here, on the coast. An old man with a cane, and carrying a bright red plastic bag, stops to stare as I go by.

Dufftown has an unfair sense of remoteness about it, as if it would be better off elsewhere. It's a spacious town with a wide main street and an old clock tower in the spacious town square. The occasional tourist rushes around in white running shoes, and blinking at a high rate of speed. There won't be a lot of tourists, however, because this is way off the tourist route: Morton, the great pioneer of tourist routes, never visited Dufftown.

In the Art Shoppe in Dufftown I confessed to the saleswoman that I was admiring rather than making a purchase, for whenever I see lovely watercolours such as she had on display I'm more tempted to take up watercolours than to buy a painting. "Oh yes, many are like that, unfortunately," she said. She seemed on the verge of tears, so it seemed best to take off before I bought something I didn't want.

In the antiquarian bookstore the short, skinny clerk, with a hyperactive Adam's apple and a penchant for telling hoary old jokes about the weather as if he'd made them up, has been talking about flying RCAF jets during the Falklands War. From the counter I picked up an old magazine with pictures of UFOs on the cover and asked if, when he was a pilot, he ever saw any of these.

"No, I was a navigator," he said. "I never looked out." He laughed. "No, that's not true," he added, "but I never came across anything that couldn't be explained naturally – except that Russian submarine that managed to get away from me." More laughter. "To be honest with you, people are becoming convinced there is something behind all these sightings. A lot of books have been written about it. In fact, we have a whole section on UFOs at the back. But I still find it odd – it seems that more flying saucers have crashed in America than anywhere else. Which says a lot more about the Americans than it says about flying-saucer navigators, I'm sure. As far as I know one hasn't crashed in the United Kingdom. But I'm not surprised, given the weather."

I asked why the streets were so wide in such an old town as Dufftown. "Oh, it's not an old town," he said, "it's a fairly new town, a planned town, built from scratch, in 1819."

People were emerging into the sunlight after a tour of the Glenfiddich Distillery, a relatively small plant with a vast parking lot for tourist buses. Like cinemas with their popcorn counters, Scottish distilleries make more money from tourists than they do from whisky sales. Across the road from Glenfiddich, a few miles northeast of Dufftown, stood the thirteenth-century Balvenie Castle, and Glenlivet Distillery is nearby on the other side of a handsome old train bridge with its tracks rusted out.

"Hi, Honey, how are you, little gal?" In the ticket office for Balvenie Castle, I'm tickling an affectionate dog behind the ears.

"Oooo, whooo!" she replies.

The woman frowning over a crossword puzzle behind the counter has trouble with my accent, as I have with hers.

"Honey's not used to having visitors," I observe.

"That's quait guid, izzen tit?"

"How are the crosswords coming along?"

"No too bawd, I git goin' an' then I cheat. Th' answers're in th' back."

"Do you ever get complaints about the Union Jack flying? Not that I wish to complain, it's just that most castles fly the Scottish flag solo."

"Eh noo, niver at all, we've niver had a complaint yait that I knoo of. But th' postman who brings oop th' meel, he cooms by an' he asks us why haivn't ye goot th' lion flyin'. Yis, an' some o' th' bats are barefaced bastards, real problems we'd poot it in th' barefaced truck." She seems to be saying (I think) that it's the birthday of someone in the Royal Family, and that's why they're flying the Union Jack.

"You don't have it up every day then?"

"Noo, we've th' floggin' it oop in th' Scotch o' Scotland, it's like this." She shows me a miniature Scottish flag for sale. "We poot it oop thair, un of the mid lots. But th' side flag was first transferred, partly in th' middle of some firstborn thair like with Prince Philip."

"Ah, that makes sense."

"So that way we niver fergit to poot oop th' Union Jack."

"Of course not. And do you live in Dufftown?"

"Noo, we jis' live back over thair." She points to a junk-strewn house fifty yards back of the parking lot.

"Oh, lucky you. You and Honey can walk to work. And with a real thirteenth-century castle in your backyard."

"Yis, we jis' look out th' window an' thair it is."

"What's the most important thing to know about this castle, if you only know one thing about it?"

"I'm no really sure, but I ken that Mary, Queen of Scots, were here a coople o' taims."

"That would be before the castle was wrecked?"

"Aye, yis. Th' byook they jis' poot it away, they poot th' candles away, they poot th' bells away, and they took th' valcobles out an' jis' wint away and leff tit."

"Were there a lot of massacres and stuff like that here?"

Her voice becomes clear and sober. "I think thair have been," she says. "Thaire've bin quite a few bottles thair, accordin' to th' byook."

"I'll check the book."

"Will, I've half read it, but it says thair were quite a few bottles. So I soopooz thair would 'ave bin. Mine ye, that'd be yairs ago."

Balvenie was a massively fortified castle; if they didn't like you, you got killed, unless you had leverage. It was built in the thirteenth century as the "mighty stronghold of one of Scotland's foremost barons" (Alexander "the Black" Comyn, Earl of Buchan, 1244–1289), and remained a "noble residence" for four centuries. It started out as a mere "defensive shield" and ended up as a "stately mansion befitting a Renaissance lord." Today it's a roofless, window-less shell – but some restoration has been done. New wooden stairs lead up to a new second floor. As you enter there's a picture showing Mary, Queen of Scots, and her entourage arriving at the castle in September 1562. It was a busy place then. Now, there's nothing going on. It's empty save for a lonesome songbird.

The quadrangular ground-floor common room somewhat resembles the much larger one at Linlithgow, but in the centre, instead of a fountain, there's the original well, which is probably older than the first building on this site. I shout down: "Hawhoo, hawhoo!" It's not that deep, only about thirty feet, judging from the echo, and from the fact that I can see the bottom. It used to be deeper, but now it's filling up with old beer cans.

The fifteenth-century "Great Chamber" would have been the main apartment. The kitchen is about ten by twenty feet and would have housed an oven enormous enough to cook an entire stag and have room left over for roast potatoes. Somewhere a duck is quacking. The original slop drain is still in existence; it runs through the wall and into what used to be the moat. Shivering, starving peasants huddled naked at the slop drain on cold nights, hoping for something vaguely edible to come sliding down, and taking turns getting a bit of the escaping heat – like homeless people today huddling in the lanes that run behind restaurants. And now a terrible ruckus heralds the arrival of three cars full of tourists, definitely not quiet, studious types. I steal into his lordship's inner chamber, built in 1410 for the Earl of Atholl.

A famous battle was fought nearby, on the other side of the River Livet, on October 3, 1594. The Campbell chief was only nineteen, but he raised an army of twelve thousand men from his own clan and from the MacLeans, Grants, McNeills, MacGregors, and Macintoshes. They met the Gordons and their clan allies at Glenlivet. But the Campbell forces panicked, turned tail, and ran. This was the last time the Highlanders took the harp into battle. After that it was pipes only.

Tomintoul, close to Tomnavoulin (base camp of the Tomnavoulin Distillery), is known as the highest town in the Highlands (though, curiously, there are slightly higher towns in the Lowlands). Off in the distance, great blue mountains lose their summits in misty clouds. The Cairngorm mountains tower above the surrounding multicoloured hills, the Ladder Hills, the Hills of Cromdale. It's like being at sea: there are all these rolling waves and suddenly there's a big wave. A big wave is when the sea tries to break loose from the earth's gravity; a big mountain is when the earth tries to do the same. Scotland is one big thermostat: when the sun comes out it warms up and starts to rain, and when the sun goes behind a cloud, things cool off and it stops raining. That's why everybody from

Tinker to laird wears warm and dry Harris-tweed jackets and caps. It's a wonder they don't make houses out of Harris tweed.

Ballandalloch Castle has been sitting at the juncture of the Avon and the Spey, in the shadow of stately Ben Rinnes ("Banffshire's landmark"), since 1562, when a laird, who claimed he heard the wind telling him to build a castle there, built a castle there. In the tourist brochure, written by some sly Kafkaesque copywriter, no doubt, it's billed as "The Castle You Would Love to Live In." As I was coming down the long, narrow, and steeply descending walled lane leading to the castle, a hefty tourist bus was coming up: no passing places were in sight, so I prudently pulled over as far as possible, to within an inch from the wall. Still, it looked as if the bus was going to hit me, so my only option seemed to be to pull over even further and ahead. But when I did, an outstanding sharp stone delivered a puncture to the outside rim of my left front tire. The bus sailed on, I pulled ahead a bit onto some flat ground, figured out how to work the jack, got the car lifted up, had the wheel removed, and was putting the new wheel on, when who should come around the corner in a spanking new top-of-the-line Land Rover but the laird and lady of the estate. They were turning down into the no-cars-allowed area. They stopped.

"I say, are you all right there? I say, are you *doing* all right there? What happened? Is there anything we can do for you?" I was on my knees with my shirtsleeves rolled up and with greasy hands.

"Thanks, but I don't need anything, it's coming along fine," I said. "I might need to wash my hands when I'm finished though."

"Oh, just come down here. There's a public washroom down here. And were you going in to see the castle? Can we give you a free pass?"

"No, thank you, I'll be okay."

The lady, who was in the front passenger seat and gawking over the laird's shoulder, had a bright idea: "Can we get you a cup of tea?"

"No, thanks. I'll be fine."

"Oh, all right then, carry on," they cried cheerily. And off they went.

Back for the night at the Blair Farm: a black-and-white border collie with intelligent and sorrowful eyes was limping badly, its left front paw tucked under its leg in a peculiar way so it had to walk, with great difficulty, using the front of the shin as a paw. I could feel the pain as he struggled to get out of my way. So I started patting him and telling him not to worry, we were going to get him looked after. And I told him to lie down, because I didn't want to see him walking on it. So he lay down.

Two farmers were sitting chatting at the back of the kitchen.

"I think we have a problem with this dog out here," I said.

"Problem? What problem?" They didn't move a muscle.

"Seems to have broken his leg."

"Och, no. He's been like that for nigh on sixteen year or more."

Turned out when the dog was young it developed a tumour on its shoulder. When the tumour was removed, the surgery was botched, a nerve was severed, and it affected his leg in some way. He hasn't been able to walk properly since.

Joining me for dinner tonight were Mr. and Mrs. Walter Morris, a middle-aged couple from Manchester, and Mr. and Mrs. Kappy Snortz, an older couple from Basel. First course was macaroni soup that tasted as if it had been made with water poured from an old barnyard rubber boot. I managed to get most of it down, and pretended it was fine. Everyone was either pretending it was good or they sincerely didn't taste anything wrong. Mrs. Blair was placing numerous bowls of food in the middle of the table, and we had to pass them around. The mashed potatoes carried the strangest bouquet of puréed tennis balls. The chops weren't lamb, they weren't pork, they weren't beef, but they were cooked to a crisp all the way through, and they reeked of that kind of grease you can get only in ten-gallon tubs at the hardware store. The broccoli tasted as if it had been boiling in the pot around the clock since last Wednesday, until there was nothing left of it, then it was left to go cold, and then it was slathered with a mucusoid farrago of assorted farmyard carcinogens. Also there was a great heaping bowl full of tiny cobs of corn, so limp and lifeless you could have spread them on your bread as margarine. With every mouthful, Mrs. Morris from Manchester kept raving about how delicious everything was.

"That were good, that were," she oinked, causing the Swiss couple to glance at me anew. Mr. and Mrs. Morris were an attractive, well-dressed, and intelligent-looking couple. They wouldn't have looked out of place perched in a Land Rover. Through no fault of their own, they didn't know verbs and subjects were supposed to agree, but they were certainly a bright couple. In fact, as we ate, they entertained us with metaphorical tales of daily life, sprinkled with philosophical ideas of great subtlety and sophistication. "We had a begonia once," said Mr. Morris. "We had it for about twenty years. Oh yes, we just went out one day and bought it. And how long did we have it, dear?"

Mrs. Morris looked around, a bit embarrassed, then said, in a lukewarm monotone, "For about twenty years."

"Yes, that's what I thought, twenty years. And we gave cuttings of it to all our friends and neighbours. And then one day she" – he jutted a contemptuous nose wife-wards – "just got fed up with it and threw it out."

Mrs. Morris looked around the table, trying hard not to look mortified. "I didn't get fed up with it, and I didn't throw it out. I just took it out and planted it in the garden."

Kappy Snortz said he'd recently taken up the study of Latin. A thought bubble appeared over Mr. Morris's head: "The bloody fool can barely speak English, what's he learning Latin for?" And over Mrs. Morris's head: "Blimey, I wish Walter was more like that." Kappy and Mrs. Snortz spoke good French with a German accent, a bit of Italian, but her English was much better than his.

We were chatting quietly about linguistics, and about the well-known phenomenon of people whose first language is English having such a hard time learning other languages, while people from non-English-speaking countries pick up new languages in a flash. Mr. Morris, who had an unpleasant, whiny, and certifiably paranoid manner of speaking, and who had a tooth sticking straight out over his lower lip (giving him the appearance of a slater's knife), listened with the gravest disapproval. He had obviously never heard anything so ridiculous in his life, and didn't believe it for a minute. How could we sit there making malicious statements about the English people, in the company of an actual Englishman? He was miffed beyond tears, but was trying not to show it.

Besides begonias and linguistics, the couple from Manchester were interested in *Coronation Street*, a television program on which this kind of radical, back-stabbingly slanderous talk about the English would not have been tolerated for one split-second. I never did find out what Mr. Morris did for a living, but his missus told us he worked shifts. He was also interested in football, but only when England was in international play; otherwise he had no time for it. And that was about all he was interested in – except that he had a tremendous hatred of anything to do with the European Union. He snarled and sneered viciously about it, and seemed to think that people who weren't English were subhuman. He did not want British money going to support poor countries.

"Oh," I said, "you mean you don't like to see EU money going to build motorways in Ireland?" He dropped his fork and looked at me in stunned disbelief. He had not heard of that, but obviously it must be true, I couldn't possibly have made it up. He was scandalized, and given more fuel, but he tried hard to pretend that he knew about those Irish motorways all along.

The couple from Switzerland said that was the reason their country refused to join the EU: they were rich and didn't want to share with the poorer countries. And since they didn't seem to agree with their country's position on that score, I managed to refrain from asking how Switzerland got so rich.

The Swiss couple retired early, leaving Mr. and Mrs. Morris to sit in the television room, swapping metaphysical insights with Mr. and Mrs. Blair. I strolled past the room and gave a big smile. Mr. Morris glared at me, pushed the door shut, and locked it. I sat down in the sunporch and began going through old newspapers, mostly containing news of the Royal Family. I could hear enough of the muffled conversation to know it was revolving around plants, bulbs, cuttings, and giving cuttings to the neighbours. Occasionally Mr. Morris would say something that would annoy Mrs. Morris.

A high wind suddenly came up over the hills and was whistling through the eaves in an unsettling manner. God forbid anyone should be in trouble in the North Sea. There was a nice little collection of books here, mostly boys' adventure stories. A few of them seemed to have been former inmates of the Dundee Public Library. I think Evelyn (Mrs. Blair) is from down that way, and one of the books was presented to her in 1938, so I imagine she's about seventy. But she can't cook worth a dang, and I felt a bit hurt by being excluded so rudely from their little soirée.

Later, when I was coming back from my walk, and was coming up the stairs to my room, I was treated to the lovely sight of Mrs. Morris in a flimsy, pink, fluffy negligée. She came bouncing out of the bathroom in this terribly intimate attire, and I stopped two steps down and lowered my head respectfully so she could slip by fast without being embarrassed. But when I looked up she was still standing there looking down at me, and she said, "Good night!" with such a sweet and sincere smile that I was touched and amazed. I said, "Good night!" and we went into our respective rooms. An unintentionally bawdy fantasy flickered through my mind. It ended with Mrs. Morris saying: "That were good, that were!"

From my window the carbonated lime of the nighttime sky is visible behind streaming flimsy little bedsheets of white cloud, and sometimes blankets of thicker grey cloud, which turn the lime into sapphire. Nothing can stop these cloud formations on their slow sail northwards. For a while there was a small black cloud, round as a soccer ball, in the middle of which the evening star was shining, but a little squad of big thick white clouds moved in and pushed the cloud away (but not the star). In this remote area the sky must be a riot of constellations and galaxies in the full night of sober winter.

A solitary truck, toy-like with red and gold lights, steams by along the distant dark highway, the sound very faint, then growing in the silence until it reaches its screeching peak and then gradually fading until it disappears again, the colours in their little oval of light moving and bending along the unilluminated highway. This long protracted twilight, this gloaming, appears to be good for the soul, don't ask me why.

SUENO'S STONE

Burghead • Dingwall • Forres • Inverness
Loch Ness • Glengarry • Tomdoun

Tuesday, June 11. I went to bed last night wondering about Mr. Morris's motives in slamming the door in my face. When I woke up I remembered: as we were finishing last night's meal, Mrs. Blair came into the dining room, looked straight at me, and said, "Well, would ye like yer braikfist at eight agin in th' morning?" I said yes, that would be fine. I figured she would ask the others, and if there was any difference of opinion we could compromise, so that we'd all have it at the same time and make things easier for our hard-working hostess. But Mr. Morris spoke for everyone, in the kvetchiest tone, "Well! I guess we'll *all* have to have it at eight then," suggesting that as usual the foreigner is the favoured guest and the English working man has to suffer for it. My blood ran cold for a moment: it was okay by me if we had it at nine or even ten for that matter. But I didn't say anything. We McFaddens have stubbornness bred in the bone. There doesn't seem to be much we can do about it. And it gets worse with age.

But Mr. and Mrs. Morris were already sitting at the breakfast table when I showed up at eight, and to my relief the breakfast was fine: porridge, a couple of perfect soft-boiled eggs with rich orange yolks right off the farm, and some blissfully good rolls Mrs. Blair made herself, whole-wheat kaisers, hot from the oven. Maybe I'd been too critical about last night's meal.

Mr. Morris was at the top of his form. "I slept like a log – and woke up in the fireplace." He looked away, feeling pleased with his joke, and for having forgiven me. His wife looked at me and fluttered her eyes.

"Ohh," she exclaimed, "that were an old joke, that were." Her eyes semaphored that she'd made him promise to be nice to me or else she wouldn't be nice to him, and he had reluctantly agreed, and now he was glad he had, if he hadn't been earlier. But the devilish McFadden genius was about to strike again, leaving me to imagine a better world with me dead and buried.

"I don't understand people having problems driving on the left," Mr. Morris said, with a flourish that emphasized his genial good spirits. "If they has problems driving on the left, why in the name of the Lord don't they just follow the person in front of them?"

I laughed, way too loud, a repeat of the disaster involving the trombonist at Jedburgh. Everyone seemed to be looking at me with terribly serious looks on their faces. Whatever could he be laughing at? They thought that the man from Manchester had made a perfectly reasonable statement.

"You've been listening to the Goon Show again, haven't you?" I said with the sweetest smile.

He looked at me. He didn't know if his feelings should be hurt or what. Oh oh, I thought. He really is serious.

"No, I'm being serious," he said.

"Oh, I'm terribly sorry," I said. "I thought you were making a joke. Yes, why indeed wouldn't they follow the car ahead? An interesting philosophical question to be sure. Let's see now, there must be a reason. Oh, I know: it's simply because they're ignorant foreigners."

He didn't like that. The Swiss couple appeared busy with the morning paper. It's true what mother used to say, an idle mind is the devil's breeding ground.

On my way out Mrs. Blair wanted to know where I was going today. I gave her a big smile and said I was off to find the Loch Ness Monster. "Ohh!" she exclaimed, brightly. That explained everything. She wished she'd known that before. She couldn't wait to tell Mr. and Mrs. Morris from Manchester, and Mr. and Mrs. Snortz from Basel, and of course her husband, and all his friends. Pretty soon the whole town will know about it. "Probably a snick from the tourist board," her husband would say, but he's always that way.

In Burghead, a late-medieval town on the coast east of Inverness, people are taking their dogs for walks along the sweeping yellow beach. I'm sitting in my car listening to the radio. A woman phones in from Dingwall.

"And how's Dingwall this morning?" asks the radio host.

"It's all right, I guess," she says. "It's dry," she adds.

"Oh, and have you got your washing done then?" he inquires.

"Most of it, not all of it yet," she says. She sounds worried, though. Her name is Evelyn MacLennan and she's having some problems with her husband. She wants to leave a message for her husband, in case he happens to be listening to the radio, wherever he might be. He's a great radio listener, and this is the only station in the area. The message is "You forgot my birthday." "What's your husband's name?" inquires the host. "Stephen," says Evelyn. "Where does he work?" "He doesn't work, he's away with his brother today, and I know he'll be listening to the radio." "Well," says the host, "to Stephen MacLennan, a wee slap on the wrist for you."

Sueno's Stone is a towering Pictish monument near the town of Forres, where Macbeth found the witches, and overlooking Findhorn Bay. The stone is richly carved, but it won't suffer further weather damage as long as its massive Plexiglas enclosure survives. On the back of the stone is carved a purely Celtic cross, a late addition – but directly below the cross is a circle enclosing two skinny, bent figures facing each other; above the circle, a pair of little people are bending down and seemingly whispering in the ears of these elongated people in the circle, as if the people above the circle are angels, and the people within the circle are ordinary mortals receiving celestial messages (sort of like Morton and me).

Anna Ritchie, who has written at least seven lucid books on prehistoric Scotland, says the term Pictish describes a relative amalgamation of indigenous tribes in the face of post-Roman invasions from the Norse and the Scotti: the Pictish tribes amalgamated only to disappear, which would serve not only as a warning to indigenous peoples everywhere, but also serves as an excellent refutation of the old slogan, "United we stand, divided we fall." Legend has demonized the Picts, but they were a "perfectly respectable population," says Anna Ritchie, and they mirrored what was going on in the rest of Europe at the time, with kingdoms emerging and drinking from the pool of cultural traditions of Rome and the Church. They remind me of the ancient Etruscans: they made beautiful walls and brochs (stone forts), and, according to the occasional portrait incised on pieces of slate, they even had the look of Etruscans. There is no real evidence the Picts were indigenous, nor is there any evidence that the Picts painted themselves blue, except for one Roman report that one naked Pict was once seen running around painted in that colour.

The earliest stones on which Pictish symbols are carved appear to be from the sixth century, and probably followed a long period in which they painted symbols, of which there are no traces remaining. In the eighth century, Christian stone crosses, like the high crosses of Ireland, begin to appear, at first with Pictish symbols, but soon with Celtic symbols only. It's apparent that the Picts were influenced by Christianity, but whether they disappeared by intermarriage or by massacre or by both is not known. Anna Ritchie thinks they were "absorbed" by historical pressures into the foundation of what is now Scotland.

A great battle scene is depicted on one side of Sueno's Stone, in four large cartoon-like panels representing cavalry, infantry, and the capture and beheading of the defeated. These solemn, silent panels are surrounded by carved depictions of vegetation, with little people standing among the leaves. The stone, obviously a memorial to a battle of extreme importance, had been buried and was unearthed in the eighteenth century in this approximate area. It is said to represent a "fine mixture" of Northumberland, Irish, and Pictish traditions. Some think the stone commemorates a battle between a Scottish–Pictish force and the Norse in the late ninth or early tenth century, others that the stone represents the vanquishing of the Picts by the Scots under Kenneth MacAlpine in the mid-ninth century, while a third group maintains the stone represents the battle, in AD 966, during which the Scottish King Dubh was killed by the men of Moray. But who buried the stone and why?

Go to National Tyre, someone told me. They always have everything. So that's where I went to get my tire (or tyre) repaired in a little rainswept seaside industrial area not far from the Inverness town centre. The receptionist was named Liz, in her twenties, thin, small, about four-foot-ten, and wearing a lipstick-red cardigan and a pair of faded and alarmingly worn bluejeans. She dropped everything to wait on me, and went out with me to the car. I opened the boot, and before I knew it she had hauled the wheel right out of there and hopped in herself.

"Take me away from all this," she pleaded, jokingly.

"Get out of there, you! Oh look, you're gonna get your nice red cardigan all greasy!"

"Oh, I'm use t' it," said Liz. "I'm use t' it."

She hopped out with a sigh, grabbed the wheel again, and this time got grease all over her hands!

"I'm use t' it," she said. "I'm use t' it."

Back in the office she made a couple of fast phone calls, then said, "Ye have t' go over t' the KwikFit." She gave me directions. "And don't say nuthin' about me hoppin' in the boot and all, okay?"

KwikFit fixed everything fast, and nobody's paying me a cent to say it. "D'you have good service like this in Canada?" asked Mr. KwikFit.

"No way," said I. They said they'd take an hour, but they only took half, and it seemed short at that.

In *The Scotsman*, there was an article about a poor misunderstood guy who ran a "luxury" hotel near Inverness. He'd been charged with harassing a lowly chef over a long period of time, until the chef finally felt forced to quit. The trial was under way, with lots of human-interest witnesses, and the boss's picture was in the paper. He wouldn't talk about the case except to say, "We stand by our reputation." In facing disappointments, my "I understand perfectly" sounds pathetic next to the unmistakable glory of "We stand by our reputation." Then on the next page there was a picture of Hollywood movie stars Jack Nicholson and Michael Douglas: they're staying at the same "luxury" hotel, and are said to be there for the golf. Mick Jagger has joined them, and the three are going to be taking lessons together.

Two ladies in the garage waiting for their punctures to be patched were looking at the paper. One said, "Oooh, look at that Jack Nicholson, he's so good-looking, and such a good actor too." "Oooh, I think Michael Douglas is much handsomer," said the other. They weren't too interested in Mick Jagger, but then again Mick Jagger's picture wasn't in the paper.

Loch Ness is speckled with boats on a sunny afternoon, and the rain-clouds have sailed away over the sea to Norway, leaving behind litters of little white clouds and sailboats. This is an area of deeply serene beauty, with a blue mist rising from the long, narrow loch, deep as time itself (as Morton would say), and ancient green hills with rocky outcrops lining both sides. On this side, numerous people peer through breaks in the trees at Loch Ness sparkling in the sun: they're having a go at monster-spotting. German motorcycle gangs, Dutch caravans, and French tourist buses are bombing along the road, with varying degrees of impatience, as they try to negotiate their way past large parties of Danish ten-speed cyclists. The loch is a silver-violet colour, and in places it's a darker purple with touches of wine.

Yet pain and sorrow are never far away: a car with German licence plates has pulled into a lookout point. A woman sitting on a bench in front of the car looks worried: her head is hanging low, she's staring at her feet and wringing her hands rather than gazing rapturously out over the lovely loch, while her husband sits behind the wheel reading a newspaper. I watch the sailboats sailing by, and stand on alert ready to report on any further developments in this tragic little scene of marital disharmony. Maybe she's upset about the clear-cutting operations on the slopes on the far side.

A French tourist bus has pulled over, and the tourists mill about, gawking at the loch and keeping their eyes out for the monster. Everyone has a camera around his or her neck, and many are flashing pictures in the sunlight. A tall, red-haired piper is playing a tuneful lament that has its source on the shore of this loch no doubt, in the days when Urquhart Castle was still the place to be. He has a flag pinned to the stone wall behind him, red lion on yellow background, and he's in the habit of patrolling the north shore looking for tourists to play for in the hope they'll be generous tip-wise and help him with the rent of his bar stool. A group of female tourists have him surrounded, and seem to be patiently waiting for him to stop playing so they can ask him what he wears under his kilt.

Suddenly there's a dramatic change in the weather: misty downpours sweep in from the sea, and the windshield wipers can't boogie fast enough for this stormcloud. Viewing of the Loch Ness Monster is postponed till tomorrow. Maybe this is the kind of weather the monster loves, so that he can cavort and frolic around on the surface, knowing that nobody can see him because of the mist and rain. Any monster would know when people were looking at him and when they weren't: a certain intuitive understanding of these things would go with the territory. It would be dreadful to discover later that there was a significant sighting of the Loch Ness Monster on the day I drove by without having seen it. I'm listening to the *Goon Show* from the early fifties on nostalgic radio. In order to save time, someone is drying himself off while swimming ashore.

Meal Dubh (2,581 feet) was directly in front of me for several miles as I drove through the rain, but has now floated over to one side and is rapidly vanishing into the swirling clouds. It's raining down here at the approach to Glengarry and the mountains of the Northwest Highlands, but up on the peaks it's likely snowing. At the lookout point there's a stone cairn with a large, flat, polished-steel disc on it, with arrows showing the names and heights of the various peaks. But you can hardly see the mountains at all in this gloom, only their bases softly blurring into the grey of the clouds and mist.

An unusual-looking couple are laughing, because they have almost the same licence number as mine. She's a short, red-haired, bottom-heavy Australian with a fairly heavy moustache; he's a Swede, tall, gangly, prematurely bald.

"Long-distance romance?"

"Not any more," says she with a grin.

The Swede stood back with rain dripping off his long thin nose. He was staring blankly off to the side.

"I had the great good fortune to meet him while I was on a tour of Sweden. I found him and liked him and got him and we hit it off – and now I'm living in Sweden."

"How's your Swedish?"

"It's pretty good."

"And his Australian?" He looked a decade younger than she.

"Practically non-existent. But I have some pretty quick students in the village where we live. I've got almost the entire village speaking English with an Aussie accent."

Alas, she knew nothing about the Highland clearances, or that Glengarry was ground zero for that particular historical atrocity. They didn't know how sacred this area is in the racial memories of Scots all over the world. They'd picked up their car at the airport this morning and were off to Skye. It was the one place they wanted to go.

In a cold, dark downpour, a narrow one-track dirt road leads deeper into the mysterious, ghost-infested heart of Glengarry. Finally, a lovely old hotel appears, the Tomdoun, with motorcycles and cars in the parking lot. With a glass of Laphroaig in hand I'm having an earnest chat with a kind-hearted bartender, a Welshman. When he took over the hotel fourteen years ago there were fifty-five people living in the glen, and since then it's gone down to thirty-two. And yet, in the eighteenth century, when Bonnie Prince Charlie was collecting men for his army, which was to come to great disaster at Culloden, so populous was this valley that he managed with no problem at all to enlist two thousand men.

But the hotel was far from empty. The Welshman had guests sleeping in the halls, and he couldn't take one more person, but he said there was a little place on the other side of the rainswept bridge over a narrow section of Loch Garry in what was the village of Greenfield a century ago. He called them and reserved a room for me.

Suddenly a tall elderly man with a military bearing was standing quite close to me at the bar. It was amazing to see such an old man with such piercing blue eyes and such a boyish look. He said, "I used to come fishing here in the thirties," which struck me as an interesting opening line. "From 1931 to 1939. My father used to bring me fishing here every summer." He had an Oxford accent, and an endearing smile. He was six-five, eighty years old, and wore a blue silk scarf under an open-necked white linen shirt.

"I bet it hasn't changed much," I said.

"No, it hasn't. Would you like to see some photographs? My wife and I haven't unpacked the car yet. We've been too lazy, you see." He went to the car and brought back a well-maintained album filled with sepia-toned photos showing him as a young man, easily recognizable by his height and bearing. He was with his father and mother. He pointed out some mountains in the pictures. Then we would look out the window and through the mist see the same mountains.

His wife was sitting alone at a table, reading a Delderfield novel, drinking a beer, and smoking a cigarette. He had told her, That man at the bar looks like he'd enjoy my stories, and had got up and joined me. We went over to the table. "My wife is unusual for a woman: she loves to talk," he said, and his wife beamed with pleasure. Mr. and Mrs. Mitchell presented me with a pint of Guinness. They came up to Scotland almost every summer from their farm near Exmoor, in Somerset. His wife had a herd of Exmoor ponies, the management and care of which was her responsibility: they ran wild. They had sheep and grew crops. I mentioned something about Paul McCartney, who now ran a farm in Somerset. "Oh yes, he's about ten miles away, but he doesn't actually live there all the time, he just lives there part-time. We've never met him. We don't like him, because he is opposed to hunting and fishing." Mr. Mitchell's great-great-grandfather was an Orkneyman who had joined an eighteenth-century invasion of England. They got down as far as Lancashire, then argued among themselves about what to do next, then split up and went their own ways. Some went home, some continued on, and some stayed put. His ancestor was one of the latter.

He mentioned he'd had six and a half years of Royal Navy service in World War II as the captain of a minesweeper. "I still have trouble believing I'm alive. We got shelled and strafed and bombed every day and every night for that whole time, all the time I was at sea." After the war Mr. Mitchell studied history at Belfast, and then he taught at Oxford for twenty-six years. His wife had served as a Wren. "I was in port one night," he said, "and of course the first thing a Royal

Navy man does when he's in port for the night is he goes looking for a Wren. And I found this one, and I've been with her ever since."

The Tomdoun Hotel was a Dickensian maze of corridors, apartments, knitting nooks, sitting rooms, reading rooms, dining rooms, and little bars here and there, with roaring fireplaces, numerous examples of the art of taxidermy, bulging bookshelves. At every landing there was a large window alcove with a couple of chairs and a table with a vase full of flowers. Paintings of local flora and fauna were hanging everywhere, wildflowers, raptors, elk and deer, photos of the area down through the century, and framed topographical maps. Odd antique tables were covered with pleasing assortments of doodads, knickknacks, and whatnots, and a tremendous proliferation of horns (both bone and brass) and antlers, going back to the Reformation.

Finally, I said goodbye to the Mitchells and drove through the gloomy gloaming to the bed-and-breakfast. I'd inadvertently drunk too much to be driving on an unfamiliar, winding, one-track road in the rain and fog, but the Welshman at the bar said, "Oh, don't worry about it, the police never bother anybody in this valley." Wasn't that an interesting thing to say? It would become more interesting in retrospect.

I was dispatched to my room by my smart, funny, youthful hostess. While resting, with the door closed tight, I heard her husband on the phone. He was talking to a friend about fishing, and he went on and on about some big fish he had discovered in a pool somewhere, and how he felt he had Moby Dick on his line. He was extraordinarily enthusiastic. I dozed off with a sense of being very pleased to be here.

THE PINE MARTENS
OF GLENGARRY

*Glengarry • Greenfield • Tomdoun • Kinloch Hourn
Glenelg • Isle of Skye • Isleornsay*

Wednesday, June 12. Over my bed is a silver-tint etching of a golden eagle sitting on a rock. He's looking off in the distance with such stunning fierceness, it's like a Scot watching the tourist invasions of early summer.

Sensuous cedars dripping with rain surround this house, which sits on the shore of Loch Garry, deep in the darkest part of Scotland. Each trunk comes up about two feet before branching into four, the main trunk transforms itself into a river delta of four branches, and it makes a perfect little seat. Louise Ferguson, my hostess, doesn't know what kind of cedars they are. On a lamp table in the dining room there's a little stuffed animal, some kind of weasel sitting there with a little bushy tail and the sweetest look on its face.

"Who shot that cute little fellow?"

"That cute little fellow ate my hens," said Louise. "And what's more, he also ate my pet duck."

"What was your pet duck's name?"

"McDonald."

"Nice name."

"It was a nice duck, but it met a bad end."

"How did this tragedy come about?"

"These little pine martens, they go into the henhouse and they kill for the sake of killing. After all the hens are dead they go. They don't even eat them. Same with my pet duck. These are murderous little varmints – these pine martens are the Nazis of the animal world."

Fly-fishing trophies fill the house: they're presented by *The Scotsman* annually, and Sandy Ferguson places first almost every year. I'm proud of him and I haven't met him yet.

What about that rack of antlers mounted over the fireplace?

"That wasn't shot," she said. "That was our dog that killed that, about twenty years ago. The dog's dead now. It was a Labrador retriever. My husband was out with it, and he saw this big stag, and the dog attacked him and killed him. Killed him all by himself. My husband was quite glad of it, because he didn't have to waste a bullet."

Their son Derek is a beefy little guy of about ten, with a scar on his chin. Does he want to leave the glen when he grows up? "No, I don't," he replies immediately.

Louise says he fell off his bicycle and hit his chin on the barbed wire. The cut was deep. They had to put stitches on the inside and outside both.

"Did you panic?"

"No, I didn't have time to panic. We just got him to the hospital in Inverness as fast as we could. I just felt sick to my stomach."

A dark green truck is parked under the light blue sky. It says FOREST ENTERPRISE on the door, with a little logo comprising a hardwood tree and a softwood tree, in a lover's embrace. Sandy works for Forest Enterprise. Louise tiptoes into the kitchen and says, "The gentleman would like t'meet you, Sandy," and he comes out and shakes my hand. The wedding photos on the mantel show him skinny, with long sideburns, checked bellbottom trousers, and a sneering look on his face. Now he doesn't have sideburns, his skinniness is buried under great layers of fat, and his sneer has been replaced by a warm, shy smile.

He calls himself an "old-time gamekeeper," who occasionally takes a week off to do some guiding for North American fishermen. I mention overhearing him last night on the phone talking about Moby Dick: "That wasn't around here, that was over on Tayside. I took some people fishing over there. You need a lot of luck to catch a fish around here these days. The reason is, it's not that they're overfishing at all, it's just that there's too many predators. In the olden days, they used to hire people to net the pike and the other predator fish, but now they don't have the money, and the conservation staff is thin on the ground. So, as the predators increase in numbers, the trout get fewer and fewer, and that's a terrible sad thing. They're restocking, but not nearly enough."

"What would the fishing be like before the clearances?"

"There'd be fish jumping everywhere you looked. There's be no end to the fish you could catch in a day and no end to the hunting you could do in a day."

"Sounds like the Garden of Eden."

"Och, you're right there."

Even twenty years ago he could go out and easily see fifty blackcocks (also known as black grouse, famous for their intricate courtship rituals) in a day. Now he can go all day without seeing one.

I mention that, in old Scottish churchyards, the occupations of people are never given on the headstones – unless they happen to be gamekeepers.

"No, that's the way it was in those days," he says. "The gamekeeper was well-thought-of. He was right next to the laird. He was the laird's right-hand man. It was the highest job on the estate, being the gamekeeper. It's not like that now, believe me."

"What's killing all the blackcocks?"

"It's the pine marten. That's my theory anyway."

"The cute little pine marten?" We both look at the stuffed sample on the lamp table.

"Aye, I see blackcocks all the time with their necks bitten off, and they're just lying around dead. And the pine marten is the only animal that does that. They just kill 'em and they don't eat 'em. They eat other things. They just kill for the sport. They're vicious little things, and we're overrun wit' them. It's unbelievable."

"You take your rifle with you on your rounds, so every time you see one you can kill it, right?"

"I'd lose my job if I did that. The pine marten is a protected animal."

"Do they know your opinions on the matter?"

"They know all the gamekeepers' opinions, and we all agree that the pine marten should be killed. But they won't do it, they can't do it. They're such cute little creatures, that's why."

"It pays to be cute."

"Aye, that it does."

Young Derek, not exactly cute but with a face full of boyish intelligence, passion, and almost-adult character, goes out to play. The chat turns to him. "Yes," says Louise, "the lad really loves it here. He doesn't know anything about the cities, but he's not interested in them. And he was saying to me t'other day: 'You know, Mother, I wouldn't want to live in a place like Fort William where all these people live so close together and everything. I like it out here where you have all this space to yourself, and you can do anything you want.' He went on a ski trip with the school and he was on the gondola with the teacher. She was getting nervous being up so high. But he kept saying, 'Oh, look down there, there's some deer tracks, and there's some blah-blah, and there's some blah-blah trees, and there's an outcropping of blah-blah, and there's some blah-blah eagle.' She got so engrossed in what he was pointing out to her, she forgot to be afraid of the height."

"He knows his birds and everything?"

"Och, aye. There's nothing he hasn't seen. He's seen ospreys catching fish, and he's seen every kind of animal there is in the valley – and he's watched them at close quarters, too. He's seen it all. He knows every footprint, everything about nature."

Later I mentioned something about retired tourists with unlimited time to wander around foreign countries.

"Oh, I don't want to do that when I'm retired," said Louise. "I just want to travel in Scotland, I don't want to go to any of those countries – Holland or France or Germany or anything like that."

"You're wise," I said. "They don't even speak English in those countries, for Pete's sake."

"Yes, and I hear they don't wear pants on the other side of France."

"Tsk, it's a terrible problem."

Louise suggested I pop in to see Dion Alexander, who lives in the old schoolhouse. She described him as a young man of scholarly disposition who was making a general study of Glengarry. Dion turned out to be quite scholarly in his manner, and a bit nervous, but kind and eager to please, and he gave me his time generously. We sat at a huge oak table in the former school classroom, now used as a kitchen–dining room. The school was dated 1840. Dion lived in it with his wife and four children, who were away today. He was gentle and soft-spoken, with bushy eyebrows, dark hair, a sweet choirboy's face starting to be wrinkled with age.

Dion was more interested in the present plight of the glen than in the historical atrocities that had taken place. His aim was to see the population grow. He served as the secretary of a committee exploring ideas of how more tourists and permanent settlers could be attracted. The committee was a "tiny initiative. If we could get one extra household into the glen, that would be a major achievement."

He described himself as "a sort of rural housing specialist," and he had travelled widely accumulating expertise in the area, even to

Canada. "Our group here in Glengarry, we call it the Glengarry Partnership Initiative. It's attempting to do something about the chronic depopulation of this glen. It has dwindled dramatically over the last two to three years. We've lost a lot of young families." As for the sudden depopulation of the clearances: "The pressures were put on them by their own clan chiefs, which is particularly sad. Their rents were put up, and notices were served on people if they didn't pay the rents. And what people did was to make a decision, which was that they were not going to be picked off individually. If they were going to have to face this destruction of their way of life and community, which they valued so highly, they would go off, across the world, to find a place where they could still be a community together, and would not be subject to the pressures that were being imposed upon them by grasping lairds – and, as I say, it's particularly ironic that the grasping lairds should have been their own chiefs. Ironic perhaps isn't a strong enough word to describe it; it was tragic."

The sky had clouded over again and it began raining heavily. We looked glumly out the window. "I'm afraid that kind of wind-driven rain gets you wet very quickly." The rain and the mournful subject matter had me almost weeping.

Dion tried to cheer me up. "But the interesting thing is that it didn't destroy their lives, did it? I mean, when these people were forced out they took their lives and their way of life with them. They weren't able to continue their way of life here in Glengarry – and more's the pity. But they did at least make a new home for themselves – and very successfully – in Glengarry County, Ontario. And they soon became pillars of the Canadian society. They went to Canada because they had to go there, and they prospered, they were courageous, brave, enterprising, they had a strong sense of values, and they took all of that with them and contributed hugely to the development of modern Canadian society. And, you know, Canada's gain is our loss." He laughed bitterly. He said he was interested in "reforging the lost links" between the two Glengarrys and had written to the Glengarry Historical Society in Canada but hadn't had a reply yet. He thought there could be value for both communities in trying to set up a kind of "living partnership."

What's with Dion's classical Greek name? "It came about because my father was a Greek scholar and he fancied calling me Dion. They ended up calling me Di and now everyone calls me Di."

"How's your Gaelic?"

"Before we moved back here we lived in the Hebrides for a number of years, in Colonsay and South Uist, so I've got quite a lot of Gaelic. There's no Gaelic left in this glen now. I'm the only person living in this glen at the moment who has a word of Gaelic – and that's terribly sad. And a few years ago there were still four or five people who had the Gaelic. That's all gone now." He added that, at the time of the clearances, the glen was solidly Gaelic-speaking. "There would be no English at all at that time."

He gave me a little lesson in pronunciation of Gaelic names. He said *Garlic* is closer to the actual pronunciation of the word in the Gaelic language. The Island of Islay, he said the locals call it *I-lah*, the rest of Scotland calls it *I-lay*. And Uist is pronounced *You-ist*. The stress in Gaelic words and place names is almost always on the first syllable.

I asked him, "What's the problem with the glen being depopulated as it is now?"

"Perhaps you're right. In the great scheme of things, is it so tragic? But certainly you feel the impoverishment of the community, because there are fewer people around to be able to have a sense of community with, so there are fewer children from the glen going down to the school, fewer families, a lot fewer older people who lived in the place a long time. So it's sad, it's the loss of community, and it gets a lot harder to make things work."

"If there were one main villain in connection with the clearances in this glen, who would it be?"

"Certainly the last of the resident chiefs of the MacDonells," he said. "Alasdair Ranaldson MacDonell of Glengarry, whom John Prebble refers to in one of his books as 'a buffoon.'" Prebble, author of *Culloden*, *The Highland Clearances*, and *The Lion in the North*, also refers to MacDonell as a "ludicrous romantic" and mentions that on at least two occasions women protesting the clearances were beaten with truncheons. "Buffoon is a fairly kind description of him. He had a highly inflated opinion of his own importance. He was adopted by Sir Walter Scott, and used to go down to Edinburgh with his piper and his bard, and whole gangs of hangers-on dressed in their kilts and their finery, and they were paraded around the city."

I mentioned seeing a magnificent full-length Raeburn portrait of him in the National Gallery.

"Yes, that's right. And he was the guy who was pushing the rents up and issuing the eviction notices. And the motive was that they wanted the land for sheep."

"Why had sheep suddenly become important?"

"Because the price of wool had shot up – and they found that they could raise sheep on these hills, where they never thought they could before. Up until the middle of the eighteenth century they really thought the sheep could only survive on the lower pastures, and they didn't think they could survive in this hill country. And then they found that they would thrive. And so that totally altered the economic potential in the area."

"This is Thatcherism two hundred years earlier – profits over people."

"Exactly. Absolutely."

He said that in 1883 a law was passed protecting the integrity of the crofters, but, unfortunately, it was too late for Glengarry. It had all been lost by then.

"It must have been a terribly melancholy time."

"Well, yes. It's quite important not to get too carried away on the horrors. Yes, it is in many ways tragic what happened to this place. But there's always a side of me that says, Well, actually, at the end of the day did the people – those who managed to get across to the other side of the water without dying – did they get a better life out of it at the end?"

"I think those who survived generally prospered."

"But they had to work hard for it. It was a brave thing they did. They got their hundred or two hundred acres, whatever it was, for their concession in the forest, and so they had to clear the forest. There were no houses waiting for them when they got there, or social security system to look after them. I mean they just had to bloody well survive. It would be the later generations who would really be able to draw the benefits. So they were hardy people. Courageous people."

"It's a fabulous story."

"It is a fabulous story, and it's a very moving story, but it's moving not only because of the sadness of the situation which made them have to leave but because of the sort of triumph of the human spirit."

Back at the Tomdoun Hotel, after a frightfully long, melancholy run along the entire lonely valley to the tiny village of Kinloch Hourn on the sea coast, I had tea with the elderly couple from last night, Mr. and Mrs. Mitchell of Exmoor, then we stepped outside for a little air. They were a romantic pair: long decades of married life hadn't spoiled their appreciation of each other. They'd been together with hip waders in the river all day, and had caught two fingerlings. ("Index?" "No, pinky!") But their only complaint was about the hotel: their mattresses were unbearable and their window faced the dump.

Would they complain to the management?

They paused and said no.

A buck and a doe came by, the buck with a couple of little feathery antlers. Mrs. Mitchell tiptoed up to them with her little camera, and she was whispering out of the corner of her mouth, "I don't think this is the right kind of camera for this kind of shot." I tiptoed to my car and silently got out my Nikon with a longer lens and popped in a fresh roll of film for her. She started firing away with great avidity. When she was finished, I whipped out the film and handed it to her.

Later, out of the glen, I stopped at the lookout point again. Now I could see the entire glen in a clear light that reflected the courageous future rather than the miserable past. A rainbow was arcing over the bridge down there, and a larger rainbow over the whole glen. When I got out my camera, a couple of Germans in a Mercedes-Benz passed me, gawkingly, then backed up to see what I was shooting, then got out of their car and came over. I wanted to get a picture of the magnificent double rainbow, but it was a difficult shot, and every time I took a step towards the spot where I wanted to shoot from, those Germans with their pathetic little Leicas would anticipate my move and step right into my way. It was frustrating; the rainbows were fading. I felt like bashing them in the face with my Nikon F3. I'd simply tell the judge I was afraid the rainbow would disappear before I got a picture of it. That's a fear Freud never dealt with. And as I drove away, one end of a third rainbow was landing in the middle of the road: it exploded against my windshield in a flurry of brightly coloured shrapnels of light.

So now I was rushing towards Glenelg to catch the last ferry to Skye. At the Five Sisters filling station and general store, one of the sisters directed me to the toilet. When I returned she gave me a maternal lecture: "Holding on like that is not good for the kidneys. Better just blast away wherever you happen to be when the need arises."

She was the only one working there. "So where are your four sisters?"

"Oh, they're at home taking care of their four husbands." She's pumping my petrol.

"Four husbands each?"

"Yeah, sixteen altogether. No, actually it's those mountains over there, the Five Sisters, that's what they're called." Sure enough there were five mountains in a row, all similar in shape. "You have them in Canada, too," she said. She was an enormous woman, twice my size and half my age, in green shorts, and she had shining teeth, red hair, and knee-length socks with pink and white vertical stripes.

"I'm afraid you've been misinformed, we only have the Three Sisters."

"Oh," she said. "I told some Canadians the petrol station was named after the Five Sisters, and they said, Oh we have Five Sisters in Canada, too."

"Liars," I said. "Canada's big as all get-out, but we only have the Three Sisters."

She gave me a schedule for the Glenelg ferry. And she did not tell me about the dangerously frightful road I was about to encounter, a guardrail-less single-track road over the top of a huge mountain range, with the sun's rays turning my steamed-up windshield into a rosy impenetrable opalescent glow.

Two young fellows at the little Glenelg ferry asked where I was coming from.

"Glengarry! That's not very far," they said, knowingly, "as the crow flies."

I told them I must have set a record for the slowest speed ever recorded through that pass. They glanced at each other and smiled gleefully.

It was a little nine-car ferry, and they asked me to park right in the middle, because I was the only car and they didn't want me to capsize the boat. This resulted in my scolding them for making fun of my fine wee car.

It was the last trip of the day. I said, "Okay, let's go." They said they couldn't take off till the ferry was full. How long would it take to get eight more cars? They said it could take all night. Had I noticed any cars behind me on the road? I said I d been too afraid to look.

Finally they said, Ah, let's go, we've been having this guy on long enough. As we took off, I went to lock the car.

"Oh, don't bother doin' that," they said. There were only the three of us.

"Stupid of me!"

"Yeah, but it's amazin' how many people do that though."

Halfway across it started to pour torrentially. Were they sure they knew where the Isle of Skye was? You could see it looming up through heavy mist, giant black rockfaces hundreds of feet high.

"Isle o' Skye?" they said, jokingly. "I dinna know why you want to go there, we're goin' to the Isle of Mull."

"Oh that's just as good. I'll go to the Isle of Mull then. I'll zip over to Skye tomorrow."

"Aye, hear that? A free spirit," they said.

"I Go by Sea to Skye, Walk Through a Gorge, Meet an Eagle, See the Fairy Flag of Dunvegan, and Try to Keep an Appointment with Prince Charlie." This is the title of Morton's chapter on Skye. What will mine be? The road I'm on now is even scarier than the one on the mainland. My hands are shaking, the windshield wipers are on full blast. Even scarier than the thought of a bus forcing me to back up are the blind summits, where you have no idea if some drunk is coming up over the top. Nobody better be there or we'll both be knocked off the mountain for sure. No wonder most take the controversial new bridge a bit further north at the Kyle of Lochalsh, or the long ferry further south from Mallaig. The horrors of the trip were even worse than described, because the Tourist Board gave me a hundred pounds for a promise not to go on too much about the roads. Just kidding! It was because almost all the way the setting sun's rays were hitting an inlet from the sea up ahead and bouncing into my eyes, as if on purpose. Then the windshield steamed up and I could see nothing but a tremendous glow.

In a little tourist haven just outside the village of Isleornsay (a.k.a. Eilean Iarmain), on the shore of the Sound of Sleat separating Skye from the mainland, I sit guzzling tea to steady my nerves, and I'm also getting a Gaelic lesson from a dark-haired beauty whose husband was away in Glasgow with his seriously ill brother. *Dreich* is a horrid, wet, miserable day, and it's only used in connection with weather. And we know it (perhaps) as *dree*, which, although it has a related meaning in English (*enduring* or *suffering*, in a fateful sense), is said to have not a Gaelic derivation, but an Old English one. But *dreich* is definitely Gaelic. In other words, *dreich* is for bad weather, and *dree* is for all the other things over which we have no control. She also informs me there are three main Protestant churches in Scotland – the Free Presbyterian is the strict, narrow one, the Free Church of Scotland is the middle-of-the-road one, and the Church of Scotland is the liberal one. Somehow I forgot to ask about the Reformed Baptist.

Marie McKay, age nine, with dark, flashing Gaelic eyes, comes into the room and announces she's going to bed. Mama tells her to say good night to the guest in Gaelic.

"Eh Cuba?" she says, to my ears.

"How do you spell that, Marie?"

"*Oichdhe mhath*," she spells.

"Could you pronounce it again?"

"Eh Cuba?" she says.

Mrs. McKay starts talking about the Tourist Board, which she doesn't believe in. It's true, she says, that the Tourist Board has lately been urging everyone in the bed-and-breakfast business to give their guests their privacy. Don't have breakfast with them, don't talk to them too much, let them be on their own, have a private sitting room for them, have a television in each room, and all that kind of stuff. She didn't like that, so she quit the board. She's all on her own. Her attitude is that this is not a hotel, and, if you want to come in her home, you have to be part of the family. And so we sat there all evening, chit-chatting about Scottish churches (and how hers is the most liberal, and how people shouldn't be all that narrow in life), the state of the Gaelic language, the IRA, Scottish nationalism, the snooty, condescending ways of the English, about her brother-in-law having severe angina, so her kind-hearted husband had to drive him the 250 miles down to Glasgow Royal Hospital and stay with him for three or four days.

"Och, aye," said Mrs. McKay. "It's true, with some English people it's just an instinct, even the English who live up in the Isle of Skye, they're so patronizing towards the natives, as they call 'em. It's just unbearable. It really gets up my nose." The English people who come into her place are often like that, but they're not as bad as the Americans. They come in, they're loud, they demand things, and they make these demands in the most unpleasant way possible. Sometimes they'll sing, "What are we waiting for?" when she's busy brewing up, or they'll complain about how small the tomatoes are and boast about how big theirs are back home. But on several occasions she's allowed Americans into her home and, after they get settled, they turn out to be lovely people. They quieten down, and they speak softly as she does. I told her it was just the power of her personality, and she smiled sweetly.

She and her family always speak Gaelic in her home. But her husband, who was born and raised on the large outlying Isle of Lewis (Eilean Leodhais), is particularly fluent and literate in Gaelic. She's fluent, but she neither reads nor writes in Gaelic. She says she can carry on a conversation in Gaelic with someone from the Republic of Ireland, but when she tries to speak with people from Northern Ireland, it might as well be Chinese. She has no idea why that would be so. She also finds she can understand some Welsh, gropingly, though she's never studied it.

As for Lewis, Mr. McKay's parents live there. It's about a hundred pounds to take a car over with four people in it. I suggest it would be cheaper to go pedestrian class and rent a car over there, as I did on my visit a few years ago. She also said things have changed in Lewis over the past decade, and Stornoway, formerly quiet as a tomb, has developed a terrible alcohol and drug problem among the young. I asked what kind of drugs. Sniffing glue? Oh no, ecstasy and all that sophisticated stuff. But when she said that, I might have detected a slightly coy look, as if she wondered about it, and was curious.

"I've got a couple of nice hits of ecstasy in the glove compartment," I said. "Shall we try some?"

"Sure," she said, with a big liberal smile.

"Just kidding. I'm in a state of ecstasy all the time, so I don't need that stuff."

"Me too," she said.

We talked till an Edinburgh couple, who had booked in earlier and then gone to the pub, came back in, woozy-eyed but on two feet (each).

Mrs. McKay, we shook hands good night and she squeezed so tight tears came to my eyes. It's true, people seem to have more time in the "Highlands and the Islands."

THE FAIRY FLAG

Isleornsay • Armadale Castle • Dunvegan Castle
Flodigarry • Portree • Kyle of Lochalsh

Thursday, June 13. At breakfast I was orange-juiced, tea'd, porridged, and kippered along with an interesting young Scottish couple. Alison MacGregor, originally from Jedburgh, was a marketer for a German computerized-shower firm in Edinburgh. She knew her family history well, and wasn't about to romanticize it for my sake. What had the MacGregors, including Rob Roy, really done to deserve such a horrible fate, being outlawed, having open season declared upon them at the hands of neighbouring clans, and coming close to being exterminated? Her answer caused my face to drop: "They were liars and cheats and thieves, and even worse they tried to play both sides of the fence."

Her partner, John Coulter, was a long-time editor and reporter for the Edinburgh *Evening News*. He was born in Ireland and raised in Glasgow. He said that Glasgow is a much larger town, more streetwise and sophisticated, than Edinburgh: he suspected I'd prefer it. The Glaswegians despise anything to do with Edinburgh, which is smaller but *much* more culturally refined and less working-class. They don't pay any attention to Glasgow's envies and resentments. He told me there were still tons of McFaddens in Maryhill, which was the one part of Glasgow that still has real character. My information, that the old Maryhill (from which my little twig of the meditative, retiring McFadden family tree had emigrated in 1870) had been gutted and replaced by high-rise blocks of flats, was quite false. There's still a lot of the old Maryhill left, he said, and they even have their own football team. And the chief counsellor of Glasgow is a Jean McFadden, who is from Maryhill. A most interesting woman, he said. I mentioned having been told that the McFaddens used to be Tinkers. Alison said all the Mcs and Macs were originally Tinkers.

John Coulter said he always liked Maryhill, even though he grew up in the east end of Glasgow. He knows lots of McFaddens and they're a pretty rough family. They and a lot of other Irish clans, reduced to toiling in the Clyde shipyards, used to hop on a bus every Friday afternoon and take off for County Donegal for the weekend. Sometimes they wouldn't get back till Tuesday. There was a lot of cross-pollination between Glasgow and County Donegal.

All through breakfast we could hear the cleaning lady working on the bedrooms and singing a special bilingual version of "The Old Rugged Cross."

Alison had a long thin nose, a narrow face, and twinkly little brown eyes, from which sparks flew when she spoke of the rotten ways of her forebears. As much as I admired Mr. Coulter, I felt he was no match for this intelligent fiery beauty. At one point, in talking about Alison's job with the computerized-shower company, Coulter referred to her jokingly as "a lackey of capitalist society."

"Journalists aren't?" I said.

"Heavens no," he said, with journalistic self-possession. "We search for the truth."

The Clan Donald Visitors Centre and Museum, which wasn't here in Morton's day, is located in the old Armadale Castle, which definitely was. The castle is surrounded by deep green parkland, generous profusions of blossoming rhododendron bushes, Methuselah-like trees, many in flower, and each hosting an enchanting choir of little warblers. But once one is inside the museum the charm erodes, with this kind of glop coming out of the loudspeakers: "The people who came together to make this culture, people with names, who kept records of their victories and defeats, were not the first. They too encountered a past, and felt the presence of others before them, in silent circles of stone, in chambers, and overgrown forts. They took that strangeness and made it part of themselves." It's the verbal equivalent of a Big Mac with cheese.

But there are some nice scraps of ancient poetry on the walls. For instance this, from "The Message of the Eyes" by Niall Mór MacMhuirich (early seventeenth century): "Silence gives meaning to the swift glancing of the eyes; / what matters the silence of the mouth when the eye makes a story of its secret?" Also, from the Clan Donald "Incitement to Battle," by Lachlan Mór MacMhuirich, written in the hours leading up to the famous Battle of Harlaw (1411): "Be strong, dealing swift blows," "Be spirited, inflicting great wounds," and "Be dour, inspiring fear." In spite of all this poetic advice, the Donalds, allied with the English, were routed by the forces of Alexander Stewart, though the museum makes no reference to that historical fact.

Waves of elderly people recently disgorged from tourist buses weave their way in. They look askance at the German cyclists, who look miserable in their gauche, glaring, garish, and gaudy waterproof uniforms, covered with Looney Toons insignia, and some with a big picture of Bugs Bunny on the back. I slip back outside.

Many of the older trees in this heavenly park would have been a fair size when Boswell and Johnson came through. The house where they would have stayed is a terrible mess, a ruined shell. On the museum wall is an interesting quote from Boswell, dated

September 20, 1773: "In the morning, we were ferried over to the Isle of Skye. We landed at Armadale where we were met on the sands by Sir Alexander Macdonald, who was at that time there with his lady, preparing to leave the island and reside in Edinburgh." Armadale Castle is in the south of Skye, on the Sound of Sleat. A much older castle, the ninth-century Dunvegan Castle, the home of the MacLeods, is way up the coast, on Loch Dunvegan, which is a great fiord separating the Waternish Peninsula from the Duirinish Peninsula, and running in from the Little Minch, which separates the Isle of Skye from the Isles of Harris and Lewis. As one crosses the drawbridge and enters Dunvegan, one comes face to face with a huge Raeburn portrait of Norman, son of Norman, the twenty-third chief, born 1781, blown up on HMS *Queen Charlotte* in 1800. This romantic young hero was a handsome fellow, slightly effeminate in appearance, and he died at nineteen.

On the way up to Dunvegan I missed the stone Morton talks about: "I passed the bloody stone where the Macdonalds were slaughtered – or was it the Macleods? – and the wind howled like the ghost of the dead." Of Dunvegan, he writes, "The castle is surrounded on three sides by water and on four by ghosts. It stands there like a grey ghost from which there is no escape. It is the Iliad of Skye: it is a saga in stone." Was he being serious or was he camping it up? You be the judge: "Everything you have read about enchanted castles, captured princesses, wizards distilling the Water of Life, victims dying of thirst in dungeons, mermaids swimming up in moonlight to lure a man to his death, men beaten back to a whistle of swords and a hail of arrows, comes true as you see the turrets of Dunvegan lifted in the dusk above the trees on a spur of rock that leans over an arm of the sea in Skye."

An impeccably dressed castle employee approaches me shyly and says she knows some ghost stories about this castle. She says her name's Dolly. I ask for the scariest one.

"That would be expensive to tell you."

"You look as if you could afford it."

"No, silly – tee-hee. I mean expensive for you." I reach for my wallet. "Nae, I'm only kidding ye."

She told two stories, but either they weren't scary or I couldn't understand them. She did say all they found of Norman was his "thumb" bobbing in the waves.

Dunvegan's famous Fairy Flag has become so badly chewed up over the centuries, it's beginning to look eerily like the map of Scotland, with intricate networks of lochs and canals, little blotches of what looks like red paint, and jagged margins. It's the remains of an ancient silk flag, and there is no impression of a design left on it whatsoever. It's framed in a glass case, and beneath it the caption reads, "The Fairy Flag of Dunvegan – fourth to the seventh century AD." It's the Fairyland version of the Turin Shroud. And it bears a terrible curse. Morton relates the story of the Flag, and its curse, but I want to hear it from a bona fide MacLeod.

Manikins languish mournfully in the lamplit depths of the dungeon, along with certain special effects for hard-working tourists who are, through no fault of their own, a bit lax in the imagination department. The pit of horror is about six feet by five, and twenty-five feet deep. Apparently, one of the barons kept his wife down there, though I'm not sure for how long at a stretch. Maybe for indefinite periods, whenever he caught her frolicking naked with the local shepherds. She had to stay there until she apologized and promised never to do it again. Or maybe she was tossed in for causing a fuss after catching *him* frolicking naked with the shepherds. This would be long before the days of pay equity.

Various rooms of the castle display fine examples of chain mail; a supposedly Pictish stone with fake, clumsily etched circles; and a stone statue of a woman in sixteenth-century dress, about three feet high, which stood for generations in the castle garden with a sun-dial on her head. An obnoxious little girl tourist keeps screaming, "Shut the door! Shut the big door!" Here's a large fifteenth-century sword without a spot of rust on it, the kind of sword that requires two hands. Lucky I'm a nice guy, or that little girl's doting dolt of a mother would quickly find herself with twin half-daughters.

A tourist film is being shown in the theatre. A moist, snooty English voice drones on about the Fairy Flag being "the treasured possession of the chiefs of the clan. . . . How it came to Dunvegan – or when – is one" (sounds more like two) "of the many mysteries of the past. But ancient legends" (this won't be the last tautology) "handed down through generations" (a lot of legends are like that) "are firm on three points" (firm legends are the best legends): "1) it has mystic, or fairy, power; 2) it comes from the east, the Holy Land; and 3) it wins battles. It was woven in silk in the fourth century AD."

At the end I watched the credits, hoping to identify the wonderful piper whose music does much to make the film palatable. It was Iain Macfadyen. A name to remember! I later discover he's famous in piping circles. As tourists file out, a man sitting behind me begins whispering in my ear: "Are you the man who was asking about the Fairy Flag?" His name is Chris MacLeod, a bona fide MacLeod in staff uniform. Dolly has tipped him off. In the still-darkened theatre, he whispers that the Fairy Flag has historically been kept sealed up in a box in the Fairy Tower. "I think it was in there for maybe as much as a hundred years. And the prophecy ran that, when the Flag was exposed to the air again, there would be certain disasters fulfilled in the family history, one of which would be the surrendering of a tract of land; one of which would be – well, perhaps not so much of a disaster, but an unusual happening – a vixen would give birth to cubs in the castle; and the third would be that there would be news of the nature of that which was fulfilled in the death of Norman the Younger" (the fellow who got blown up). "And in fact Mr. Buchanan was in charge of family affairs at the time and he, presumably under his own authority, rather than under the chief's authority" (that's right, blame the Buchanans), "opened the case containing the Fairy Flag. And a vixen gave birth to cubs in one of the turrets of the castle; the news came through that Norman MacLeod had been killed at the age of nineteen, his ship went down off Genoa during the Napoleonic Wars; and the third thing is that a certain tract of land had to be sold to the Campbells." At that point harp music signalled the resumption of the film for a fresh audience. The conversation didn't resume.

At the gift shop I bought an Iain Macfadyen tape, and marvelled at his music almost non-stop for the rest of my Scottish wanderings, causing natives to stick their fingers in their ears as I went by with my car windows rolled down.

Was Morton right when he asserted that Dunvegan Castle is "the oldest inhabited dwelling in Scotland"? Nobody knew. They all thought it sounded right, but nobody had heard that before. And they seemed a bit embarrassed when I asked.

Oh Skye, Skye, beauteous Skye. I dip down into a little glen, and the blue sharp-peaked mountains looming on the horizon slowly sink into the earth. And I come up out of the glen and the mountains rise up out of the earth again. There's a waterfall off to the right, and to the left a single solitary small white house surrounded on all sides by an ancient stone wall. There's a blue sky over Skye, and Skye really does mean *sky*, even if it does come from a Norse word meaning *cloud* (its Gaelic name is Eilean à Cheo, "Isle of Mist").

The Skye Museum of Family Life (a.k.a. the Skye Croft Museum), just south of the twin northernmost points of Skye, Rubha Hunish and Rubha na h-Aiseig, is a darling little cluster of old stone huts on a cliff above the sea, with stones hanging down from stretches of chickenwire covering the thatched roofs, to encourage them to remain in position during the wildest storms. On display is a set of pistols belonging to a landlord a hundred years ago: they'd be handy to have on hand while collecting rents. Here's a 1953 National Bank of Scotland five-pound note, six inches long and four inches high. Here's a pot that was used to make a meal for Bonnie Prince Charlie in the home of the landlord Donald Campbell, for it was on Skye that Charlie first landed in Scotland.

Hanging on the wall is a framed certificate telling the where-abouts of the remains of someone's son killed in World War I. It tells where he's buried, and it says his name is carved in stone and gives the name of the cemetery. His medals are here, along with a snap-shot of him standing in a garden dressed in full Scottish regalia, kilt and all, and surrounded by black and white flowers, and with a mournful look on his face.

Crofters borrowed each other's horses during ploughing season. Here are parts of the harnesses and the saddles. And here's the turnip sower. And a potato hoe. And a potato hook for digging pota-toes, especially in sandy soil. These are still being used in some of the smaller islands of the Hebrides. A family of French people are fol-lowing me everywhere and, for reasons unknown, they keep making barnyard noises – mooings, oinkings, neighings, and even the occa-sional quack when I least expect it.

At the museum I bought a tape of Gaelic singer Christine Primrose and another Iain Macfadyen tape. Macfadyen is billed as "Scotland's premier piper." Which one to play first? Probably the Primrose, because this is her island. Primrose can bring tears to one's eyes, even if one doesn't understand a word of Gaelic: one of her songs is "Oran do Mhac Leoid Dhun Bheagain" ("Song to MacLeod of Dunvegan"). Her work is known by Gaelic speakers throughout the world, but there are so few of them that she's still working full time as a receptionist at the local college.

Bobbing gently in Portree harbour are a couple of cabin cruisers, an old fishing boat, an old nine-car ferry, a couple of spiffy new good-sized fishing boats, and some rowboats. A brightly painted pastel row of waterfront shops, many catering largely to the tourist crowd, face the harbour: the Lower Deck is a fish-and-chip joint, and it's painted blue on the first floor and white on the second floor, where there are offices of some sort. But Portree is packed with snappy, stressed-out tourists. It's not that there are too many tourists as much as that the only visible people are tourists. The locals are waiting on tables, standing behind cash registers and sales counters, and dreaming of winter. All these tourists want to say to the people back home is that they were over on the Isle of Skye. As for the Isles of Mull, Harris, Lewis, they don't have that ring. But the Isle of Skye! How wonderful!

Numerous fatsos are gasping with asthmatic attacks on the narrow cement staircase leading from the lower town to the higher town, causing tourist gridlock and the occasional outburst of tourist rage. Portree is full of bed-and-breakfasts, bars, bistros, boutiques, and irritable tourists with cigars desperately trying to manoeuvre their big cars into tiny parking spots.

The volcanic Cuillin Hills (also known as the Cullens, the Coolins, which was Morton's preferred spelling, or the Red Cuillins), further south on the island, look strange and unpleasant in this late-afternoon light. There are twenty sharp mountain peaks, fifteen of them over three thousand feet high, with the highest, at 3,257 feet, being Sgurr Alasdair. They are of extremely hard granite, some of the slopes are rather smooth and rounded, and there are countless foothills. But the peaks themselves exhibit twenty different ominous ways of being sharp and forbidding. This is where climbers get lost and are never heard from again. These mountains resemble hungry wolves with sharp teeth, they're a dark blue colour with grey in it. They're like blue-faced giant Pictish vampires, with their huge forty-pound two-handed swords over their shoulders and ready to start whacking at you for the joy of seeing how far your blood will spurt. The mountains are so close you can smell their breath. I'm in a rather small deep glen surrounded by the Cuillins, and I hope these sleeping giants don't wake up: any time these mountains have a mind to wake up and start a war dance, that's the time I get out of here at top speed, scattering loose chippings at their ankles. Wrote Morton, "I can imagine a neurotic person flying from these mountains as from the devil."

At the Kyle of Lochalsh, on the mainland, after crossing the new little bridge that has caused such outrage among the good people of Skye (it's too expensive, for one thing), I stopped and ordered deep-fried scampi with french fries.

"Easy on the batter, I'm not supposed to eat fried foods," I told Mrs. McScampi.

"It's okay 'cause it's made with bread crumbs," she replied. And all the time we're standing there, some lonesome, homeless mutt is cringing at the front door with its nose stuck in and sniffing, twitching, sniffing, twitching.

With my little package nicely wrapped up, I noticed the gleaming, handsome *Royal Scotsman* about to pull out. So I scamper over to have a look at it, but it's just two old passenger cars turned into a bar and grill. Tourists surround it with videocams on their shoulders, but they miss the interesting shot, the one of this ugly mangy mutt trotting along beside some guy with scampi, and everybody in town looking out the window, praying that the mutt and I will form a permanent attachment and they'll never be pestered by her ever again when they go to the scampi store. But what a nice dog: she takes the fries out of my hand without slobbering and without biting my fingers. Dogs are like people – it's the homeless mutts, despised by the world, who are actually the most intelligent. I try a scampi on her, but to her it's just another chip. I leave her the entire mess and go back for more for myself.

Mrs. McScampi makes good food. It's not the place on the main street; it's the one that's tucked behind the main drag, behind MCFADDEN QUALITY BUTCHERS (the Q is missing) and facing a parking lot, the sea, and the *Royal Scotsman*. But you have to really want scampi in the first place and be ravenous, otherwise you won't experience true scampi ecstasy. The scampi is so light and juicy, and although it's almost bedtime, it's still bright as day in the Kyle of Lochalsh, except there are longish shadows cast by cars, trees, mountains, dogs.

> *The world is still beautiful though you are not in it,*
> *Gaelic is eloquent in Uist though you are in Hallin Hill and*
> *your mouth without speech.*
> — Sorley Maclean, "Elegy for Calum I. Maclean"

I asked Mrs. McScampi what she thought of the music of Christine Primrose. She said she liked her, but here on the mainland they're not really that enthused, because they took Gaelic in school but they didn't get fluent. And the mainland isn't a real Gaelic area. So now they've books and tapes at home and are trying to brush up. But they're not getting far for some reason. I suggested English translations of the lyrics should be included with the tapes, so you would know what she was singing her heart out about. Mrs. McScampi looked shocked.

"Oh no, you couldn't translate those songs into English, you couldn't. It'd sound silly, because in Gaelic you say everything backward."

"Like, give me an example in English."

She started scratching her head and couldn't think of one.

"Like, would you say, 'In English an example give me?'" I said.

"Nope, that's not it." She couldn't explain, but she said, "It's well known that you can't translate Gaelic into English." She's obviously never been to the Clan Donald Museum, or read the beautiful poetry of Sorley Maclean in English translation.

"It's not that we don't like Gaelic. It's that we're not fluent in it yet. It's a strange language. If you translate it directly into English you get garbage. Nobody would understand it."

When you go to the tavern
Drink only one drink
Drink your dram without sitting
And be attentive to your men.

– From an old Gaelic poem, translated by Sorley Maclean

THE VIEW FROM
DUART CASTLE

Fort Augustus • Loch Ness • Corran • Ardgour • Fshnish
Isle of Mull • Duart Castle • Kinloch

Friday, June 14. "Few travellers bore me more," wrote F. V. Morton, "than those dull fellows who explain in great detail the mere machinery of their progress." But Mull was drawing me towards it, and Iona, too. And to avoid confusion I should mention that, to get to the ferry to Mull, I had to head inland quite a bit, in a southeast direction, and sweep around Loch Glengarry. In Newtown, a few miles southwest of Fort Augustus, young, handsome Mr. MacKnochen, in the temporary absence of his wife was single-handedly running a bed and breakfast out of his home. He said his mother always thought their name was a misspelling of the more usual McNaughton, but nobody knows for sure. He adds that a friend has traced it back to a similar name in Ireland. His hobby is reading history books about Scotland.

I asked an innocent question: why did the Highlanders sign up in droves with Bonnie Prince Charlie? His answer was very impressive. He said it was because the Highlanders were pretty well all Catholics then. They didn't change till later. British historians tend to down-play religious differences, it's safer that way, and this only adds to the confusion. It was also a crusade, a romantic, sentimentally misguided thing. There had been many Highlanders on the government's side as well, of course. He was pleased to know I'd asked others the same question, and had looked it up in various books, but this was the first time an unambiguous answer was forthcoming.

He works on the oil rigs in the North Sea. He's off three weeks and on three weeks. Good money? He said it'd have to be to com-pensate for being away from home for so long. His wife is away for a few days, something for the church. He gets out his photo albums. He looks exactly like his father. He told me he never knew anyone before who was interested in other people's family photos. I said I know, it's strange, but I've always been that way, born with an unquenchable face fetish.

In the morning I zip up to Fort Augustus. Two elderly Scottish gen-tlemen are strolling in the parkland bordering Loch Ness and sur-rounding the abbey at Fort Augustus. "Och, the peace and quiet of the Benedictine life," says one.

"Yes," says the other, "even we non-believers can grasp that aspect of monasticism."

A winding, treelined footpath descends to what is signposted as the "world-famous viewpoint," and that's no exaggeration. The view has been seen hundreds of times hanging framed on walls, embroi-dered on dishcloths, painted by numbers on black velvet. There's even a clever postcard depicting a coffee mug with a picture of Loch Ness from the abbey stamped on it. It's a view straight up the long, narrow loch, with hills and mountains arcing down on both sides like multiple rainbows of all the thousands of pale-blue tones in the spectrum. This is the place where two giant land masses collided. A small group of elderly Scottish people, their bones creaking, crane their necks and take pictures, thereby saving money on postcards.

They're being relatively well behaved, but one mischievous old lady suddenly yells out at the top of her lungs: "Oh, he's going to pop his head up any moment now, I can feel it. Oh, there he is." And as soon as everybody turns to look she says, "Oh, you're too late. you missed him, he's gone now." Everyone laughs. With jokes like this, we know we're among Celts.

I whispered in her ear, "You're a terrible leg-puller, aren't you?" The others heard and smiled sweetly.

"Oh, we'd get a terrible shock if he did pop his head up," said another sweet old soul, with a quavering voice.

The songbirds resumed their lovely chorus.

A couple of guys who run the tourist boats show up too late for the merriment. They look world-weary and particularly tired of tourists, but not of their money. It's a long cold winter.

"Are you fellows believers?" I said.

"Yes. We know people that have saw it," said one, instantly.

"You do?"

"Less than a month ago really." His voice was flat and matter-of-fact, but not bored. He seemed serious.

"And I know other people that have saw it too, you know," said the other guy, who seemed to have gone to the same grammar school. But both seemed to be telling the truth.

"Geez," said I.

"They know what, ehm, the waves are," he said.

"They do?" said I.

"And they know what the wakes of boats are, and that," he added.

"Aye, and it wasn't that they saw, you know." said the other.

"If you'll be here in twenty minutes, we'll talk to you about it," said the first.

"We're in a bit of a rush right now," said the second.

Headphones are mandatory for the tour of the abbey. First come the relics, "parts of the bodies," as the audiotape advises us, of a vast slew of saints, if you can believe: Saints Vincent de Paul, Brigid of Sweden, Agatha, Francis of Assisi, Clare of Assisi, John of the Cross. Little bone slivers are displayed in gold cases behind glass.

About thirty of us shuffle our way through the various galleries like exercise hour on the lobotomy ward, with the headphones clamped to our heads playing bagpipe music, with pleasant pauses to tell us when to stop, where to look, when to go fast and when to go slow, when to proceed to the next exhibit. This makes high school seem like fun. Give me a book any day. The others seemed to be enjoying it, but I dropped away and returned the headphones. The fellow was pleasant in spite of his why-does-this-always-happen-on-my-shift? look. He directed me to a section of the display he thought I'd be able to enjoy without the headphones. The others in the death march, resenting that I had bolted ahead and changed my place, seemed about to tear me apart, so I slipped out the side door, which had one of those fake NO EXIT signs.

Such places at such times get so clotted with tourists that the staff doesn't have any energy to do anything but the mundane rituals of their job. I wanted to speak to a certain monk, who knew everything about the monster, had devoted his life to it, and lived in the abbey. They said yes he lives here, he loves visitors, but they were too busy to get around to arranging a meeting. I understood perfectly.

I feel like Jacques Tati in *Monsieur Hulot's Holiday*, in this tiny four-wheeled motor scooter, the Fiat Cinquecento 500, with Iain Macfadyen's bagpipe music blasting out. Blame it on the bagpipes: they had me racing around corners and going flat out on the bends, and now here I am in a lineup waiting to get on the Corran Ferry to cross over to Ardgour, drive along the shore of Loch Linnhe, then across the very remote Morvern Peninsula to Lochaline on the Sound of Mull, then a fifteen-minute ferry to Fishnish on the Isle of

Mull. As soon as one gets off the first ferry, the Corran Ferry, there's the whitewashed, thatch-roofed Ardgour Hotel, temptingly located directly facing the ferry dock. An invisible arm comes out of the hotel, grabs me, tries to pull me in, but I resist. Mull is calling, and Iona too. I'll be coming back this way.

A young, bright, and terribly tactless German student is taking tickets at the entrance to Duart Castle, the home of the dreaded MacLeans, in a glorious setting on the Isle of Mull, overlooking such vast bodies of water as Duart Bay, the Firth of Lorn, the Sound of Mull, the Lynn of Morvern, the Lynn of Morn, and Loch Linnhe, and the Isles of Lismore and Kerrara, and a wonderful range of mountains receding back from the mainland coast. "Ah, the hangers-on," said the student, when I gave her my name. I stared in dismay. Apparently that's how the MacLeans, as unpleasant today as they always were, describe the role of the McFaddens in their life down through the ages We chatted for a while, and I brought the chat back nicely to the McFaddens.

"The Rankins were the hereditary pipers of the MacLeans?"

"That's right," she said.

"And the Beatons were the hereditary physicians of the MacLeans?"

"That's right."

"And the McFaddens were?"

She lets out a hoot of laughter. "No idea," she says. "But I know that they are considered, uhm, I think it's called an 'adjacence' to the clan. A hanger-on, let's say. And as such they are allowed, or are considered, a member of the clan, or can join, for example, the clan association."

I had the unusual sense of feeling my ancestral blood simmering.

"It's my understanding," I said, and I wish now I hadn't, because I was dead wrong, "that this was originally the McFadden castle."

"As far as I know, you would be dead wrong on that." Another peal of laughter.

All the little cells in my body were waving the McFadden coat of arms.

"And the original MacLean tartan was originally a McFadden tartan."

Ancient hatreds began to make sense.

"I wouldn't know about that, but I do know that the MacLeans can trace their lineage back to 1250 when the walls of the castle were first built, by a fellow who answered to the name Gillian of the Battle Axe." My knees trembled in terror. "The walls would have surrounded a little village of cottages and thatched huts."

"I see," I said, my passion genuflecting to her knowledge.

"I don't know, you could be right," she said, with sudden sympathy, "but that's what we know. Mind you, that's the MacLean story. Losers write little history."

"Losers? Do I look like a loser?" Oops, I shouldn't have said that. The joke's on me. She doubled up with laughter.

"What you should do, when you go inside, there's a guard up in the C-room and, if you get her to look up *Macfadyen* for you, she can tell you where it comes from and why you are a hanger-on."

The big feature of this castle, besides its glorious view out over the Sound of Mull southeast to the Mountains of Lorn, all the way up to Ben Nevis (4,406 feet) in the northeast, Aonach Mor (4,006 feet), and dozens of other mountains over three thousand feet, is the collection of silver candlestick holders, which use, as their bases, hooves cut off small deer and horses. And they say the clans weren't classy. There's a small inkwell made from the tiny hoof of the two-day-old foal of Sir Fitzroy's Crimean charger, Sir Fitzroy being the twenty-sixth chief of the MacLeans. On the wall is a framed note in his hand explaining the "origan" of three of the mounted hooves. It illustrates how civilized the Highlanders had become, and how unctuous. "Before sending my chargers home, I wrote to Colonel Maude, the Crown Equerry, to know if H.M. Queen Victoria would like to have the last trooper that was in the Charge of the Light Brigade at Balaclava. H.M. graciously accepted it. I sent her" (the horse, not the Queen) "to Buckingham Palace Mews. She ended her days at Hampton Court Paddocks, in company of the late Prince Consort's favourite charger. The Master of Horse sent me the hooves when she died." He had three of the hooves mounted, and the fourth he presented to the brave trumpeter who rode her in the charge, Henry Powell. The hooves were mounted "on the occasion of F.M. The Duke of Wellington's funeral." The note signs off with: "X [large cross] all men who were in the Charge at Balaclava." One hoof forms the base of a small clamp for holding music. Another has a small silver statue of a horse on it. The third seems to have galloped away.

From the castle the sound silently sparkles an otherworldly silver blue in the mid-afternoon sun. A few hundred yards out is a shoal, visible at low tide, with a tragic history that would have been worthy of Shakespeare's attention. The story relates that, some time in the fifteenth century, one Lachlan Cattanach MacLean, the eleventh chief, was hoping to bring an end to his unhappy marriage, because it had failed to produce an heir. And so he had his wife, Lady Elizabeth, marooned on the shoal, expecting her to drown as the tide rose. But her cries were heard by a passing fisherman, who quietly carried her off to the home of her brother Colin Campbell, third Earl of Argyll, whose fury, when he was apprised of Lady Elizabeth's near-death experience, can only be imagined.

Then imagine his delight when he received a letter from Lachlan, the swine, announcing the sad news of his wife's drowning, offering his condolences, and offering to bring her body to the Campbell home in Inveraray, so she could be buried among her own kin. Colin craftily agreed, and when Lachlan arrived at the castle with a well-sealed coffin, he was ushered into the dining hall. Seated on the right hand of Colin was Lady Elizabeth herself, alive and well, peeking out from behind a veil, teasing her husband, till it gradually dawned upon him that he'd been exposed. She must have begged that his life be spared, for the rotter left Inveraray unharmed. There's no reference as to what was in the coffin: perhaps the body of some unfortunate McFadden.

184 ◆ AN INNOCENT IN SCOTLAND

Lachlan recovered from the shock, arrived home unscathed, married twice more, with his third wife, Marian MacLean, of Treshnish, giving birth to a "much-wanted heir," Hector, in 1497. However, the Campbells had not forgotten his treachery, and much later, on a visit to Edinburgh, just when he was beginning to feel safe, Lachlan was ambushed by another of Elizabeth's brothers, Sir John Campbell of Calder, and killed.

"I would like to see Iona before I die" is something the British are fond of telling each other, but the taste for travelling tends to taper with time. And, although there are many tourist buses heading for Iona today, they're almost empty. When the bus stops here and there along the road, it's just to drop off a parcel.

A young woman, with long blonde hair flying, speeds by on her bicycle as I'm making a right turn. She sails by with a friendly red-lipped smile. Maybe she thought I was the new minister, the new bartender, or her mother's new boyfriend. Maybe she said to herself, here's a guy who's going out to Iona for a weekend of spiritual solace. She was obviously local and not going far along a line of blossoming trees that come right down to the side of the road.

Numerous little islands, populated by colonies of puffins and the occasional sea eagle, appear in the sea off Mull. These islands, Lunga, Bac Mor (the Dutchman's Cap), and the Treshnish group, are oddly shaped, geometrical in fact, betraying their volcanic origins. They rise from the sea, with perpendicular cliffs, and one or two terraces, and are capped with flat tops, so they would be a perfect setting for a sci-fi movie, and could serve as landing pads for inter-stellar vehicles.

I managed to get all the way to the Ulva ferry before beginning to suspect I was on the wrong road. The map, which I've been blithely ignoring, now indicates that, instead of going to the southwest tip of Mull, I've been zooming up the west side towards the northern tip, and suddenly the map of Mull turns into a map of Britain: the Ross of Mull is a mini-Cornwall, Iona is Land's End, and to extend the comparison I have very stupidly driven all the way from London up to Glasgow instead of out to Land's End. As for the Hebrides, the Isle of Ulva is a mini-Skye, proportionately speaking, the Ardmeanach Peninsula could be a stand-in for Wales, the "Waist of Mull," from Salen to Gruline, looks like the perfect spot for Hadrian's Wall, and above it the entire northern chunk of the island looks a lot like Scotland. Mull is a scrunched-up, depopulated Britain. Am I the first to notice this?

On the way back I seem to have made another unnecessary turn, for I'm passing a village with a filling station and a church, which I definitely didn't see on the way up. It's embarrassing to be lost on such a small island with only four roads. Somehow I've crossed the island to the east side, to the two-lane road running from Tobermory to Fishnish, and am now bearing down on Fishnish, from the north, but I don't want to go all the way back there, so I make a U-turn and then a left. An elderly farmer and his wife are out for a stroll. The farmer is ahead of his wife by several yards, but they're both walking at the same speed and she's making no effort to catch up. A dour little West Highland white terrier is trotting along behind her. I slow down and stick my head out the window:

"This wouldn't be the road to Gruline by any chance?"

"Oh yes it is," he said. "It most definitely is."

On two previous trips to Scotland, circumstances not entirely of my own making prevented me from getting to Iona. But this time I was going to make it.

Already Mull appears to be more interesting than Skye, but that could be an illusion caused by the absence of tourists here. Skye's no fun when you're in tourist gridlock.

At the Kinloch Hotel, back on the road to Iona, the lovely young woman behind the bar gives me a glass of Laphroaig. I tell her about having made the wrong turn, and getting lost.

"Oh, I saw you," she said. "Where you made the turn. I was coming by on my bicycle."

"Oh, that was you. You gave me a big smile and I didn't smile back."

"That's right."

"Were you smiling by any chance because you knew I was making the wrong turn?"

"Oh no," she said. "I had no idea. I'm just a friendly girl."

I said I remembered her long blonde hair streaming out behind her as she flew by. She laughed. Her hair was a sort of vitamin-enriched lemon meringue, and contrasted startlingly with her black, bushy eyebrows. Her name was Terry.

She said I shouldn't worry, I had finally done the right thing: I'd arrived at the right place, I'd be well taken care of here. I asked for the menu. She said, "Oh, I hate to tell you this, but the kitchen is closed." I put on a tragic look. "Wait a minute." She came back and said, "All you can have is the steak-and-kidney pie or the chicken-and-mushroom pie."

We chatted merrily until I began to sense everyone else in the pub was quietly listening. The other drinkers seemed to think I was taking up too much of her time: it appeared she was coveted by many of the locals. So I asked if she'd serve my pot of tea and chicken-and-mushroom pie at the table in the corner, by the window. She seemed to have lost her friendly manner. Could she have felt I was scorning her?

"Lancashire's flat, no mountains like around here," the couple at the next table were telling me.

"If you want to meet the English, come to Scotland," I observed.

"We watch the same television programs, though. And that's the main thing," he said, shrewdly.

"But we don't dream the same dreams," said his wife.

I've never seen a woman with a more expressive face than this Lancashire lady. Every time her husband said something, she would twist her face into a look of amazement, as if she had never heard anything so brilliant in her life. Sometimes, when he said something critical about anyone or anything, like about the tax on wine or whatever, her face would adopt a look of extreme disapproval. It was hard to say if she was mocking him or simply being supportive. "That's an expressive face your wife has," I said.

"Oh yes," he said, in less-than-admiring tones, "if looks could kill." She made a whole series of comical faces while he told me she used to be a schoolteacher and that might have something to do with it, for she knew all about the art of using exaggerated facial expressions to encourage children to be well-behaved.

She made an expressive face and said, "Yes, that's true. These campy theatrical facial expressions have become completely ingrained. I can't help myself. It's just me."

Meanwhile, Terry's shift was over. She put on her jean jacket and off she went to cycle home. As she was leaving she said goodbye to the new bartender, an Englishman with a curly beard who happened to own the place, she said goodbye to the Lancashire couple, and she said goodbye to several locals – but she noticeably didn't say goodbye to me, nor did she even look at me. Oh well, mistakes come in clusters.

By this time, lots more locals were streaming in. It was nice to be in a place that was overrun by locals rather than by tourists. The new bartender took a break from pouring drinks and ushered me up to a spacious room on the second floor overlooking the road, Loch Scridain, and a pair of lovely pointy and sensuously curvaceous mountains off in the distance. I sat there in silence for an hour. At one point, as I was breathing in, I heard a squeak, and when I breathed in again I heard another squeak. I'd been smoking a bit in recent days, and figured it must be the onset of emphysema. But the next time I didn't breathe, and there was a squeak. It turned out it was a squeaky little wren just outside my window.

Loch Scridain was at low tide, with extensive mud flats stretching up almost to the road. On the other side of the loch another band of mud flats gives way to brilliant green grass, then the land goes swooping up the sides of a foothill, over which loom the two afore-mentioned enormous volcanic breasts, like a pair of Vesuvii. One would have been Ben More, at 3,170 feet the island's tallest peak. The other might have been Coirc Bheinn, at 1,837 feet. From this angle they both seem the same height. What if they both started erupting at the same time? Red-hot lava would come rolling down almost to the front steps of this hotel. I was later advised they both have the potential to become active, and it could happen at any time.

Meanwhile, some bird over on the tidal flats is going "Ker-PEEP, ker-PEEP, ker-PEEP," at a fairly slow tempo, and then the same bird starts getting excited, ups the andante, and starts going "PEEP-pop, PEEP-pop, PEEP-pop," at an ever-increasing rate, until at a certain point numerous other birds join in, all going, "PEEP-pop, PEEP-pop, PEEP-pop." I've been advised these are oystercatchers. Apparently there is a dominant bird that gives the intro solo, "Ker-PEEP" – and then all the other oystercatchers join in for the "PEEP-pop" fun. But sometimes the chief oystercatcher gives a slightly different intro – something like a long-drawn-out "Brrrrrrrrr" four or five times before all the subordinate oystercatchers join in with a chorus of "Ker-PEEP." The chief oystercatcher goes, "Okay, where are all youse guys?" And they start going, "We're here, we're here," from all directions.

When I return to the bar, a man in his twenties is rolling his own cigarettes at a table by the door, his woman's not smoking; the man is drinking a Coke, the woman a Guinness. They're dressed in an unwashed proto-punk style from about 1972, very Brit. They play a quick game of backgammon. When they leave, one of the regulars at the bar says, "That was funny rules for backgammon." Another replies, "Och, there's all sorts of different ways of playing." Another fellow says, "There's the French rules, the German rules, the Italian rules – all really different." The first guy says, "I think they were playing hippie rules."

I DISCOVER IONA

Isle of Mull • Isle of Iona

Saturday, June 15. I'm interested in people, almost pathologically curious, and so people sense that quickly and tell me the strangest and most personal stories. I love reading fiction, but nothing I could invent could be as interesting, fresher, or more real than simply writing about the people I happen to meet in my wanderings. Also, this sort of factual writing is full of the elements of randomness, which often seems to have an intelligence all its own.

As we ate a large breakfast I hungered to know how the Lancashire couple had met. Mr. L. said, "Oh I picked her up at the Saturday-night dance." Mrs. L. pulled an expressive face.

"Sparks right off the bat?"

He was about to agree when she jumped in and said, "Oh no, absolutely not, I don't think so, no, not at all."

"Oh, I don't know," he said, charitably.

"It was more his mother wanting us to get married," she said. "She'd had enough of him. She wanted to be spelled off, and I was her choice." Her face went inexpressive all of a sudden, and an awkward silence ensued. But then Mr. L. spoke of his work: he was a production engineer in a machine shop. I asked about "deference," a major subject on Scottish phone-in shows. People phone in and say there should be more deference: they complain people don't know their place in society any more. Is there anything that can be done to bring the old system back?

Mr. L. didn't want to see the old system come back. He said twenty years ago there were certain kinds of hotels you never went in unless you were well-dressed. And even then you might not, depending on your social level, because you just felt it wasn't your place to. And there used to be a lot of tugging of the forelock to indicate respect, right up to the late seventies, when you encountered a laird or even anyone who happened to be wearing a pinstriped suit or driving an expensive car.

The curly-bearded Englishman came over to tell us about Mull, to which "people from all over the world were moving." Skye gets the tourists but Mull gets the settlers. "We have the Canadians, the New Zealanders, the French, and the Germans – all living here permanently, as permanent as life can be." On Mull there were two religious communities – the traditional Presbyterianism, with a sprinkling of Catholicism, and the New Age religious community, which has taken over a small island just offshore: he pointed on the map to the tiny island of Erraid, off the coast of Mull, and told me how to get there, or how to avoid it. As for the Isle of Iona, he said there were many on Mull completely ignorant of what goes on at the world-famous religious community there, "but it's a matter of them never having visited it or not having visited it in a long time. There was no real resentment because, without Iona, Mull would be much quieter than it is."

He also pointed out the location of a castle on Lochbuie, a stronghold said to have been owned in antiquity by the McFaddens, and showed me how to get there. The chapel nearby guarded a burial ground for the dreaded MacLeans of Lochbuie, who had moved in without invitation and dispossessed the McFaddens.

Terry from last night, was she a permanent resident? Yes, she'd moved up years ago from Glasgow and seems to be permanent now. I told him I liked the local weekly, the *Mull Newsletter*, and admired the writing. He said it was one of the many things that made him proud to be from here. He said there were no Tinkers permanently on the island, but they come over from the mainland when the winkles are in season. They park their caravans by the shore and collect winkles non-stop for three weeks or so. Then they take these "Tinker winkles" back to the mainland and sell them. And they get quite a good price for them too, he said, and with the profits they go off to Spain, Portugal, and all over the place.

This fellow seemed untroubled. He was a man who felt he had made the right decisions in life so far, and would probably continue to do so. He said he was originally from the Lake District of England. "But now I like to say I'm from Mull. It sounds nicer. And it's true. I am from Mull." There was hardly any crime on the island, not that gets reported anyway, particularly at this end, on the Ross of Mull. A couple of years ago a desperate young fellow went wild on Iona and stole a lot of stuff, and the mainland police helicoptered straight to Fionnphort (pronounced *Feen-a-fort* locally, and meaning "white port" or "fair port," because of the white sand), and waited for him there. When he got off the ferry, they collared him and said, "All right then, you come with us." When there's trouble with people on Mull they get deported to the mainland.

On Loch Scridain, a saltwater inlet from the sea, sometimes referred to as a sea loch, inch-high waves about thirty feet long come in to shore and break as if they were huge rollers in miniature. A tiny island in the centre of the loch has a single tree on it. The road is studded with ancient milestones. At the end of the loch, as it opens up into the sea, tiny flat-topped islands abound: one of them is completely flat on top except for a little rounded button of a hill right in the centre that would be fun to climb some lazy afternoon. Without stretching it, the island looks like a broad-brimmed flat hat on a little head.

In Bunessan, an almost-busy little town, small groups of tourists wander around, looking in windows, staring out over the water, saying "Hoot mon," and not spending any money. Now and then little groups of fishing boats can be spotted tranquilly moored among the sandy coves. Black-faced sheep graze around miscellaneous piles of ugly dirt and gravel, the houses are badly overdue for a paint job, and there is no shortage of microwave towers and transmitting towers with red lights blinking in the sun. A woman on a loud-speaker recites haiku in Gaelic. There's a curvaceous little bay here, with pure white sand made from the shells of land snails, according to no less an authority than Mr. Morton. On the far side of the bay two men, two dogs, and two sheep are having a terrible shouting, barking, and baah-ing match. The dogs are rebelling; they won't collect the sheep properly, and they run up and down the rocky-grassy hills. I can hear every word the men are screaming, and it certainly isn't Gaelic. "He's a fookin' eeeevul doog, that un." "Coomon, coomon, git back here you you you fookin' oogly indolent sluggish creecher." They get the sheep back to the house, with precious little help from the rebel dogs. And now the dogs snap to attention and take off looking for more sheep in the hills – but there aren't any more. No, the dogs aren't so hopeless after all, for now they're making a move on some sheep that have gone too far beyond the house, owing to a fence being broken. Now the sheep are running back to the house. The dogs go up to the shepherds for praise, but get none. "Git away, doog, git away," they say. Now the sheep are running around the back of the house, the dogs run around the front; one of the dogs stops and looks back to see if the other dog's still running. These are dogs that would clearly prefer to be having a snooze about now. The dogs are border collies, a breed renowned for its intelligence, black with bands of white around their necks. The two men appear to be father and son. They're now laughing. The crisis seems to have passed. They'll probably have to do this every morning until they get the fence repaired.

Iona is a tiny island, just over five square miles, with an amazing history and amazing legends. It's said to be the first piece of land to come up from beneath the sea at the beginning of the world, and will be the last piece to go beneath the sea at the end. Before the time of Christ, it was a centre of religious learning for the Druids, who, along with their solar deities and other mysteries, were exterminated by the Romans, but not here (their last stand was on the Isle of Anglesey, in Wales, in AD 60). Saint Columba arrived from Ireland in AD 563 to found a monastic community, and lived on Iona until his death in 597. Between 795 and 986, Christian-hating Norsemen attacked five times, with much slaughter, pillaging, and destruction. Saint Margaret, Queen of Scotland, rebuilt the monastery in 1074. Reginald of Islay, King of the Isles, again rebuilt it in 1203, and he also built the beautiful stone convent that is now a picturesque ruin. Numerous ancient kings of Scotland were buried here, including Macbeth and Macduff. The modern Iona Community founded in 1930, is an evangelical mission with members around the world. About 150 members live on the island, living the contemplative life.

I'd been waiting for the ferry and happened to say "Lovely day to go to Iona" to a lovely old lady who was standing next to me. Her husband turned around. He was carrying an old Nikon on a spiffy heavy-duty tripod. "Looks like your husband is a serious photographer," I said, and he came over and gave me a few tips on taking pictures. They were Eric and Joyce Greenberg, from the Lake District. They used to bring their three children up here, but now they come alone. Eric knew the works of H. V. Morton practically by heart. He recited a list of titles and said he'd read them all. He said Morton was a terrific writer, and we discussed his pros and cons and why he isn't being read now. The Greenbergs are great friends of the people who give the boat rides over to Fingal's Cave on Staffa Island, to the Treshnish Islands and to other tourist sub-destinations.

Eric and Joyce were insistent I come with them to Staffa right then and there, and listen to the sea making strange noises in Fingal's Cave, the "melodious cave" made famous by Felix Mendelssohn in his Hebrides Overture, after his 1829 visit. Jules Verne also visited, and featured Staffa in his 1885 book, *The Green Ray*. The tourist boat was about to leave. It was such a gloriously clear warm day without a cloud in sight, and you never know in the Hebrides, it might be the last lovely day till next year. Unfortunately, I didn't feel in my heart the timing was right. I wanted to visit the abbey community centre first, get a place to stay for the night at the hostel there. Eric and Joyce wanted me to take a room in a little house by the ferry dock, as they didn't think I'd like the church accommodations, but I insisted on going to the abbey first. So they ended up accompanying me, forgoing their trip to Staffa for now.

When we entered the ancient abbey, we encountered Fawn, a middle-aged lady from British Columbia, who said I would have to sign up for three days, and I had to share the room with three or four others. Eric and Joyce stood there in silence, but it was obvious they didn't think it would be right for me. I had innocently thought that it would be nice to be at least temporarily connected with the highly regarded Iona Community and have my money go to them. The Greenbergs took me to the canteen for a cup of tea. Faded BOYCOTT NESCAFÉ posters covered the walls, along with posters of starving children covered with flies. We popped into the bookstore, and instead of a "feminist fiction" section they had a "womanist fiction" section. "We found that *feminist* sounds a little too aggressive," said the clerk. I told her I suspected I'd be hearing the word *womanist* a lot in the future, and whenever I did I'd remember I heard it first on Iona.

But the whole atmosphere was actually a bit on the sanctimonious side, and I sensed the food would be ghastly too. This was a missionary outpost, and I was a little African boy in from the bush.

A thousand years ago perhaps Iona was a beacon of light in a dark world, but it seems to think the same situation still prevails. In a thousand years a beacon can become a bank.

The ferry dock seemed more my idea of a cultural focal centre. Alongside the dock was a little green-painted row house. It was the one that Eric and Joyce, who had by now given up on adopting me, leaving our next meeting to chance, had earlier pointed out. They had said, "Nora doesn't advertise, she doesn't have a sign out, but she's a lovely lady – and she does a lovely B & B. And her husband is the uncle of the man who gives the boat tours to Staffa." As I was going past the house this time there was an elderly lady mowing the little lawn in a nice pink dress and matching slippers.

"A little birdy told me you did a nice B & B," I declared.

"Oh no, we're all taken," she said. "No vacancies at all." She was lying.

"How many rooms do you have in that little house?" I queried, perseveringly.

"We only have the two doubles," she replied, with a slight emphasis on the word *double*. But her voice was softening; she was being won over.

"You're not being prejudiced against single people now by any chance, are you?" I said, with a slight emphasis on the word *prejudiced*.

Nora's husband, who had been tying up the roses, heard that last remark and didn't like it. He left the roses with a "Hmf," and walked around the back of the house.

"Oh no, not at all. Where are ye from?"

"I'm Canadian."

Magic word! She focused her eyes and gave me a good looking-over.

"Wee-yull, y'know, we do have a double vacant. An' I kin give it t' ye for the price of a single. An' ye can stay one night or two nights but then we're booked after that." She said she decided to change her mind because of my being Canadian. She likes the Canadians.

She doesn't like the Americans; oh, they're okay singly, but in groups they're far too loud. She said she had some guests only last week from Canada – from Detroit, she thought it was. I told her Detroit used to be in Canada, but since 1812 it's been an integral part of the U.S.A.

She looked down at her pink fluffy slippers and apologized for wearing them outside, but she always liked to wear these slippers while she cut the lawn or else her new shoes would turn all green. The slippers showed no sign of turning green. As we went into the house, there was a big cast-concrete boot on either side of the front door. Geraniums had been planted in them.

"Are those your good shoes?" I said.

"Those are the ones I wear in the winter."

I made some mild comment about the air of sanctimony at the abbey.

"What religion are you?"

"Buddhist."

She blinked nicely. I'd said another magic word. The Dalai Lama had stayed at her house. My mind boggled. Maybe he too found the abbey a bit too stuffy.

"How did you like him?"

"Oh, he was a lovely man!"

On the wall of the sitting room, in the place of honour over the fireplace, she proudly pointed out the picture of the Dalai Lama. Except it wasn't the Dalai Lama at all, it was some other lama in orange robes, and a shaved head, surrounded by adoring young women, and, a smile on his face, pointing his finger amusingly at the camera.

An old church, newly stuccoed and turned into a private residence, is surrounded by songbirds, and still has its stained-glass windows in place. Extensions have been added for a growing family. An old rusty bell sits on top. The church faces out directly across the bay to Fionnphort, and there's a terrible stench that rises from it when one is a bit downwind: they must be having trouble with their septic tank.

I'm sitting on a rock and the tide's coming in. Fingal's Cave on Staffa can be seen clearly from here. The blue of the sea is delirious, and with the sound of the waves, and the little sailing boats way off in the distance, it's like one of those lost afternoons from the fifties in the Mediterranean, and you can never recover it. It's strange to think of the Vikings suddenly appearing on this lovely horizon studded with islands, then coming ashore and massacring your fellow monks, and then, finally, you, right here, on the beach, by the rock where I'm sitting, on Martyrs' Bay, on a day otherwise much like any other day. The screams must have been heard over on the mainland, if there was anyone there to hear them. Anyway, it's unthinkable, and thank God it's been a thousand years. Was there anything the monks could have done to appease these brutes? Apologists for the Vikings maintain they were driven to travel over the seas because of the encroachment of Christianity in their own country. So when they hit an island in the Hebrides and saw signs of Christianity, it was their chance to get even.

A large raptor stands tall atop the tallest rock in this general area, strewn as it is with igneous rocks of various sizes and shapes. She's maintaining a solemn stillness, except for her ever-watchful, all-seeing head, which points in one direction for ten seconds, then slowly swivels to another direction and points there for ten seconds, and on and on. She swivels her head slowly and knows exactly when to stop. The sun sparkles on the waves: the light bounces all over the surface of the water, so that at times it seems there's more sparkle than water, it's almost complete illumination, and then beyond the rocks the reflected sunlight goes out to sea, getting thinner and dimmer as it goes. I have the beach to myself today, the white land-snail sand sweeps up from the sea and becomes capped with grassy green peaks and numerous little hills and holes, tiers and tors. We're surrounded by gently rolling farmland and odd-looking hills, and the land is more restless than the sea.

How many monks were put to the sword on this lovely little beach? The locals say it happened over and over again, and always in the same spot, but according to the books, the Norsemen raided in 795 and 801 without killing anyone, and then in 806 when they massacred sixty-eight monks at Martyrs' Bay. In 986 the abbot and fifteen monks were slaughtered at the White Strand on the other side of the island. Life is simple, but thinking about it isn't.

A fishing boat goes by with three guys in it, the captain steering and two men in the back. One of the two just stands there, but the other guy bends down, picks something up and throws it overboard. He keeps doing this as the boat passes from the extreme right to the extreme left of my swivelling viewpoint. I thought it might have been the guts of fish, but they don't clean fish at sea: that cuts the weight down – and the profits. Besides, they have to save the fish guts for catfood, and there were no gulls following them, so it couldn't have been fish guts, or anything organic.

The sun is definitely not getting any higher, but it's taking its time setting. It's sitting there as if stuck, suspended, not wanting to say goodbye to such a lovely day, one that it had such a big hand in making. The waves are moving in a wonderful conglomeration of ever-changing patterns in a long harbour which is composed of giant, irregularly shaped rocks. I'm standing on one right now the size of a beer truck. The waves arrive in an orderly fashion then bounce all over the place as they strike the chaos of the shore: they start eating each other like too many rats in too small a cage. A needle-like cormorant flies by, thin, svelte and aerodynamic, three feet long and with a humped neck. If there were hundreds of people strolling up and down, I'd enjoy this beach as much. But there's nobody here. Oh, waves, I love every green-backed one of you. It's a whole universe of waves, foamy white and deep emerald.

I hate to have to walk across this meadow of brilliant, juicy green grass with hosts of tiny white daisies (some of them are pink) and big fat buttercups. The flowers are so thick among the grass that it would be impossible to walk without stepping on hundreds of them. But what pleasure it is to be here, for it's not every day you get to walk across a bright green meadow full of blossoming wildflowers, with the ocean sparkling and sighing in the distance and the songbirds pouring their little hearts out so earnestly. There was a path but it died out. The sea and the sky mesmerized me for a couple of hours and now it's the birds and the wildflowers. Here's a park bench, in the best British style, overlooking sea and setting sun. There's a memorial plaque on it: in memory of "Hugh D. B. Morton, who loved this island – The Family." Could he have been related to H. V. Morton, who also loved this island, and raved about its beauty?

Now I'm standing atop a hill. The map has it down as Cnoc Ard Annraidh, the Height of Storm Hill; it looks like a top hat, straight up on all sides, but there are lots of little toeholds and fingerholds to assist the unpractised climber. It shoots up out of nothing in the middle of a gently rolling meadow, and it seems to be a great pile of rocks topped with gleaming thick grass. It's a geological, bubble-like, natural hill, and there are a number like it on this island. It's high, about eighty or ninety feet above the meadow, and it offers an exhilarating viewpoint for drinking in this gentle, modest, but heavenly landscape. I'm watching a herd of sheep below. These sheep are not clustered, they're fairly well spread apart in a most pleasingly civilized fashion, and they're doing their best to make a dent in the buttercups and daisies, which outnumber them a million to one. It's like a field of candy.

Off in the distance a lady carrying a purse is making the speediest beeline across the buttercups without even looking where she's stepping – and the beeline is leading her to the Morton bench so lately sat upon by me. You can tell she's dying to get there before anyone else, as she wants to watch the sun set, but she doesn't notice the buttercups: all her attention is focused on that bench.

Back in the village I sit on a ruined wall of Reginald of Islay's early thirteenth-century nunnery, the ruins covered with clumps of green grass and wildflowers, and watch a full cast rehearsing *The Tempest*. At precisely 11:26 p.m., I enter the pub. There are dozens of people sitting around drinking, but no one's bartending. A table full of women is busy drinking and chatting. A sixth sense tells me one woman, the one giving me the once-over, is the bartender.

"Is there any possibility of getting a pint?" I inquire.

"We closed at eleven," she says in an unapologetic voice with a Kiwi accent. She seems miffed because I picked her out.

"What if I get down on my hands and knees and plead with you?" I query.

"Particularly not then," she says, with an edge to her voice as bitter as death.

"What if I promised you a huge tip?" I pull out my wallet, and pretend I'm counting fifties.

Her eyes meet mine in a spirit of rancour.

"How huge?"

"Huge enough to turn you into a human being, at least temporarily."

"I'm sorry," she says, uncertainly. "It's been a long day and I'm tired."

KAMIKAZE CROWS ON DUN BHUIRG

Isle of Iona

Sunday, June 16. It's breakfast-time at Nora's place. Beverly and Kevin are from Bristol. Beverly teaches a course in the history of computing at a small college. These big football players, she says, they simply cannot stop hitting the keys with excessive force, and sometimes they'll hit a key so hard it goes flying across the room. Then when they put the keys back on they put them in the wrong place, so that when somebody goes to hit a j they get a k. Kevin is a tall, skinny fellow with black hair who, when he's not talking non-stop, is eagerly waiting for a break in Beverly's conversation so he can continue talking non-stop. His words pour out at a breathless rate, for if he leaves the smallest gap Beverly will start up. They always travel by train, and Kevin launches into a complex explanation of how the train works, along with lengthy descriptions of every station from Bristol to Oban. Without being obliged to take part in this competition, it's rather pleasant to hear them taking turns spouting information like a pair of intellectual firehoses. At one point they were discussing the ecumenical services at the abbey, which is becoming less and less interesting the more one hears about it.

Kevin knows a ferocious amount about everything. Until the end of World War II the British rail service was the greatest in the world, bar none. Then they started taking out little bits and pieces here and there and now there's not much left at all. When a line isn't considered cost-effective, it gets taken out.

"Now, who would have thought that?" I offer.

"Right you are. And if they were building a tourist attraction," says Kevin, "they wouldn't build one way out here on Iona, because that wouldn't be considered cost-effective. They wouldn't have the imagination to build it here."

Kevin said, wrongly, that all the monks were slaughtered in Martyrs' Bay.

"And that's why they call it Martyrs' Bay," said Beverly, causing Kevin to wince. "And what about that cuckoo, is it still around?" she added.

I said everywhere I went last night there was a cuckoo.

"Oh, there's only one cuckoo on the island," said Kevin. "It must have been following you around."

"How did that cuckoo get here?" said Beverly, with a sweet glance at Kevin.

"Probably on the ferry," said he. "Yes, he's been around for two years now, and he's driving everybody crazy."

A tourist comes up and looks in the window. Then she walks away. Very rude, I thought.

"Amurrican," said Nora, quietly.

"How can you tell?"

"Och, they're forward, the Amurricans. They come right up and look in the window. And I could tell she was Amurrican because she looked foreign."

"But how could you tell she wasn't foreign French or foreign German?"

"They're forward too. They're forward and they're foreign."

She later found out the woman was Irish.

I ask Nora about local amateur historians. "How about Mrs. Beaton?"

"Och, aye. Ooh, noo, Mrs. Bea – but she's too long gone, that one."

"Long gone, eh? Any others?"

"Well, there's Johnny Dougald, an' Charlie McPhail, an' Willie Cole."

"They know the history of the island?"

"Aye, aye, but they're all long gone, too."

"And there's nobody to take their place?"

"Noo."

"What a tragedy! How long have you been here again?"

"I'm only here twenty years retired."

"But your husband's been here forever?"

"Och, aye, David was born here, yis. He was born here, retired twenty years ago."

"Do you think he'd be willing to have a chat about the history of the island?"

"Well, see, he was away in the navy, then he wint to the Glasgow police. So he hasn't been here a-tall."

"Maybe we could have a chat about growing up on Iona."

"Well, their days were spent in Oban in the high school. They were away all the time. They only got home three times a year. Nowadays they go home every weekend. But in David's days, well, it was private digs an' ye had t'pay fer everythin', an' they jis' didna get home, an' the connections were no what they are today anyway."

The front parlour, which doubled as a breakfast room, was decorated with a vast collection of brightly painted ceramic statues of old pipe-smoking one-eyed fishermen, farmers, soldiers, sailors, little people sitting on mushrooms, travelling salesmen, con artists, lairds and ladies, kings and queens.

"These are my friends. Aye, I like faces," says Nora.

Next to her friends is an original oil painting. "An' this is by Charlie Badding, he used t'come in an' git a wee cup of tea an' things like that. An' one day he give me this paintin' as a gift, it was the first one he ever did. Isn't it lovely?"

"It's beautiful. What is it, a cow?"

"Noo, it's a horse."

"Lovely colouring."

"He's dead now."

"The horse?"

"Noo, Charlie Badding. He worked in th'Argyll Hotel. He was sitting out there doing this painting, and he thought that I had seen 'im, but I niver seen 'im. So he gave me this painting when he went away, an' when he came back he died."

Daphne the Kiwi (not the one who refused me the pint last night), pronounces her name Deaf Knee. She is leaving tomorrow, for Skye, after seven weeks on Iona. I was in the convenience store–souvenir shop where she works yesterday, and after only a short chat she kindly offered to lead me to the summit of Dun I, at 101 metres the highest part of the island, and her favourite spot on the island. I accepted gladly, for she could direct me to the hill fort up there, and the Well of Eternal Youth, and she said we might get a bottle of whisky and have a drink or two under the stars. But we left it open as to when and where to meet.

This morning I ran into Deaf Knee in the village but didn't recognize her at first. "Oh, it's you!" I said, brightly. "Yis, a'im Deaf Knee," she said. She gets off work at 9:15, and she'll be looking forward to climbing Dun I with me. I didn't recognize her because she wasn't wearing her working duds of tartan skirt and white blouse. She looks quite sporty in a pair of dark green shorts down to her knees. This is more my style, she said. I told her she looked terrific in both styles and I'd do my best to be there with a bottle of Scotch.

Now I'm resting on a bench above the ruined nunnery. Female voices with Kiwi accents float up from the beach: "So he saiz to me, he saiz, what if I get down on me knees and plead with you." "Tsk, the nairv!" You can see for miles in all directions and everything is appealing visually – there is nothing harsh, everything is gentle here. The map says this is Monk's Meadow. The occasional cyclist flutters by. The sea is milky green and clear where there's a sandy bottom, then darker where there's a rocky bottom, and then there are alternating and irregularly shaped patches of intense green and intense blue all the way out. Seabirds are piping back and forth with the most piercing clarity in the entire world.

Around the back of the island I can't resist climbing Dun Bhuirg, the Hill of the Fort. I've got a tenuous toehold here, and I'm finding myself slipping. Almost straight down there's an inlet from the sea, and it comes almost up to the base of the hill. A few tiny people down there are leaving their footprints on the clean white land-snail strip around the inlet. I feel like an angel in a Wim Wenders film. Little purple flowers are growing out of crevices in the rocks above me, and they're telling me to take courage, I'll soon be at the summit. There's an ancient hill fort up here, or traces of it.

From the top there's a wraparound view of the entire northwest quarter of the island, or whichever quarter you choose. There's not much left of the fort, just a few stones that, because of their geo-metric layout, must have served as some kind of foundation for a hut that provided protection for a small group in times of trouble. On closer inspection, the remains of a circular wall appear, the con-struction technique being to put two stones together as close as can be with no mortar. The walls would have been about eighteen inches thick. These stones and a few shards of Clettrabel pottery dating to the first three centuries AD are all the evidence we have of these people: they might have been slaughtered by the Norsemen, for we're told that Iona was uninhabited when Saint Columba arrived from Ireland in AD 563, the Druids having long gone by that time.

Because of the mist, mountainous islands seem to be floating above the water, an effect one never tires of seeing. A crow and a duck call out at exactly the same time, way off in the distance, at almost exactly the same pitch. Oh, if the heart could leap where the eye doth see! A bit over from the foot of the hill can be seen the remains, all covered in grass, of a stone circle: the individual mound for each stone is clearly visible. There's nothing about stone circles on my map. I suspect I might have discovered something. I'm sitting here absorbing the view and wondering how secure I'd feel if I were a Bronze Age man on afternoon watch – and all of a sudden a man's head, with a badly sunburned nose and a herpes sore under his left nostril, pops up right in front of me, followed by the rest of his body. He has quietly climbed the hill without my hearing him. He was from Aberdeen and wanted to know where the hill fort was. So I showed him and gave my interpretations and we seemed in agreement.

After he went, I picked up for examination an egg-shaped stone, marble white, with tiny yellow spots all over it. A crow came flying by and began circling me angrily, squawking its bloody heart out: the nutty thing was so upset because he thought I had an egg in my hand. I held it up to him and he had a good look, seemed satisfied it was a rock, and flew away. But then he came flying back, diving and screeching, and with a partner, double trouble. These kamikaze crows were flying straight at me, screaming their guts out. I pretended I had a gun and pointed my arm straight at them as if about to fire; they vamoosed so fast I had to laugh.

Somehow I manage to get back far too late for Deaf Knee. I feel badly about that, because it would have been a lovely little trip up Dun I, and she could have given me all her acute and penetrating observations on her time on Iona. So I don't know if she went up there by herself to say goodbye to Iona, or if she took another friend, or all her friends, or what. At the pub I get both a pint and some fish and chips. A Maori girl waits on me.

"You wouldn't be from New Zealand by any chance would you?"

"Why?" she says, suspiciously. The Kiwis seem to have a bad reputation on Iona, probably because there's so many of them. "Is it all right? Have you met too many of us?"

No, not at all; I mention having met Deaf Knee.

She said, yes, she's leaving us tomorrow. She looked sad. I should have asked where I could find her, but I was too shy.

CHAPTER 20

THE TIPPER
COMPOUND

Isle of Iona • Isle of Mull • Calgary • Dervaig

Monday, June 17. At the abbey I had a final chat with Fawn, the woman from British Columbia. I asked her where Macbeth was buried. A painful, confused silence ensued. It had never occurred to me she wouldn't know. She looked at me as if I were mad, as if nobody had ever asked such a silly question.

"Who?" she said, finally.

"Macbeth? Eleventh-century king of Scotland? Shakespeare wrote a play about him. Had witches in it."

She looked at me as if I were too smart for words, as if she doubted they had kings that far back. She seemed never to have heard of Macbeth.

"All the old stones," she intoned, "have been lifted from the graveyard and taken into the cloisters in the abbey."

"Not Macbeth's. I was just through the cloisters and there were many interesting stones but there was nothing for Macbeth or

Macduff, both of whom, according to my information, were buried here."

"Ah, that's the story anyway. But we wouldn't have a stone that old even if the story were true." She looked horrified at the thought of a stone that old. "Any stone there would have been from Macbeth is so ancient that it just wouldn't exist any more."

"There are a lot of stories," I said. "But in the Infirmary Museum there are several stones that go back six hundred years before Macbeth."

She looked as if she thought it cruel of me to have pointed this out. A fellow who had been listening in the other room came into this one with a great smile on his face. "Maybe some rich foreigner from America bought it and took it to Texas with him," he said.

This fellow was from Orkney, his name was Hourston, and he came to the Iona Community as a volunteer for a month or so each year. "It makes a nice change to be asked about prehistoric things. We're always asked about John Smith, the Labour Party leader. And if there's any controversial burial, everyone wants to see it. Few ask about anything that old."

John Smith (1938–1995) was a politician who had pledged his life for Scottish nationalism – and for fighting for a legislative assembly for Scotland. At Smith's funeral Tony Blair said that, if Labour won the next election, "I will be the prime minister who does it." Meaning give Scotland its legislative assembly. Of course, Labour did win and he in fact did do it.

We talked about what a wonderful funeral cortège that would have been, winding along the single-track roads of Mull and all. John Smith died young and had in his will that he wanted to be buried on Iona.

"If I put that in my will, do you think I could get buried here?"

"Och, ye'd jis' join a long list. Apparently there are not one but two Americans lyin' in the deep freeze jis' now waiting for the relaxation of the burial restrictions so they can eventually be buried on

Iona. But it is restricted to islanders and those resident on the island, you know, because it's a restricted burial area. And of course there are folk all around the world who fancy being buried here."

Coincidentally, in the churchyard there was a great crowd of English people huddled around John Smith's grave, and not a damp eye in sight. It seemed they came all the way to Iona to see this. And they were saying, "Ah, but there was a fence around it on television." They were disappointed it didn't have the fence around it.

"Didn't you see that on television? There was a fence around it!"

"That's right, I saw that. There was a fence around it. I remember seeing that very well indeed."

"But there's no fence around it now."

"Why not?"

"I don't know. It's terrible."

"More's the pity."

The woman who takes tickets at the Heritage Centre said, and I quote, "It's a known fact that there are no stone circles on Iona." I told her I'd found one and I pinpointed it on the map and showed her where it could be viewed from. "I can see you're an expert," she said. Not in the slightest, I said. She said nobody on the island was a bit interested in whether or not there was a stone circle there, except for herself, and she knew there wasn't, so there. I didn't know what to think, so I didn't think anything. I slipped down to the ferry, and back to Mull.

Sitting around the house reading a book, playing Scrabble with your spouse, or videotaping the cat is a whole lot better than looking for a place to stay on Mull at midnight, even if it's still light out. The little road is traffic-free, except for my funny wee Fiat. Everyone's sitting quietly in their kitchen drinking tea and listening to the breeze in the trees. There are lots of birds, sheep, cows, and lots of spiritually uplifting natural beauty. I drove along one section of the road where huge stones had fallen off the tops of the mountains like bombs, some landing in the sea, some right on the road. It's amazing they found the room to fit this road in. In places the road becomes a causeway, built over the sea to avoid having to blast away at the base of the mountains.

A sign says PUBLIC FOOT PATH TO CALGARY. A big black cow takes her own sweet time crossing the road, causing me to sit there twitching in my Fiat, then as soon as she's almost out of the way the grey one starts its stroll down the runway. Cows know how to torment us when they put their mind to it. And now here's the brown one. They cast shadows a mile long. There are plenty of signs saying PLEASE CLOSE THE GATE and KINDLY REFRAIN FROM COLLIDING WITH THE SHEEP, but no tourist-home signs, and then . . .

An English couple, the Tippers, Philip and Christine, both with a great sense of humour and enough intelligence to share it, have built a large single-storey house in a deep blue hollow down a steep unpaved lane from the main single-track road. It's called Croit Glack Gorm (The Croft in the Green-Blue Hollow), and it sits on a large lot, with many outbuildings and gardens full of flowers. Phil's a laid-back, funny, generous, retired policeman, and Christine's a smart little ex-schoolteacher. They also have two dogs, eighty chickens, and a whole coop full of assorted rare birds. First thing Mr. Tipper tells me after I dump my bag is, "I'm sorry we can't supply a young lady for you," to which I reply, causing a thoughtful look to pass over his friendly face, "How about an old lady then?"

He insisted I head down to the pub at Dervaig straightaway and have a pint of Caffrey's. It's just a mile down the road, and then come back in an hour, or two hours even, or any time I want, because they can't go to bed until it gets dark, and it won't be dark for hours yet. They can't go to bed until the rare birds return to their coops, and they don't do so till it gets dark, which can be a problem in the summer.

I try to get Mr. Tipper to come with me, but he insists he feels too dirty. It's a country pub, they won't mind, say I, they'll all be dirty. No, they wouldn't mind at all, but he wouldn't feel right. Have a pint or two, take your time, but make sure you drink Caffrey's. It's the best. Then his wife pulls up and she starts raving about what a wonderful colour my car is and how it's so feminine. When I get back I can have a cup of coffee with them, "and maybe we'll crack open a bottle of single-malt Scotch." There's never been a happier reception since Morton arrived at Dunvegan. I'm certainly glad I didn't stop at that pretentious art gallery–hotel with the Jaguars and BMWs parked out front, and, as for Calgary, it was only two houses and a fifty-gallon oil drum.

As I was leaving the Bellachroy pub in Dervaig, a fellow who'd been at the back all along (listening avidly, no doubt) came out, a tall, skinny guy, with great hairy ears sticking out: "Eeeh, y' forgot yer, is that yer cap there?" I put it on and looked at him. It was my Isle of Mull map cap, purchased from Deaf Knee on Iona. "Och, the map of Mull!" he said.

"Yes," I said, "whenever I get lost I take my hat off and get oriented straightaway."

The bartender, about twenty-five, is off to Calgary, Alberta, come November. She's going to stay in Calgary for a while, then she's going to work her way to Vancouver. Her big ambition is to work at Whistler. I chatted with her and with an Englishman who's been doing some fishing up here and some roadwork as well. He's busy right now expanding the road from one to two tracks up in the major urban centre of Mull, the Tobermory area, Tobermory being most famous for its tiny but renowned distillery. The roadworker confirmed that sections of the road had been built out over the

water, on a sort of causeway, and, as for accidents, he had just had
the one in all the time he was up here and that was when he hit a
tourist who had parked illegally in a passing place, which happened
to be atop a blind summit, the most dangerous kind of passing place.
A third car suddenly emerged at full speed coming over the hill. So
my friend had no choice but to slam on his brakes and hit the tourist,
just as the poor fellow had a camera sticking out the window and was
trying to take a picture, without getting out of the car, of a sign
saying HORSE-DRAWN CARRIAGES AND ANIMALS.

The bartender was saying her one brother married a Spanish
woman and lives in Spain, her other brother married a Finnish
woman and lives in Finland, and now she's off to Canada to see what
trouble she can stir up there. Her parents are sad and lonely, devas-
tated, out of their minds with Gaelic grief. And they're saying,
"Please, don't go, don't go. What will the neighbours think?" With
three out of three out of the country, the neighbours will think they
haven't been good parents, when God knows they've worked their
fingers to the bone.

But she has to go, her destiny is calling her: it's saying, "Cowboys
galore!" and "Come to Lonesome Cowboy Country" and "Pretty
Scottish girls are always welcome in Wild Rose Country." So I said,
"How could you do that to your parents after all they've done for
you? You shouldn't go. Stay put, you'll feel happier in the long run.
You can have chats with Canadian tourists and watch the Calgary
Stampede on the all-sports channel right here in this remote corner
of Mull." But she didn't waver in her determination.

The trouble with Mull is that, with all the English settlers, like
the Tippers, nice as they are, moving in, it pushes up the price
of real estate something fierce, and people born here can't put
together the scratch for a down payment on an old wrecked croft,
never mind the handsome villa they visualize owning in Canada,
Finland, or Spain.

Back at Croit Glack Gorm, the multicoloured rare birds, sensing darkness won't be all that long now, have started to retire into their little pigeonholes, and the crows are flying around making subdued *pcaws* as if they know that, if they let out a full-blast PCAW!, they might get shot. I'm bedazzled by the bounty of beautiful flowers in special little cultivated plots throughout the garden, the blossoms swaying on top of their slender stalks in the perilous gloaming. The delphinium blossoms are two feet in length for instance. It must be the long days of sunshine.

"Good morning!" A door slams and Mrs. Tipper comes wandering through the blossoming gloaming in her nightclothes. She looks as if she's been dozing. It's almost two in the morning. She mumbles, in a slow, yawning, sleepytime voice, something about the garden, her voice like an oboe over a symphonic background of subdued crow pcawing.

We wander around. The sun has now set, but there is still that midsummer quiver in the night air. "These are peas. An' they're broad beans. An' then two rows of tatties. An' Philip's got cabbages down at the back there. I've got fennel there an' we've got onions there an' Jerusalem artichokes there an' spinn-itch." She opens a squeaking gate into a sub-garden.

"What times does it get dark at night?"

She looks up. "Oh, about now. It doesn't get any darker now. This is it." Not even dark enough to see a star. The entire surrounding countryside and inland hills are etched in the gloaming like an old lithograph.

"And in the winter?"

"Well it gets light about nine o'clock. On a good day it should be dark by about quarter past four. But if it's a dull day, from two o'clock onwards you need the light on." She stops. "This is our polytunnel." We peer inside. "Yep, an' I got lettuces growing in there an' I've got all Chinese vegetables growing here an' I got strawberries up there. But unfortunately, this big sheep that's coming to us now" – I look, it bleats – "because he wants to get fed – again! You've *been* fed!"

Some serious bleating ensues. "This is Rodney, an' that's Rodney's mum over there. An' the other one's Teddy an' he's adopted. As soon as they hear that gate here they come looking for handouts."

"What would that tree be with the white flowers?"

"That's hawthorn. An' the red ones outside the kitchen windows are red hawthorn. An' they're called mayflowers here, because in Scotland they don't die until June, but in England they're a mayflower, you know, a true one."

THE SCONE
CONVERGENCE

Isle of Mull • Dervaig • Gruline

Tuesday, June 18. Blissfully brewing tea and chatting about the business of running a bed and breakfast is Christine Tipper: "We're not desperate for business. But because we're fairly isolated, it's nice to get to meet with the people," and so on. There's no word on Philip's whereabouts. He doesn't seem to be in the garden. "Sometimes people knock on the door an' ask for the rates, which are reasonable, an' they'll be responding by saying, 'Oh, that's too dear.'" But this doesn't bother Mrs. Tipper. She says, "Well you've missed out, mate," and closes the door behind them. "Tea?"

"Thanks. Those hawthorns, how high do they grow?"

"Well, that white one, I think that's probably its full size."

She spreads out her topographical map. There's a Loch Cuan and a village called Cuin on its shore. Mornish, Mishnish, and Quinish are the three northern peninsulas of Mull. "They were estates originally. Quinish is still an estate, an' Mornish would have been another estate, an' Mishnish, too. There used to be a school at Mornish, and another at Kilninian, but now Dervaig's the only one. Quinish is still owned by one person. His name's Jones, an' he lives in Hong Kong. He's a banker."

"Does he have a manager running the estate?"

"Yes. Delbert is quite good. He's not so much a manager, he carries out the jobs that he's told to do. But Mr. Jones is definitely in charge. He had him take down all the no-trespassing posters because in Scotland you're allowed to walk on the land anywhere, wherever an' whenever you want."

The house is comfortable, spacious, furnished in the most mainstream, middle-of-the-road, up-to-date U.K. style imaginable. The Tippers built it from scratch six years ago. "There was nothing here but undergrowth. It was all blackthorn bushes that were matted together. An' we had to cut our way through right up to the house site from the road."

She gave me the stats on the population of Mull – 1821: 10,612; 1841: 10,064; 1871: 6,441; 1881: 5,624. "An' today it's 2,700. But we're growing! We have babies now. We're beginning to get a younger population on Mull. It used to be an aging population."

"Transplants are welcome?"

"Yeah. Transsexuals an' everything." She was referring to a fellow in the area who had changed his name from Eric to Erin. In the pub last night he was dressed up like a woman. He was a hefty six-foot-eight and badly in need of a shave, but he wore a nice dress and heels. He was balding, with his hair at the side of his head sort of pulled down into a pair of braids, with two red velvet ribbons, and he was nicely made up. "He takes these giant strides," she said, "an' his little wife, a perfectly ordinary housewife with five kids, walks along behind him, trying to keep up." The family had recently moved to Mull from Leeds. "It's the strangest thing, by

Mull standards, an' it gives everybody in the community topics of conversation."

Lachlan "Lachy" MacLean, in his seventies, has farmed on Mull all his life, and is known as the foremost local folk historian on the island. He lives near Gruline, on a narrow isthmus between Loch Ba and Loch Na Keal. It's obvious he was a pretty swift guy in his day, and a well-spoken man, but he has now become hesitant and scattered in his speech. "I'm havin' trouble with my head." There are great pauses between each word, and lots of unnecessary repetitions, but he can still think, and ponder. His face is a little baked apple, but merry and full of smiles, and with diamond eyes. He has a lot of self-understanding, he's not burdened by excessive egotism, he's sure of himself. He's drinking tea and sitting on a chair he won't rise from for the duration of our chat. His daughter takes a break from playing hide-and-seek with her kids to put fresh pieces of rich chocolate cake on my plate. They weren't expecting me, and I'm thrilled by their hospitality. Soon I'm buzzing with chocolate overload.

"Eh, we have a lot of monolithic monuments, we've got standing stones, and we've also the cairns which are obviously prehistory. On the farm we've got four cairns. And that Dr. Clegg in Tobermory, he did a study of these monoliths, you know, the standing stones, prehistoric. I myself haven't seen it, but I believe it would be worth your while getting that. I know him when I see him in Tobermory. He has his books on show there. I thought he would have been the best person. I myself don't know much about the old cairns, they're quite sizeable things, obviously. I think all of them have been pilfered, or there's usually a hollow on the top, like it looks as if they've been explored."

I mentioned finding a submerged stone circle on Iona.

"I would be amazed if you did. But I don't know anything at all about Iona. I don't know if ye've heard of ley lines." He meant the mystical lines of natural energy, which dowsers claim to pick up, and along which antiquities can be found. "A gentleman came around and said he'd traced one standing stone by using ley lines. All these stones and such are on ley lines. Jesus, I'd defy anyone to find that stone unless you'd done it with some means like that he had; he just walked to it. And he said we've got thirty-two ley lines passing this farm. And they're all major. He reckons the terminal of all these ley lines is a clamshell cave which lies off the Isle of Staffa. You know, have you heard of Staffa? It's a cave called the Clamshell Cave. And most ley lines that pass this way end up at the Clamshell Cave."

"Good heavens."

"Most people pooh-pooh it, but if I was in their place, I'd be apt to have done the same, had it not been that the man came and said to me, 'Have ye a graveyard around here?' Yes, I said, there's one in the wood over there. So he said thank you and he went off and he came back the next day and he said, 'Ye'll either believe me or else think I'm jis' a nutcase.'" The fellow told Lachy that every holiday he goes walking with his dowsing rods, following one or two ley lines and seeing what he finds. The major ley-line convergence in Scotland is at Scone: "That's where they used to crown the kings and queens of Scotland. The ancients chose that because of the power that lay there, and not because it was the centre of Scotland. It was because they had some belief in this power. And he said that every holiday he takes, he chooses a couple of ley lines and follows them. This particular ley line that he was following, he looked at his notes and found that he was going from a Campbell stronghold to a Campbell graveyard. And he came to a Campbell stronghold near Oban, and the ley lines pointed across the sea, and he spent a week trying to find them, trying to pick them up, across to the islands. There's one across the road there, in our fields. And then he got divining, and he followed it and found the other one, which is in bushes down below."

"When you say he found it, you mean traces of the ley line? Standing stones, or old cemeteries?"

"No, the actual ley line took him to this standing stone. And then, which he said he wasn't surprised at, it took him to the Clamshell Cave." He laughs. "It makes a good story there anyway."

"Had you heard of ley lines before this fellow came around?"

"I'd heard of them, but I'd never given them any credence. I think I asked a scientist one time and he said it was absolute rubbish. But how did he find that particular stone? And he also asked if I knew of anything else, and one of these cairns, one that's been demolished with people taking the stones for the buildings. I knew of it, and I said yes. He said, is it that direction? I said yes, so he said, 'I felt there was something else in that line.' You couldn't see it because it was covered with grass at the time. Most people would say you have to be pretty gullible, because you obviously can't get them corroborated. I mean, history, you can get songs, or something like that, which can prove the folklore ye've been told. You can always check it by other means of cross-dressing, I mean cross-checking" – he lets out a big laugh, as if he'd had Erin/Eric on his mind – "but with prehistory there's not much chance of having it checked."

Besides, Lachy was too busy: even at his age, he still had a few projects he was working on, and this took up all his time. He was mostly interested in the local history around here, the Waist of Mull, because this was "the centre point of Mull civilization. But it's taken me all of the time I have to get what I've got."

I remarked about a phenomenon in Ireland, where people seem to find megalithic monuments invisible. "They could have a stone circle in their backyard and not know it's there."

"You know," he said, with great wisdom, "there's not only that. There's a Celtic tradition that if you didn't know about it you kept quiet. I don't know whether it was a belief or not. You know, even about the clearances, which was a tremendous upheaval in the area, people didna want to talk about them, yet maybe half their family would be away to America or Canada or Australia and that. They would rather forget about it. So you don't talk about these things. Forget about them. For instance, I was never told about the Highland clearances."

My jaw dropped. "You weren't?"

"Oh no, you were never told this. Always the glory of the British Empire. You know, the sun never sets on this glorious British Empire and that. And anybody that kept pushing the history of the place was always regarded maybe by some as being a bit of a bolshevik. No, we were never told about the clearances and that. Except that there were quite a few well-educated old men in your path through life who were interested in that sort of thing and were good storytellers. We were lucky we had a few of them back then, and they used to tell us stories. Some of it stuck. And that's the only reason that they call me a historian in this way, because I was told these stories by these old men. I don't know if this is much good t' you."

"Why don't you tell me one?"

"Oh, Gaw'! One old man meeting us going home from school, he asked us what we were doing in school, and we told him history. And he said, What area of history? So we showed him the book. And he looks up Wolfe in Quebec. And he says that's a lot of rubbish. You know, he says, Wolfe was the biggest rascal that was ever let loose in the Highlands after Culloden. He was Cumberland's right-hand man. And he gave licence to his men to do anything they liked. They slaughtered dozens of people. And, he says, you know when Wolfe was shot after climbing the Heights of Abraham? You know who he called for? He called for Dr. MacLean, who came from Kilninian down the road here. And he was the man that was with him at his last, and tried to do something for him."

"You mean Dr MacLean was in Quebec with him?"

"Was in Quebec in the army. He was third in line going up, in scaling the cliff. And when Wolfe was shot he called out, 'Get me MacLean!' That was just one of the stories I was told, but I always remember that one, which of course made us a bit more interested about Wolfe."

Lachy MacLean was amazingly generous with his time, considering there was a barbecue going on tonight and he had a lot of work to do to get ready. He was a little late and wanted to get changed. We had a good chat, in retrospect, but at the time I was burdened by feeling I couldn't quite find the right questions to ask him.

But then we got talking some more. Lachy told a good story about the role an oxhide had in the dispossession of the peaceable, friendly, co-operative McFadden clan of Mull.

"Is that a story that is told, or is it something that you read in a book?"

"No, it's just passed down. All my stuff is just stuff that I heard from old people. I can go back about sixty-five years of listening to folk. Where I was brought up, there was one old lady and there was a minister and myself; we're the only ones who's left from that area, the Lochbuie area, end of the island. And it gives you a shock when people say to you that you are the oldest one from that area we could find."

"When you were growing up in Lochbuie were there any McFaddens around?"

"Yes, there was two families, but they were related. I don't think there's anybody still living. There's a grandson of theirs, but he's a MacPhail. And I don't think he's got any interest in the family. The McFaddens, they seemed to be all tradesmen – joiners and masons. They were a very nice, very quiet family."

"Would they have been my physical type in general?"

"Yes, I would say that. A little stoutish. Short legs. They wasn't terribly stout, but one was bordering on it. Colquhoun was his name, they seemed to have that name in the family."

"Colquhoun McFadden?"

"Aye, that was the name. They seemed to have plenty of them from Lochbuie. I often wondered why there was no more of them left.

But this happened in twelve- or thirteen-something when the MacLeans took over Lochbuie from them."

"They cheated them out of their castle?"

"I think MacLean built the castle, but they cheated them out of their land. All these castles are built on a place where there was prehistoric forts. Aros Castle, every castle I've ever seen, was built on a prehistoric fort."

"You say the McFaddens of Lochbuie didn't have a castle, the MacLeans would have built that one?" The ancestral humiliations were accumulating fast, but they all had the ring of truth about them: a little like astrology, it couldn't be true but it often feels true.

"I would think that they probably had a stronghold of some kind there," he said, "because it's an ideal place for a castle. And you know they must have been there for quite a while, because the story goes that one day a McFadden was sitting eating a bone, you know, the marrow of a bone, when MacLean told one of his henchmen to fire an arrow at him. The arrow, I don't know if it struck him or missed him, but he thought it was time he was taking off. So he gathered his people around him and moved out of Lochbuie. Accents were put on different deeds, but mainly the story was always the same: after MacLean got established he got rid of the McFaddens Don't ask me what he was doing eating a bone."

"It says a lot. Before they were evicted from Lochbuie they had become reduced to the status of dogs, sitting around gnawing on bones."

"Probably it was a natural thing to be doing, because food would be scarce. If McFadden wasn't in control of the food, he had to take what he got. You often get people having to eat the marrow of bones. But the McFadden history was pretty short."

"So this MacLean went up to a McFadden and said, Would you give me enough land that I could cover with an oxhide?"

"That's right, and the MacLean, he cut the hide into strips and he covered so much land the McFadden and all his people had to clear out. And there was a story about a McFadden who was hung. He met MacLean of Lochbuie in the forest one day. P. A. MacNab has got that story in his book on the Isle of Mull: I don't think he mentions it was a McFadden, but I was told by local folklore for sure it was a McFadden. The McFadden met the MacLean o' Lochbuie and Lochbuie happened to hang the McFadden on the cliff. And it's a complicated story. And it's kind of an amusing one."

"Those are the kind I like," I squeaked, feeling the noose around my neck.

"He was hung. And at night, when they were carousing and wining and dining, somebody challenged one of them that he wouldna go and cut that man down from the tree. But also at the same time there was a McFadden and a friend, and they decided they were going to steal one of MacLean o' Lochbuie's bullocks. When the fellow came to cut 'im down, this other McFadden was sitting at the fire warming his hands up, and the fellow who cut the McFadden down, he thought this was the man that was hung. So he bolted and ran home. And the end of the story was that Lochbuie thought it was a great joke, and asked that a sheep be given to the McFadden family, every year on the date of that hangin', and also a sheep to the family o' the man that cut 'im down."

"I didn't know the McFaddens were famous in folklore. And then they became goldsmiths or silversmiths."

"That's right."

"They wandered all over the Isle of Mull. They were dispossessed, like Tinkers."

"Dispossessed, that's right. Tinkers, more or less. They lived in a place which was called Scallastle. There's a farm there called Scallastle – you can see it from the main road. You can see a lot of old buses out there. And that's where the McFaddens went after leaving Lochbuie. They went to live in Scallastle, but I don't know how long they lived there. And there's a bay there called Scallastle Bay."

Lachy couldn't recall the name of the ley-line fellow, but he gave me enough hints to think it might have been Archibald S. Thom, who collaborated with his father, Alexander Thom, on a widely respected book, *Megalithic Remains in Britain and Brittany* (Oxford, 1978). The elder Thom is also listed as the author of *Field Computations in Engineering and Physics* (Van Nostrand, 1961), *Megalithic Sites in Britain* (Clarendon, 1967), and *Megalithic Lunar Observatories* (Clarendon, 1971).

At precisely 5:52 p.m., I phoned Dr. Clegg from a lonely phone booth at a lonely crossroads near Gruline. He seemed impressed I'd been talking to Lachy and asked me to call him at 9:30 tomorrow morning, then come around to the house. I told him I'd made an interesting discovery on the Isle of Iona, and I wanted to discuss it with him. He didn't hesitate to completely ridicule the idea. There are no stone circles, as such, on the Isle of Iona, and he knows because he's been researching this for thirty years. As for his book that Lachy had mentioned, it hasn't been published, it's merely a collection of clippings, photocopies, and photographs, a research volume for his own pleasure and the pleasure of friends. It must be difficult to be in the field, if only as an amateur, for thirty years, and have some guy like me come over and think he's found something major thats never been known before. Yet I would phone him in the morning, I would visit him, and he would turn out to be a terrific fellow.

CASTLE MOR AND
THE LOCHBUIE
STONE CIRCLE

*Isle of Mull • Dervaig • Tobermory • Strathcoil
Ardurd • Lochbuie • Castle Mor*

Wednesday, June 19. Last night, by the time I found my way
out of the densest, darkest forest, where I'd lost my bearings exploring the spooky remains of Kildavie, a mysterious moss-covered
seventeenth-century settlement, it was after midnight. When I
pulled up to the Tipper Compound, their lights were out. When
I phoned this morning, from the pub in Dervaig where I'd taken a
room for the night, to apologize for having been too late (not that
they were really expecting me), Christine said I could have rung the
bell and they'd have let me in. She had told me that, but it had
slipped my mind, unfortunately.

Dave, the bartender, was saying last night that when he was in
France he felt proud to hear Scotland referred to as "the Land of
Ghosts and Castles." He also spoke about the "Gaelic mafia" on the
Islands and in the Aberdeen area: "It's no really the Mafia, like with
cement overshoes and all that. But they're nasty people – they want
to force other people to speak Gaelic. It makes things unpleasant. It's

a pressure group." He was a foe of Gaelic linguistic nationalism, but he was definitely a nationalist: up until about ten years ago you could pour a shot of Scotch for a customer by eyeballing it, he said. But now the government is insisting all drinks be measured exactly. "As always, the English are mucking things up." I couldn't resist telling him that in Ireland they give you the bottle, which has been marked, and you pour your own drinks, then hand back the bottle for them to determine the charge. He said he'd only been to Northern Ireland and hadn't heard that. Wait till he finds out I made it up!

An ugly young fellow was crouched sullenly over his rum and cola. He had a ragged little beard, with bare patches, and dozens of pimples. He couldn't understand why anyone would want to search out his roots: "The roots are always the same. It's just some family climbing out from under some damp rock and finding someone else who's just climbed out from under a damp rock – and biting him on the neck and sucking all his blood." The fellow was only about eighteen, porcine in appearance, with a snout-like nose and the air of someone who had recently climbed out from under a damp rock himself. He was planning to spend the major part of every day and night for the rest of his life in the pub. But his vision was compelling and passionate: "The human race is slime." The bartender and the regulars were amazed. They'd known him for years, but this was the first time they'd heard him speak, except to grunt for another rum and cola. He had a thin smile. He was a philosopher who had never read a book, but he'd developed a intellectual framework that seemed right for him.

After phoning Mrs. Tipper, I drove off to Tobermory. Dr. Clegg had a Hollywood quality about him. In his red velvet smoking jacket he resembled Cesar Romero in his later years. He had a beautiful, charming wife, twenty-one years his junior. They'd both been married before, with kids from before but none between them. He raved about the "Celtic walls," said he'd love to do some excavation work on them and find out whether there would be any way of ascertaining when they were put up. They're all over Mull, they're all over Scotland, and nobody knows what they were put up for, or even when. He thought they were border markers. But they certainly weren't animal enclosures, as Morton, who had little patience with mystery, declared them to be. I didn't tell him that in my opinion they should more rightly be called "Pictish walls." He spoke about the tall stone that would often be found on either side of a gap in the wall. Also here and there along the wall there would be built into it a structure that resembled a fort. Or who knows what it was?

The doctor's place was near the golf course, in a modest subdivision of newly built houses, all in dull colours, so as not to clash with the bright surroundings. He was originally from Yorkshire, but had been on Mull thirty years. An ardent golfer, he's busy editing his father's memoirs, and at the same time he's writing the history of the Tobermory Golf Club, which displays itself in green splendour outside his rear window. He showed me some pages of the book he's putting together on the monolithic monuments of Mull. His smiling wife wore a colourful dress. The house sparkled, with not even a dustball in a corner or a nose-smudge on the window from looking down the road to see if I was coming.

But nothing's perfect. The doctor was doing so much that nothing was getting finished. That's the dark side of bliss – being comfortably retired but with too much on your plate. He said there were so many things standing in the way, he didn't know when he'd ever finish any of his projects. I raised my coffee mug and wished him a long life. He needed to sit back and figure things out, make sacrifices.

He took me for a fellow who could handle disappointment. He kept saying, "I don't mean to pooh-pooh what you're saying, but . . ." and then he'd launch into a calm and reasonable pooh-poohing of what I'd been saying. He for instance brought out a huge tome which claimed my "stone circle" was the remains of an ancient building. He gave me a list of books he suggested I read in preparation for writing the book I hadn't told him I was planning to write. He said he's passionately interested in the monoliths, but he pooh-poohs all the mystical side of it.

In spite of his anti-mystical stance, he had the soul of a mystic. He'd been researching the Beatons, the famous faith-healers of the MacLeans of Mull. He was rightly proud that, although it was thought they had died out in 1750, he'd recently found a document indicating they existed up to a much later date. They were sometimes sent for by French royalty to treat their aches and pains.

The Cleggs were once travelling in the Sutherland region and came across a holy well with a tree on which people had attached rags – a rag well, as they call these things in Ireland. Her daughter had been feeling ill, and it was noon. So Mrs. Clegg put a rag on the tree by the well, and later found out her daughter's health had improved considerably at that time. When I was pleased with that story, the doctor ventured to tell me his daughter had at the same time been ill with cancer, and he placed a rag on the tree as well. That day, she had a major remission.

Dr. Clegg also spoke of a certain beautiful three-stone alignment, which I'd visited, on the side of a hill near Dervaig, overlooking the River Bellart where it flows into Loch Cuan. He mentioned that there had been a fourth stone but it had sunk beneath the surface of the earth. When I'd told him I didn't know how big the stones would be on my "stone circle" on Iona, because of the rate of sinking, he had pooh-poohed that notion. But why would this fourth stone on the dry downward slope of a hill near Dervaig be sunk, but mine in a sunken soggy bog on Iona couldn't possibly be?

Then again, stone circles are usually not set in a boggy hollow. So I merely asked him what was on the top of the mountain those Dervaig stones were pointing at. He looked it up in the big tome. He said there was a hill fort up there, but it had been badly disturbed in recent years by some hill walker who built a sloppy cairn right on top of it.

In Tobermory Harbour two large fishing boats, pulled up on the beach and covered with festive balloons, were being transformed into tourist boats. The hulls were being sanded and painted. The whole lower town was painted in an amazing variety of pastel shades. This is a familiar tourist promotional scene; it's in all the brochures. A MacLean get-together seems to be in full force. An obese American man with a small camera was walking down a hill, completely out of breath, and had a hat on saying MACLEAN. I even saw some German tourists getting out of a car on the rear window of which was pasted a bumper sticker saying MACLEAN CLAN.

All in all, I think I'd rather be a McFadden than a MacLean. Think of the guilt the MacLeans must feel for having ripped off the McFaddens so badly. The McFaddens don't have the blood of any MacLeans on their hands, but the MacLeans will never erase the blood of the murdered and dispossessed McFaddens – sweet little people, humble people, bone eaters, tradesmen, good people, funny people, smart as a whip in their own way and slow to anger. And here I am heading down to their ancient stronghold.

A glorious sight loomed up at the cutoff to Lochbuie and Croggan from the main road, at a point by the twin villages of Strathcoil and Ardurd, twenty-nine miles from Fionnphort and twenty-three from Bunessan, six miles from Craignure and seventeen miles from Salen, and with a view out over Loch Spelve and the nicely wooded Illean Amalaig. At that point stands a twenty-foot-high stone cairn memorial to the poet Dugald MacPhail (1818–1887), and engraved on the plaque are a few beguiling and intriguing quotes from his poetry in Gaelic, and then in English: THIS CAIRN IS ERECTED WITH STONES FROM THE DWELLING OF THE BARD. Would it have been common in those days to tear down a Bard's house when he died? The cairn's a massive square tower of complex and thoughtful design. They must have loved Dugald in these parts. He wrote Mull's

Gaelic anthem, "An t'Eilean Muileach," at a time when it was considered dangerous even to speak Gaelic.

This narrow, winding, up-and-down, unpaved, rocky (in places), and decidedly intermittent road to Lochbuie is lined with brilliant gorse and rhododendrons, the latter probably descended from those planted by the McFaddens, who are definitely the non-threatening sort. The McFaddens aren't big winners of knighthoods, Nobel Prizes, and such like, their poets are more likely to be hanged than to have statues built from the stones of their houses; also they can be stubborn and opinionated. But I've never met an unlikeable McFadden, so it's painful to ponder some McFadden being hanged on a whim by a MacLean. Whether my gang was from the Ayrshire branch, the Donegal branch, or the Mull branch, they're bound to have a single root way back in the mythological era, probably in Donegal.

This part of the island, with its tree-dappled roads and glorious vistas, is awakening in me little feelings that can only be called ancestral memories – deep inner moans and tingles of semi-recognition, the ancient déjà-vu experience that can be interpreted in so many ways. I'm surrounded by BEWARE LAMBS signs (they can be nasty when riled), and a great multitude of small oak forests in deep glens and along winding rivers, as well as sprinkled along the side of the road and up the hills. There are even deeply knowing little patches of oaks along the shore of the loch. In Scotland, even the landscape seems intelligent.

Out in Loch Spelve can be seen dozens of prosperous-looking salmon farms, right where they should be, within sight of the sea, instead of on a little lake that feeds into a tender trout stream. In each farm there are eight compartments, two sets of four, each about forty feet square, with a walkway down the centre and narrower walkways around the outer edge. The salmon leap into the air. Would any of them ever jump high enough to get out, which they are definitely trying to do? Great gangs of gulls are circling, looking for something dead to eat.

Loch Buie is a huge sea loch surrounded by Highland cattle grazing on gentle slopes. Ben Buie, directly above us, is a pyramidal volcano, 2,355 feet high, that at one time looked down on a teeming, squalid Jurassic Park of life forms. On its lower slopes grows a forest of those small, twisted, unusually shaped trees: some think it's the wind that twists them like that, but I think they grow that way. If you see one that's not twisted, it means the wind untwisted it. Along this part of the road, which would be unchanged from the days before anyone had ever heard of a MacLean, runs an old Pictish wall that would excite Dr. Clegg; it's covered with thick moss. In a glen like this, time doesn't have much of an impact.

When the MacLeans were digging the foundation of the unusually quaint and colourful Saint Gilda's of Lochbuie in 1876, they found a stone carved in the shape of a cross, about eighteen inches wide and forty inches high. It's badly discoloured – green-, orange-, and red-stained – but it's dignified and solemn. It was probably carved by an early Christian, or perhaps some crafty scoundrel wishing to sell it to a Christian for food. Discovering an ancient cross while digging a foundation for a church must have caused quite a stir. In the wall to the right of the altar is a piece of the altar of the Church of Merry-le-Hart, a slab that covered a relic of a Bishop of Metz, in Germany, who died in 1851. The church was set afire by the retreating French troops in 1870, and a French priest risked his life by rushing into the burning church, breaking the covering slab, and rescuing the relic. The late MacLean of Lochbuie, being at the time the war correspondent with the German army for the London *Times*, "acquired" the piece. It was eventually installed in this church, which was built after MacLean of Lochbuie had a serious disagreement with the minister of another church over the cleric's habit of herding his ducks onto Loch Uisg and spoiling the fishing.

The small, dark, squat, moss-covered, turreted stone tower of Castle Mor stands rooted in the heart of Mull, on the shingled shore of tidal Loch Buie. It's so decrepit that light shines through it; the construction techniques are a few centuries behind the refinement of the thirteenth-century Duart Castle, for instance. But it's handsome, romantic, and not in complete ruins. It could be repaired as a dwelling place for some meditative recluse. This is the ancestral land of the McFaddens, now referred to contemptuously by the MacLeans as "hangers-on." This castle is little known and seldom visited. It's not signposted at all. It just sits there: a clever old pile of rocks at the side of the sea, a single tower really, about four storeys high, and with the narrow irregular slits for windows we know from numerous other defensive fortifications of the era. The MacLeans say they built it, but to my eye it looks much older. There's a single wooden door, securely padlocked, but the castle is said to be built around a well, which is always completely full of pure, fresh water, even to this day; the more one takes out, the faster it fills up. No wonder the MacLeans coveted it.

Two hundred yards back from Castle Mor, on the other side of a handsome, low-slung, porticoed estate (until recently owned by the MacLeans of Lochbuie), is a splendid and little-known stone circle from remotest antiquity, erected long before Stonehenge, by people unknown. With plenty of room for viewing, the stately circle is graciously surrounded on three sides by a tall, thick hedge of hawthorns, pink and white intermingled, purple rhododendrons in great profusion, and, beyond and above, the looming pointed purple peak of Ben Buie. A separate stone, off by itself, stands about seven feet tall; by its positioning and shape it subtly causes one to notice another larger stone, about fifteen feet high, on the opposite side of the circle and equally distant from it. The nine deeply serious, deep-brown, squat stones of the circle are smaller. They're all relatively smooth, they were all quarried at the same place, as the stones of every stone circle seem to have been, and some of them have pointed tops, while others have square tops. Each stone is said to be planted in a pit filled with football-sized boulders to ensure that it will stay standing until the end of time.

This is a splendid sight, something to remember forever, the best stone circle on Mull, bar none. In fact, I'd put it in category A for sure, along with all the more famous megaliths. It would be a magnificent sight for even the most knowledgeable and experienced connoisseur of stone circles, and it was obviously erected for deeply shamanistic reasons, somewhere around five thousand years ago. It makes modern works of art, even the greatest, seem shallow and insipid by contrast. The effect it has on me is indescribable: it's as if my subjective apprehension of the present moment has expanded to take in five millennia.

Before I left on this trip, my friend Ian McConnell of Victoria, B.C., instructed me to urinate on the stones for good luck. Dr. Clegg instructed me rather to pour a little libation of good Scotch on each one. I have a bottle of Old Mull with me, and I go around, touching each stone, and pouring a bit of whisky down its side until the bottle is emptied. If I had drunk the bottle myself I wouldn't have felt this way, almost high enough to fly.

Hats off to the hated MacLeans for having kept their hands off these stones, and for having honoured them by keeping their location so beautifully maintained, and for having boxed them so intelligently in this spacious meadow dedicated to their beauty. Within the hedged area the grass is Iona-like – rich green and dotted with wildflowers. There's no livestock around. Thank you, God, for bringing me to this place. It's glorious. And I had it all to myself! This circle will be with me forever. In fact, it seems to have been with me since day one. There's also a strong sense that the circle would have been very much venerated by the ancient McFaddens of Lochbuie, and they must have suffered greatly when they had to leave this area.

The MacLeans aren't in Lochbuie any longer. It's said they lost this estate through gambling. Kenneth MacLean was the last MacLean to hold the Lochbuie estate. He toured Britain and North America as a singer, before World War I, giving concerts in Gaelic and English. He later won a military cross at Ypres. But he ran into financial difficulties after the war through gambling debts. He went on another world tour but was unable to raise enough money and was forced to sell the lands stolen from the McFaddens eight centuries earlier.

SETTLERS' WATCH

Isle of Mull • *Dervaig* • *Tobermory* • *Fishnish* • *Ardgour*

Thursday, June 20. I'm back at the Tipper Compound, but how did I get here and how did I get this woozy headache? My memories of last night require some sorting out, perhaps with the help of an independent witness. Some couple from Florida were here (and still might be). We all got plastered on Phil Tipper's Old Mull, and the Florida folks were drunker than we were, because they were down on their knees hollering, screaming, demanding we accept the Lord Jesus Christ into our lives. Scary? You bet! It was Dick and Connie's first time out of the U.S.A. They won this trip in a contest, you could tell, though we didn't like to ask. They'd spent their entire lives snoozing in a remote backwater of old Florida, and suddenly they were in a remote (but wide awake!) backwater of old Scotland. It was just too much for them to take in! They'd never even heard of culture shock before. Maybe they'd never even heard of Scotland. It was so unlikely for them to be here. It's now 11:16 a.m. and they've managed to get away on their trip into further areas of godlessness.

236

Christine has everything under control in the kitchen. It looks like a nice day, but Mr. Tipper still hasn't woken up.

"Do you think maybe you should check to see whether he's dead or not?" I queried.

"Oh no, he's snoring in there," she said, reasonably. "He's just doing all the things men do when they've had too much to drink."

Over tea Mrs. Tipper further relates the saga that brought Phil and her to Mull, and why they stay here in spite of a certain amount of local resentment of their presence, their integrity, their industry, their pioneering spirit.

"We lived in a village in England, an' all our neighbours were Scots, really." There were forty houses in the village, and she went through every one of them, telling me who lived in each house, and why, and how they related to the whole, and if they were Scots or not, though most of them were. "In fact, there are two million Scots in England and nobody says the Scots are taking our jobs. The equation doesn't make sense," she says. "The Scots obviously feel threatened by the English in some ways, an' it's probably because of history – but we English are so unaware of it."

Phil got up and staggered around, bumping into doors and walls, groaning. Fifty-seven years old and still treating himself like that! Christine helps me confirm my wildest jagged impressions of the night before. Phil actually was down on his knees and praying along with the Florida guy, but I steadfastly refused. He was siding with them because they shared his interest in firearms. In fact, Phil had been showing them his hunting rifles and whatnot. "These two have their heads screwed on straight," Mr. Tipper kept saying.

In Mrs. Tipper's view, Connie had been noticeably sober and stone-faced throughout the festivities because she was stressed out from having to endure Dick's driving. Dick told us that he didn't even know they drove on the left in Scotland until he pulled out of the airport parking lot and everyone started honking at him. He still hadn't figured out how to use the passing places. "It must have been absolute hell for her," she said. "Also, he had no idea where he was going or how to get there." She'd noticed that, though Dick had been laughing about it, Connie didn't crack a smile.

At one point I had asked Dick and Connie if they did much reading. "You know," Dick said, standing up and pointing his finger heavenward, "my poor old pappy, God bless his soul, always said that the only thing worth reading is the Holy Bible, and the older I get the more I think he was right."

"Don't you even look at the occasional skin magazine?" I said, to the mutual glee of everyone – except, of course, Connie.

They lived in a place called Turnip Key, down around the Everglades.

At one point Christine, in a lull in the conversation, said, "I'd better show Davy his new room, because you two are in the one he was in last and we wouldn't want him wandering in there and sleeping three in a bed."

That was a bit too naughty an idea for the likes of Deadeye Dick. "He'd be dead," he said, with the meanest look I've ever seen.

But things really got serious after Dick and Connie went to bed. Mrs. Tipper was checking on the lambs, and Mr. Tipper got a bit emotional. He started talking about his mother, who had died of pernicious anemia at the age of thirty-seven. He was about eighteen at the time. He confessed he had great difficulty getting his mind around that. He had to raise a bunch of younger siblings practically single-handedly, and it was "extremely difficult."

Strangely, his mother's name was Christine, and both his wives were named Christine. His first wife, to whom he'd been utterly devoted, died of cancer at the same age as his mother. "That was a monumental coincidence that shook me to the very foundations of my being," he said. He spoke movingly and at a very personal level about his first wife. The mourning never ends.

Now that Tobermory is all spruced up with bright pastel paint, it's become a featured fixture of the Beautiful Scotland books, and it's spawning a whole school of imitators on the islands and up and down the west coast. On the narrow sidewalk of the main street of Tobermory, to which I've returned to say goodbye to Mull, someone is painting a baked-goods store lime green. The ladder goes right over the sidewalk and everybody's walking under it. One merry old guy catches my eye.

"You know, you Scottish people aren't superstitious, are you?" I told him.

"No. We're Christians, that's why."

"But everybody's walking under the ladder."

"Aye, it's only Christians who walk under these things. They don't believe in superstition." His flat tones were testing me out. Some of these single male tourists are right barmy.

"So you can tell the true Christians from the Christians in name only by who walks under the ladder."

"That's right. Oh yes."

"One young lady I noticed, she wasn't quite sure whether she was a true Christian or not because she *ran* under it."

"Eh eh eh eh." His tone brightens. "Is this yer ancestral home?"

"Ah, the Scottish McFaddens haven't heard a word from the Canadian McFaddens for a hundred years."

"Yer jis' diggin' 'em up now?"

"With extreme caution."

"That's wise."

An indignant waitress in a haggis shop disabused me of my scurrilous notion that Tobermory had been painted such outrageous pastel colours only in the past few years. She claimed to have been in Tobermory twenty-six years, and the buildings along the main drag, with certain understandable exceptions, had always been painted in pastel shades. How did people figure out which colour to paint? Do they have committees in charge of such things? "Oh no, they just stick their heads out of the window and see what their neighbours have got and they choose something different. It was all done on an individual basis. One person started doing it and pretty soon everybody was doing it. Like just about everything, I suppose."

And then she said, "Did ye go in the Island Bakery?" I said no, but I had looked in the window. She said, "That's no enough. If ye go in there ye'll see a cake that's been baked in the form of the town, with the yeller icing, and the orange icing, and the pink icing, and the lime-green icing, and whatnot." So I went and sure enough it was one nice cake. It looked like a miniature version of the town. Every little window was in exactly the right spot. They even had grey icing for the bank and the church. The cake was about eight feet long and about two feet high and it was baked by Fiona MacLean, whom I never had the opportunity of meeting but whom I'd like to give a little tip of the cap to, because this cake was a true work of art by any criterion.

"Do you mind if I take a picture of your cake?"

"Go for it," said the wee lady in the shop.

I picked up a knife and pretended I was going to cut myself a piece. She became alarmed: "Hey, that's not how you take a picture."

The time had come to get off the island. I was second in line at the ferry and sat quietly watching the young couple in the car ahead smooching and sweetly romancing. When I got out to check the ferry schedule, they got out, too. They were English, a friendly, animated, easygoing, and highly intelligent young couple in their mid-twenties, John Chalcraft and Fiona Arnold. As we chatted away I happened to glance into the back seat of their car. There was a large rusty-brown metallic ball the size of a basketball, and next to it was another one which had been shattered, as if it had somehow been blown apart by a force inside it.

"We've been on a mission," John said.

Their trip to Mull had a sentimental component. When he was a kid, John had been on a camping trip in the area and was involved in a terrible accident, with serious injuries, though he had since made a complete recovery. There were five kids on the trip and they had a fire going on the beach.

"It was the Isle of Lunga, the middle one of the Treshnish Isles," he said. "They're the small islands only to the west of Mull by about ten miles into the Atlantic. There were five of us camping on this uninhabited island and we were putting things in fires, like fifteen-year-old boys do – to watch them explode. So we put this marker buoy in the fire to watch it explode, and we moved away from the fire, and it didn't explode. So we went back to the fire, and it did explode."

He must have told this story numerous times. He had it down pat, but he was still thrilled to be telling it.

"And what it actually did was hit me in the face here" – he pointed above his right eye – "and it scarred me and stuff. I've got a scar here and a scar there. And then while I was lying there unconscious, I woke up and it was there burning against my arm. But I didn't notice it was hot, because you feel a lot of nausea, and also I think because the nerves were burned away, so I touched it and realized it was hot, so I said, Oh, get it off. And then we were very lucky in that a yacht was visiting the island and the crew were on the beach. And the crew were able to radio for help, for a helicopter from one of the ships at sea."

"Wow!"

"So they radio the Coast Guard, and the Coast Guard then assesses what's going on, and in fact there was a helicopter in the area on exercises from a Royal Air Force ship, and it came, and it was there within about two hours that night, at eleven."

"That couldn't have been a pleasant two hours for you."

"Nope! I had to walk – a mile actually – to a place where the helicopter could land, and I was covered in blood from head to toe, and I had bandages and all sorts of stuff. So it was quite a significant experience, you know. You're fifteen years old, and you don't think anything nasty can happen to you, and then suddenly, you know, you really mess up. So I get helicoptered out to this hospital."

"So you've come up only now to gather the pieces of this object which had suddenly become important in your life."

"We tried to get it last year. We knew that this thing which had exploded, we knew it exploded into two pieces, because the people who were with me said the one piece went out to sea, and the other piece was the thing that burnt me. And, yes, we came back last year, me and Fiona actually" – Fiona's smile acknowledges the mention of her name – "but we failed to get to Lunga, because the guy who ran the pleasure boat wasn't going there, because it was the wrong time of year. So this time, yeah, we got on the boat, and we went out, and we found it in the gully."

"Two pieces," said Fiona.

"Amazing! What a great story!" He probably wanted a bit more than that, but I was speechless. He went in the car and got out the old marker buoy – both of them, the intact one and the shattered one. He had found the actual piece, I was convinced. The intact ball was to show what it had been like before the explosion.

"Yeah, it was good fun, but we're not sure that that is the actual thing that we've discovered. But it was exactly in the right spot – in the gully. But it's the right size, and they don't make them like that any more."

"So you found both of these?"

"Fiona just wants the intact one as well." He lovingly stroked the piece that hit him.

"And it hit you in the head —"

"Yeah, like that." He taps his head with it.

"With the sharp edge?"

"Well, we're not really sure, but it managed to create a scar which was black and started here and went down to here, and I was pretty swollen up."

"Let me see how that fits?"

I put the fragment to his face. It was the right piece all right. It fit the scar perfectly.

He took the intact ball and tossed it up in the air and let it drop to the concrete with a great clang. It bounced heavily a couple of feet and came to rest still intact.

"So you must have been a big hero when you got home."

"No, not at all. Not a hero. I was the laughingstock. I was the idiot. No question, it was either irresponsible idiot or unlucky boob."

This is what I love – a hotel room on the seashore with the windows open, the moon shining in, and the sound of waves smashing, swirling, cascading, and generally having a big night on the rocks below. This is the rather decrepit but once-handsome (and may be again some day) Ardgour Hotel, on the north terminus of the Corran Ferry. From my window I can look further up Loch Linnhe, a Norwegian-style fiord, towards Fort William at its end, the lights of which sparkle like a demonic little string of fake diamonds way off in the distance as far as you can see, beyond the last of the mountains. It's a clear night and the moon is a thin crescent, but it is helping illuminate millions of mountains, including the fifteen I can see from here, seven on the one side of Loch Linnhe, and eight on the other, all outlined against the darkening turquoise sky, and the moon is sitting up above Fort William like an angel. There's nothing like a room with a view, especially when there's a bar downstairs filled with lots of strange and wonderful Scots. In fact, I think I'll go back down.

Wild and loud seventies Pink Floyd-type instrumental rock is sucking up all the sounds of normal human discourse. You have to plead with your ears to figure out what people are saying beneath the din. There's a huge bottle of McKinley's, about waist-high, filled not with Scotch but half-filled with money. The bottle is

marked FOR SCHOOL KIDS' OUTINGS, ETC. A sign over the bar says:
PLEASE DO NOT ASK FOR CREDIT AS A PUNCH IN THE MOUTH
CAN BE OFFENSIVE.

The guy standing next to me is Wally Cooke (pronounced *Koo-wick*), a tipsy Welshman. I can't understand much he's saying, but I like him a lot, and luckily he's not saying much just now. He's a pudgy, lovable-looking guy, with an amazingly thick accent, and with that familiar Dylan Thomas look of the Welsh, and he's holding up, by its long, thin rat's tail, a horrible prehistoric animal he calls a thornback skate. It's diamond-shaped, and it was once alive, and despite its extreme ugliness appears as if it might be good to eat.

"Och, yeah, y'eat the wings," says Wally.

"It's like a manta ray or something; it swims by moving its wings?"

"Yis."

"Kind of an ugly-looking colour."

"Evil-looking eyes," offers Billy the Bartender, an English Scotsman (been here a long time), who also does some serious fishing on the side. "They've got black eyes, wif this gold fiery ring around them. It gives a sinister look to them." Curiously, both he and Wally had a similar problem with the *th* sound at the end of certain words.

"That helps scare off the predators, I guess."

"What they do, they bury theirselfs in the sand," says Wally.

"It looks like a rock at the bottom of the sea."

"Yeah, they do. They got sharp thorns or prongs on their back. If you look carefully, you'll see I'm holding it wif a rag. They got spikes on 'em. They got powerful jaws as well."

"What depth would this be from?"

"About 120 feet," says Wally. "You should see the horrible things we pulled out of its stomach."

Wally pulls another ugly thing out of the bag at his feet. "It's a dogfish, a member of the shark family."

"Do you eat them?"

"Aye, they do eat them here. And the common skate; it's about a hundred pounds, but just as ugly. The thornbacks don't git that big. Ye could look it up."

"Hey, he's got white eyes," I observe, inaccurately.

"No, that's not his eyes, that's his fake eyes. His eyes is just there. Yeah, he's an evil-looking git. He'll sink 'isself till jis' 'is eyes show. They come out on tubes "

Billy the Bartender tells me about the ugliest fish of all. He occasionally catches one, but I didn't catch the name of it, which is all right, because he didn't have one on hand to show me. "It's a pear-shaped sack wif a red colour to it, and it has textured spots all over it which are black or red, and the bottom of it anchors to the pebbles at the bottom, so the bigger it gets the more pebbles it will anchor itself to. And then right on top is a mowff."

"A mouth?"

"Yis, a mowff. And this mowff, it takes the bait all the way in. And you actually hook them in the mowff when you catch one of 'em."

Wally says, "And they have long feathers all around their mowff."

"I can't remember those," says Billy. "What we reckon is that, when you bring them up from the depths, they get bigger because of the change in pressure, so they might not be so inflated on the bottom, they might be small things like this" – he cups his hands – "but as they go up they get bigger and bigger" – he spreads his hands wide apart, dramatically. "They're about the size of a camel's heart" – a delicacy long favoured in Scotland – "when they come on to the boat, from 120 feet."

"And they're sorta like a drawstring purse, eh?"

"Yeah. But no neck at all. Wif this mowff on top of it. It's just one bulbous mass, that's the best way to describe it. It's not a jelly, because it's firmer than that; it's almost leathery to the touch."

"Maybe they're delicious." When you're that ugly you've got something special to protect.

"Maybe they are, but they're red and that's usually a sign of danger, isn't it?"

"But then all the other species that taste good would become red to save themselves."

Wally dozed off standing at the bar, but he woke up and said something semi-intelligible: "You took the hook right inside it, but not such depth as to go on through the flesh. It just took this massive bait on the hook and drawed it in. So it must have tentacles or somefing like that."

"I reckon there's patches of them on the bottom," says Billy. "Quite interesting. You either get a ton of them or none."

I say I'd like to catch one, and they say it could be arranged. We listen to the music for a minute or two, then Wally says, "Somefing like a sponge or somefing like that. Uglier than a sea cucumber."

The bar is jammed and I am the only non-local. We ultimately get talking about other things besides fish, and I ask about the relations between the locals and the incomers.

"Around here," says Billy, "a local is somebody who's born here and everybody else is an incomer." He says there's something called Settlers' Watch, and although it's not like the IRA, and probably never will be, it's still scary. It's directed towards the English newcomers mostly. He says he, as long as he's been here, still gets anonymous hate mail and phone calls telling him to get out of the country. "It's not somefing you want to take seriously, but it really makes you feel miserable when it happens."

A sweetly handsome young fellow named Simon MacGregor shows up. He works in the local hardware store, but his big thing in life is the dangerous Highland sport of hotdog kayaking down rapids with great waterfalls. They call them canoes, except they look like kayaks with blunt and highly reinforced noses, for when they hit the rocks at the bottom of a waterfall. They look like bullets and they come with airbags. "The Scots call everything a canoe just to keep it simple," he says. "Every one-man boat is a canoe."

Simon says he's gone straight down 150 feet and suffered no damage to the canoe, and only a bit of hoarseness from screaming all the way. He plans to study pharmacy should he survive his current hobby. He's from Grafton-on-Spey, and his dad's a pharmacist, too. Simon is up here working at the hotel so he can get in as much canoeing as possible before school starts. Billy puts my Caffrey's under the counter and Simon takes me out in the moonlight to show me his two canoes strapped to the roof of his car.

"Have you just got back from canoeing or are you about to go?"

"Oh, no," he says, "that's just where I store them – on top of the car. They're always there, except when they're in the water."

"Couldn't they be nicked?"

"They could be nicked, but I don't have any safer place to store them."

He said he had one special oar that cost a hundred pounds. He was going down the river, he hit a rock, and the force of it caused his body to fall against the oar, which snapped right in two. Did he get his money back? "Oh, no, they'd just say it wasn't built for that sort of treatment."

Back inside, one bright young female, who has been drinking with a bunch of ugly louts, suddenly ups and gathers fourteen (by actual count) empty pint glasses in her arms, and brings them up to the bar in one trip. She puts them down one by one on the bar, then looks at my astonished face and says, "Once a barmaid, always a barmaid."

Simon mentions that the waterway the ferry crosses is a narrow part of broad Loch Linnhe, and Robert Louis Stevenson calls it the Corran Straits in *Kidnapped*, though the maps have it as Corran Narrows. This hotel, the Ardgour, 350 years old, actually gets mentioned in that book. Simon is a bit more informed than most of the others here, and it was interesting to see him explaining patiently to another Scottish fellow, about twenty-five, who Robert Louis Stevenson was, and basically running through the plots of his various adventure stories, with special interest in *Kidnapped*. This was after the fellow heard him telling me that Robert Louis Stevenson had visited this hotel. The fellow saw that I was impressed. "Robert Louis who?" he inquired.

When I first came in there were fishing rods all over. It's quite a messy and chaotic sort of place. A great storm of crudely handwritten signs point to the long march to the washrooms – turn left, turn right, go up, go down. There's a messy lounge bar, a messy dining room, a messy residents' TV lounge. Definitely not five stars in the Michelin guide, but the locals like it fine and so do I.

I go in and see all this fishing gear and say, "You must be doing a lot of fishing around here?"

Billy the Bartender must have misunderstood me because he replied, "Saltwater or fresh?"

"I was going to ask you that."

"Oh, we do bof around here. If you don't mind the climb the freshwater fishing is real good because you get these brown trout – brownies we call 'em – and they fight like mad." In case I might be interested in doing some saltwater fishing, he says I might get Wally to take me. Wally's got a boat.

Another fellow tells me he works part-time at the salmon farm and was getting tired of all the complaints about fish farms ruining the sport-fishing industry, because of disease. He said this particular salmon farm "supports five families, not just five people but five complete families." He says the worst thing is the gulls. You have to take a .22 rifle to work with you. The gulls dive in one after the other, and no matter how many you shoot they keep coming, sometimes so close the wings knock your hat off. It's like they're lining up to be shot, as in, "Okay, my turn, shoot me next." Of course the gulls are protected, he says, so don't tell anybody. I didn't promise not to. Also, when they outlawed the mink farms around here, the owners let all the minks loose, and now they're multiplying rapidly and causing all kinds of damage. "And you know, it's a crime to take living things from the sea and feed them to the pigs. This happens a lot."

"Also it makes your bacon taste fishy," says Billy.

One fellow comes up to the bar with a ten-pound note. "Gimme a heap o' coins will ye, Billy?"

MACRO-FISHING
WITH WALLY

Ardgour • Argyll • Dalmally • Ford

Friday, June 21. Very suspicious! There's a nice rack of antlers on the wall – six points on one side and five on the other, and with the skull intact. There's a large marble fireplace and two ornate antique china cabinets. But the place is grungy with dust and assorted unlikely items stashed in corners: messy stacks of scrapbooks, billiard cues, rakes, and so on. Why is this once-stately dining room of the Ardgour Hotel in such a mess? I'm about to find out.

Among the scrapbooks is a large, glossy black-and-white photo of two little girls smiling and holding their McDonald's Hamburgers' Childhood Achievement Awards. These would be the children of the Englishman who owns this hotel but is currently absent from the premises. In another photo, he has curly hair, an orchid in his lapel. He's standing behind the two girls, who are still holding their awards and smiling. The two girls would be ten-year-old Kate and her sister, eight-year-old Lizzy, for there's a stack of articles about them clipped from various papers. On January 9, 1993, in the *Weekly News*, a full-page article was devoted to their story, which happened to have been written by their mother (with numerous quotes from their father), and the headline was TOP BRAVERY AWARDS FOR SISTERS. Little Liz came down with a rare and often fatal disease, and older Kate became a "tower of strength" and an "incredible support," nursing Liz back to health 'against all odds."

Their parents, a former airline pilot and his wife John and Madeleine Burgess, were running their sailboat to Sark in August 1992. Liz became ill en route back to Portsmouth, and the doctors were baffled. Soon the tyke could barely speak and was unable to walk. It was suggested she might be suffering from the rare Guillain-Barre Syndrome, a post-viral condition that causes the virus to attack the body's nervous system. It kills one in four. Breathing and swallowing are affected. Liz was put in intensive care. Kate refused to leave the bedside, and "she read and drew pictures for Lizzy to fill the endless hours." It was a serious and critical situation for quite some time; they had to do a complete change of blood. There is also a lengthy recovery time.

Mrs. Burgess portrays her husband as becoming highly involved with his daughter's health, spending entire days in the hydrotherapy pool in a local school for the handicapped, "stretching out those crippled muscles until they worked properly again." The mother wrote, "The condition certainly brought us closer as a family, and we decided to move from the south of England. We now run a hotel in the Scottish Highlands. There are plenty of wide-open spaces for our two brave girls and their new puppy, Sophie, to begin to enjoy life to the full all over again." What a great story! Handsome family! Except that they're nowhere to be seen and the hotel is falling apart already.

The story becomes more complex. In another full-page article, which appeared in the Glasgow Herald, a year later, on August 7, 1993, Mr. Burgess states that "just because the clan chiefs were busy wining it and dining it in London, running their estates into debt, and then found that people cost them money while sheep earn them money, is no reason to blame the English for the Highland clearances." Mr. Burgess apparently had been getting some flak from the locals, and was lashing out via the press. "They came, they saw, and they settled for a better life," stated the article. But because of certain comments he made, in the press and out of it, the better became bitter. Comments such as this annoyed the locals, who took to standing outside the hotel late at night and chanting, "If you hate John Burgess clap your hands." Burgess had infuriated the people he had come north to serve. He had to retreat to his private office in the hotel, and finally he was forced to move, with his family, back to England. So the hotel is now being run by Billy and his partner, Yerik Struan Kellet-Smith, though Burgess is on the phone a few times a week.

"When we came here first," Mr. Burgess is quoted in the *Herald*, "there were some who thought they had a right to tell us how to run the hotel. That wasn't on. If they'd wanted to do that they should have bought the hotel."

Early one morning, some aggrieved locals, thirsty for revenge, broke into the hotel, and apparently spent several hours sitting there drinking for free. They couldn't drink it all, so when they staggered out they left all the taps wide open. "The place was flooded," said Burgess. "That's why the place is like Fort Knox now." Apparently, he began having the door checked, to make sure only trusted people were allowed in.

The Burgess girls, even after all their problems, were taunted by classmates for being English. "There's no place in this world for racism, it's a load of nonsense," said Mr. Burgess. "I would stress that we have not seen any sign of racism from the indigenous Highlanders. There are only a few of them around here, and quite frankly they are the nicest people I've ever met. The people who have given us most trouble appear to be incomers themselves – although from other parts of Scotland." His rejection by the locals hurt all the more because he considered himself a Scot: "Okay, so I speak with this funny accent, but you wouldn't go to the Duke of

Argyll and say to him he isn't really Scottish because he speaks with the same accent as I do." Burgess claims direct descent from a large number of famous Scots. "I've travelled the world – Egypt, Vietnam, everywhere – but this is the first time I've felt discriminated against because I speak with an English accent." He was particularly miffed to have been singled out as the major cause of the clearances.

Burgess background file: He was born in Cheshire, his dad being a Shell Oil executive. "I spent my childhood having a wonderful time living beside the swimming pool in Borneo, Indonesia, Nigeria, you name it."

An ethically instructive local legend tells of the Corran ferryman who was killed by the MacLeans for being opportunistic. He'd been running that ferry back and forth across the strait all his life – and suddenly his big moment came, as it must to all men. He had a huge moral decision to make, and he chose wrong. The MacLeans had moved into Ardgour, and the local chief, McMaster, was on the run. He jumped on the ferry going across, and the ferryman, who had been of McMaster's clan all his life, nevertheless decided the thing to do was to capture his clansman and hold him for the MacLeans, thereby earning brownie points, and get off to a good start under the new regime. But the MacLean chieftain, when he got there, was so shocked by the moral opportunism and betrayal of this lowly ferryman that he had him hanged from his own oars then and there.

When I woke up this morning my watch said 10:08. The clock on the bureau also said 10:08. Showered, dressed, went downstairs for kippers and tea, read the newspaper (especially the *Scottish Independent* with its page-one headline, LIZ TAYLOR ATE MY PORCUPINE), then got interested in the clippings and the story of Lizzy and Kate. Wally wants to take me out in his fishing boat. He was thinking we could go to Seal Island. The ferry has left the pier and everybody aboard is waving like mad at the shore. But I'm the only person standing on the shore. So I wave back, and immediately everybody stops waving. Strange country, this. Where's Wally? Back in my room my watch says 11:45, and the clock on the bureau still says 10:08.

I go back down, and Wally's there with his car. I get in and he takes me home. You can't see Wally's place for the hedge surrounding it, which is a good thing because it's a terrific hedge and a dilapidated house. If you peep out through the hedge you can see two little islands, with seals basking on each beach, and the mountains all around, and lots of islands way out at sea. Wally whips out his binoculars: we can see Duart Castle on the Isle of Mull. In fact, he shows me five distant castles, right from his front yard. Wally's wife is noticeably overweight, and has epilepsy and various other ailments. Wally is also stout, but he assures me he used to be in much better shape than he is now. His car is the most incredibly messy car I've ever seen, even messier than the hotel. Wally's a short, squat, stout, sloppy man with a heart of gold, with a sloppy car, a sloppy boat, a sloppy house, and so on. He probably descends from a long line of sloppy people. But according to Billy, Wally wasn't always like that. "I've seen old pictures of him in a suit and tie and wif his hair combed," he said, with a sigh. Apparently Wally's hair hasn't been combed since he got married twenty years ago. It sticks out in all directions. Wally is a humble man, with a humble family in a humble house, and he makes it seem easy to be humble in a proud world.

We're going fishing: we've got a can of petrol and a fresh pack of tobacco. We've seen the seals, all twelve of them, through the binoculars, so Wally gives me an option: we can spend the time fishing for mackerel out in front of the hotel, or we can use the three gallons of petrol to go down and see the seals close up. I said we already saw them through the binoculars, and they looked nice, but let's catch us some fish we haven't seen yet, and any I catch he can have for dinner for his wife and teenage daughter. So let's go macro-fishing. Not macro, he says, mackerel.

The boat is *Justine*; it's a Shetland dory, with a handsome little cabin for riding out the storms. Wally's hand is too shaky for him to be pouring petrol into an outboard motor. I tell him he needs a funnel. He says he had one till the sea took it away. Wally gets in the boat, bends over scandalously, and starts yanking on the starter cord.

"I see you like to show a lot of cleavage on the backside there, Wally," I observe.

"That's called the builder's bum," he says. "Made known by the builders' trades in Britain."

Wally gets the engine going. "It's all tightened up nice as can be now," he says. "Are we moving?"

We're cutting through the waves and making a few of our own. Wally invites me to take over the controls. I'm worried about tangling with the ferry, which is on its way across the loch. "If that ferry bumps into us it'll have a big lawsuit on its hands," I think out loud.

"If they can find us," says Wally. He looks serious, his face is in the wind. "We're actually going the same speed the water is," he says. "Nine knots wi' a good forewind." He suggests I head due north-northeast.

"Sorry, I've taken over and we're headed for Cuba, like it or not."

"Bloody hell," he says.

And the motor goes dead. I think somebody's put fish guts in the petrol line. Wally's muttering about how he goes out fishing by himself every day and nothing goes wrong, but he gets to take a nice Canadian out and everything goes wrong.

"Don't worry," I said. "At least you got a backup motor."

"That thing? That doesn't work."

Finally, the motor that works starts working again.

"I'll take ye to a point where you can see Ben Nevis as well," he says. Wally starts singing a song of his own composition: "*Happy to be / Sailing up Loch Linnhe.*" He's a natural-born rhymester with a shipping trunk full of poems. His poems spring from a philosophical stance that is as old as the lochs: an absence of striving, living in the moment, a serenity that withstands all life's shocks and horrors. He has his dreams, but he doesn't see the point of lifting a finger to realize them. You might be dead tomorrow.

"I was potholing one time, and I went up there on my motorbike, and as I rode along I'd do bits of rhymes in my head. And I went home one day and I wrote this one down. I changed it; it's not the same format as the original one. It was a lot different from what it is now. I call it 'The Secret World' and it's been published in *The Other Side of the Mirror*. And it was published fourteen days ago."

"Have you got a copy of the book yet?"

"Uh, no. But I got the main copy of the poem at home."

"Is *The Other Side of the Mirror* from the States?"

"It's being printed in England but it's owned by the States. I'm a major runner-up in the contest, and possibly a winner."

"And what's the name of the organization?"

"The International Society of Poets. It's a U.S. company. But they also publish in Great Britain and all around the world, real international, it is. And they've got four of my poems – 'The Secret World,' 'I Dream,' 'Time,' and the other one is . . . I forget just now." He starts reciting: "I dream of a cottage all in white / I dream of a cottage wif the sea in sight / I dream of a cottage where deer pass by / I dream of a place where eagles are free to fly / I dream of mountains . . ." He runs out of steam. "I'll have t'show 'em t' ye. The one that's actually in the competition goes: 'Down below the sea / Seen only by the élite / Is an unlit world. . . .'"

Wally says this loch marks the spot where two great land masses, one from the north and one from the south, came together a billion years ago to form what is now Great Britain. "This is the Great Glen. You can sail from here all the way to the North Sea." We let the dory drift for an hour, but the fish aren't being fooled. We lie back with our feet up and watch the sky and the mountain peaks. Wally gazes at the hills lining the loch and says things like "There are thirty shades of green, maybe more," and "You can close your eyes and almost see the clans fighting each other." I suggested the clans were crazy. He didn't like that. "They were warlords, that's all. Like what's going on in the rest of the world nowadays." He takes a deep breath. "What happened yesterday will happen tomorrow in a different context." I began thinking of him as some kind of untutored seer.

"You'll get a little doggy," he predicted. "Either that or a small cod." But an hour later there was still no action. He said one in twenty trips he doesn't catch any fish, and this was the one. We pull our lines and Wally starts the motor. He's going to take us to where we'll catch a fish for sure. "Everywhere around here there are different places for different fish. We're going to what I call the cod bank. This side of the bank is shallow, but you get a lot of cod here, all sorts, including doggies." He cut the motor and let out the anchor. "It's deeper than you can see; it's about thirty feet down. Now let's relax. Fishing is like life: you can enjoy yourself or you can be miserable."

I asked him about the Englishman, Mr. Burgess, who owned the pub. Would he be described as a guy who enjoys life?

He paused. "He's too much of a bigot."

"Did you get along with him?"

"Ah, he's not a bad lad. He thinks he's Prince Charles, though. They went to the same school. And he's too money-mad. Some folks don't like him at all, they don't like the way he runs the pub."

He told me a story about how things first started going wrong in the pub. The pub had one terrific night, after Mr. Burgess had taken over. He took in about nine hundred quid. And a lot of whisky was drunk. And about midnight one of the boys got boisterous and tore down the Union Jack. Instead of laughing it off and putting it down for expenses, Mr. Burgess took it personally, got upset, started screaming, called the cops. The fellow had to spend the night in jail, was fined 150 pounds, and got a criminal record.

"You're not supposed to take that sort of thing seriously, are you?" I said.

"No," said Wally. "But John does. Now when he comes up, the locals disappear. Nobody comes in but the odd tourist or whatever.

So he knows it. The locals, they'll never forget him, and they'll only show up when he's away. They've lost faith in him entirely."

There were fishermen on shore with binoculars checking for action. If we were to catch a fish there'd be all kinds of boats out here before we could rebait our hook. "You either get one or you don't," said Wally.

Wally shrewdly had me down as a guy with a taste for local gossip. "In a pub like we have here, you get to hear all the gossip from the area, in a bed and breakfast you hear the problems of the family circle and the immediate neighbours usually. In the big hotels you don't hear anything."

He agreed that, generally speaking, the people on the east side of Scotland, it's hard to get them talking and it's easy to get them to stop, but the opposite situation prevails on the west side of the country. But he didn't have any theories as to why that would be. "I don't know much about the east side," he said, "except that they have more problems regarding the English over there."

"How do you mean?"

"Well, they have settlers and the Settlers' Watch and all that, anti-English and all that lot over on that side."

"Settlers' Watch is more active over there?"

"Yeah."

"But they haven't resorted to any violence yet."

"Well, it's happened wif one or a couple of MPs, they've had problems. Dirty letters through the door, that sort of thing. And they're starting to call it English Watch instead of Settlers' Watch. Makes me laugh really. Because to me there's no such thing as a purebred Scotsman, because they've been invaded that many times. I mean, Mull was actually owned by the King of Norway. And a lot of the west coast was. There's a lot of Viking blood the further north you go. It's nearer to Norway than it is to London. So they've got nothing to fight about, though there may be one or two direct descendants of the Picts and that around still. It's like most of Great Britain, they've been invaded by the Germans, the French, the Spanish. It's all mixed up. The Vikings, they used to carry their longboats overland then put them down in a loch and invade all the little settlements around the loch, and any inhabited islands there happened to be in the loch. Any woman they liked the look of they'd take back to the Scandinavian countries wif them. It's all mixed blood. Wif history you can read the books, but you have to read between the lines."

As we drifted under the fluffy blue sky, Wally philosophized, recited poetry, sang songs, and told stories, including many about his father, who was a Marine Commando during World War II. He survived the Dieppe raids, the landing in Sicily, severe fighting all over Italy and Libya, and the D-Day landing at Normandy. And then, after the war, as a Welsh coalminer, he survived numerous major mine collapses, only to be blown to bits when a truck he was driving, full of raw latex, exploded.

As we made for shore, Wally said when he was a lad they used to see a blood-drenched ghost running around the house, or rather bouncing around the house, because it had its arms and legs cut off and was carrying them, with one of its arms in its mouth and its legs and other arm draped over its shoulder. Everyone in the family saw it on many different occasions, and it terrorized the family for two years. It finally did go away, but not before his father was killed. He hadn't wanted to drive that truck, he knew it was dangerous, but the boss had insisted. He was within five hundred feet of where he was supposed to park it when the explosion occurred. His head was found 150 feet from the truck and the rest of his body, in pieces, was found under the wreckage. The ghost never returned. In some inexplicable way it was foretelling his father's fate. There was no other explanation.

When we were docking, we looked up at the ferry about to take off, and in one of the portholes a little boy was staring straight at us and serenely playing a violin. We couldn't hear it at all, but he was certainly playing it, and everyone aboard the ferry must have been listening. He was staring at us and playing with the strangest expression on his face. He was about twelve.

"Lucky Luke lacked a lock, so he liked to look at the lake while licking his lips," Wally said as he handed me a book on foxes as a farewell gift. We locked eyes. He said that, in addition to writing poems, he liked to make up alliterative sentences.

"Wally waddles when he walks," I said, causing him to laugh good-naturedly.

That was my way of saying, "Goodbye, I won't forget you."

Life holds few pleasures as profound as coming across a megalithic monument when you weren't looking for it, expecting it, or didn't even know there was anything like that in the area. Under those circumstances to come across a whole series of them is akin to Columbus discovering several New Worlds, all at the same moment. After a long drive through Glencoe, through the deep, dark Glen Orchy, and along the River Orchy to Dalmally, then along Loch Awe, I was heading south, just past the tiny old village of Ford, at the lower tip of Loch Awe, driving into the central Dalriada part of Argyll, and there was a Pictish wall, in excellent shape, lining the road, indicating the road was an ancient trackway. Suddenly, a tall standing stone appeared, rising from behind the wall. I pulled over.

It was a thin, tall, broad stone, standing at quite a precarious angle. Next to it was one almost exactly like it, but lying flat along the ground, and pointing towards the first, as if its angle had become progressively more precarious until it collapsed. I looked around and the entire area, from the road to the foot of a steep hill half a mile back, was studded with ruins from various eras: more standing stones scattered among great sycamore trees; a dizzying array of geometrically interconnected earthworks, some straight and angular, some in circles with the earth rising like a spiralling pyramid to the centre; the occasional stone circle; the remains of prehistoric huts; burial cairns; some unexcavated, unusual stone walls; and the ruins of a two-storey stone house with eight fireplaces. Some of the standing stones were eight feet high, and four feet wide at the bottom, tapering up almost to a blunt point at the top. The numerous magnificent old trees with human-like branches, along with the strange mystery of the ruins, gave the area a depth of dream-like beauty.

I returned to Ford and managed to squeeze into a crowded pub. The proprietress, Elizabeth, patiently listened as I told her what I'd seen. She said this area was the old Dalriada Empire, which was founded by Fergus More in AD 498, and most of the people who live here today are well aware of it and take great pride in living here. It's the site of the first Celtic colony in what is now Scotland, created by the first wave of immigration from Ireland, in the Dark Ages, shortly after the Romans went home.

The bartender was a lonesome type, with close-cropped hair and one of those soulful I'd-like-to-be-your-friend faces. He said it was the pre-Pictish Beaker people who put up these stones, which rings bells with me – though the books say it's not known if anyone preceded the Picts.

A tall, distinguished-looking black man was standing on the other side of the pub, so I wormed my way over. He laughed when I told him he was the first person of African descent I'd seen in three weeks of touring Scotland. He was born in Jamaica, but he grew up in England, and was now studying at Glasgow University. He said he finds Scotland a "disturbing" country, burdened with tremendous problems with the way males and females relate. The women dominate easily, he said, but the men desperately try to become dominant, and the harder they try the worse they fail, because of their jealousy and irritability. Women go to great lengths not to annoy their husbands, because they are so easily annoyed. For instance, it's hard to have a conversation with a woman, even the most banal conversation, he said, even a simple thing like asking directions, if her husband is anywhere in the area. He is likely to become jealous, because she's talking to another man. I admitted to having noticed that, and was pleased to have my impressions confirmed.

"There's a strong sense in this country," he said, "not of male domination but of women conspiring to let men think they are the dominant ones." It's a role women play and one can sense it every-where in Scotland. "It's ugly, it's unpleasant, and it's tragic," he said, "because it means that, if you're going to be married for life, you're going to have to endure that kind of tension and that kind of strug-gle every day of your life. It's just not right."

He said he'd been living in the United Kingdom for so long he enjoys the company of white people more than black people. He went to Jamaica recently to see the country he was born in, and in which he had spent the first few years of his life, and he said he had a terrible time. In a Kingston bar he saw a white man and instantly made a beeline for him and started up a conversation. I told him that was like me coming over in this crowded pub to talk to him.

There were numerous women standing and sitting around, for it was the annual Ladies' Night. By closing time I'd been invited to a party. "We'll take all our clothes off and dance under the midnight sun," they exclaimed. Elizabeth, who seemed the soul of sanity and stabil-ity, said I should go, because "it'll be an interesting experience."

At the party, which was halfway up the east side of Loch Awe, the men were saying to me: "You know, all these beautiful, interesting-looking women, they're all married." I said I thought they'd all be single, since they seemed to be at the pub looking for men. I was then informed that the women from all around get to come to the pub for one night a year without their husbands. "They're not single, they're all married, but they still might be looking for men," they said.

Under the magical spell of the radiant summer night, a bit of innocent flirtation on the shore of Loch Awe was nothing for their husbands to be jealous about. In this strange light, everything glowed with a pearlish rosy flame – a duck floating in a pond, an old stone bridge, whatever. There was a strong rosy glow in the lower sky and the rest of the sky was like a giant opal. Everything seemed unnaturally still. The rhododendron blossoms seemed to have been there forever, and would stay there forever. One's ego dissolved; one's identity became irrelevant. It was like a glimpse into the tremendous stillness of eternity. Two women drove me to the party, and the three of us were under the spell. We kept stopping the car, getting out, walking around for a while, then getting back in the car. It took forever to get to the party.

Once there we drank beer, chatted, strolled around the grounds, and I met lots of people who hadn't been at the pub. One woman was tall, elegant, and beautiful, with a shockingly deep basso voice. "To look at you, one would think you'd have a little high-pitched voice," I told her.

"Aye, strange isn't it?" she bellowed. Her biggest desire was to go to Alaska. She said people had been after her to emigrate to Australia, but she's not the slightest bit interested in that. The only place that interests her is Alaska.

In general, the main preoccupation among the women was how possessive and jealous their husbands were. They didn't actually like or admire their husbands, but they had no intention of leaving them. Perhaps they knew they'd be unable to pull it off, or else they knew they'd be going from one trap to another. Their men were not the sort of men they thought they were marrying. They have not turned out well.

ANCIENT MYSTERIES
OF ARGYLL

Ford • Kilmartin • Lochgilphead • Ardrishaig • Cairnbaan
Dunadd • Kilmichael Glassary • Portalloch

Saturday, June 22. Each room at the Ford Hotel is charmingly named after a different island in Loch Awe. Mine is Kilchurn, and there is also Innishearraich, Rudhedubh, and several others. Fox-hunting scenes decorate every wall, along with other nineteenth-century prints, including some sport-fishing cartoons poking fun at fishermen in top hats. In the dining room there's a carved wooden rocking pig, life-size, and the heads of wild goats with intricately curved horns.

One of the islands in Loch Awe was the site of the origin of the Campbell clan. In the early Middle Ages an incomer arrived, according to the tale. He had a *cam-beul*, or crooked mouth. He married the local heiress, Eva O'Duine, and their descendants retained the nickname Cam-beul, or Campbell. They took over the island castle of Ard Chonnel, midway up the loch. Soon they were instigating boundary disputes with their neighbours and in a few generations they were lords of Argyll and the Western Highlands.

Another in a series of sporty roadsters from the twenties stops at
the T-intersection outside the hotel, then turns left with a great
cello-like crescendo on the way to Kilmartin and Lochgilphead.
They must be having a Saturday-morning rally. All these immacu-
lately restored roadsters, each with a man driving and a female passenger, both in fashions of the twenties, are going by one every five
minutes or so. One of the drivers was wearing a black-leather jump-
suit with attached black-leather hood and goggles – all one piece.

Elizabeth brought in a huge piping-hot bowl of oatmeal. The tea
was served in a great silver pot, and the perfectly cooked kippers on
a matching silver platter. Tea always tastes better when brewed in a
beautiful pot, I declared. She said, "Not only that, but we also have
fresh spring water in this area. That makes it taste better, too. And
also it's good for the whisky." She said she wouldn't change my
sheets, on the off-chance I'd be back. I said that'd be fine. She said,
"I'll leave your room as it is. You're not under any obligation. And
that way I'll save on the laundry."

I stick my head into the bar to say goodbye to the lonesome bartender from last night. A few minutes later I'm sitting in my car
looking at maps and scribbling in my notebook, and he comes out
and says how much he enjoyed meeting me. I tell him I might be
back tonight. He says I'll have a good time if I do come back, because
they're planning a barbecue. And the proprietress is getting in fresh
venison steak and two kinds of fresh fish.

The Ford Hotel is the cultural centre for the area. At one o'clock
on a Saturday afternoon, the bar is jammed with locals. But once
outside, it's so quiet you can walk across the road without looking.

In the town of Kilmartin, a few miles south of Ford, the venerable
Kilmartin House is being transformed into an interpretive centre for
this area of immense archeological interest. I was reading the sign
and along came one of the women from last night's party, Kay by
name. Kay pulled over and yelled out, "Eeh, Davy!" She was taking

her kids down to the community swimming pool at Lochgilphead. She admitted that things were a little cool this morning, because she was so late getting in last night. But these things go up and down, and she expected things would be smoothed out soon. I think her husband was particularly angry because he woke up at about three in the morning and went to the bathroom stark naked, with the moonlight shining through the windows on his pure white skin, and was shocked to see that Kay and I were sitting side by side on the sofa and examining the family photo album. The party was straight out of Bergman's *Smiles of a Summer Night*. But usually it's the husband who finds his wife naked with some guy. Here the wife and the other man were fully dressed and the husband was the naked one, an interesting twist to an old story. Under the circumstances, what could he say, even if it was three in the morning? If he'd got down his shotgun and shot me, a naked husband wouldn't have a leg to stand on in court.

Someone suggested a copy of the local guide to regional antiquities might be available at the Kilmartin post office, but they were all sold out, and the woman there was complaining, as people were similarly complaining all over Scotland, that every year she puts in an order for the tourist season, and the books never arrive till the tourist season's over. Also, they get only about one-third of the number they order. So the books sit there all winter, and usually by the time the tourist season starts they're all gone. Also, I signed the Dunblane Snowdrop Petition, to ban handguns from Britain. I asked if there were any farmers in the area who were opposed to stricter gun laws, and the woman said no, she didn't know of one, everybody's totally in favour of it.

A huge man came into the tiny post office, local author and bon vivant John Leese. He overheard me asking about books and the woman saying they were out of them. "Why don't you sell him my book?" he roared. He pointed it out. It was called *Great Scottish Recipes: From the Laird's Scots Larder*.

"Does it have a recipe for Arbroath stovies?"

"There's one for stovies, but we didn't have room for regional variations."

The book includes hard-to-get recipes for Whim Wham, Tweed Kettle, Crowdie and Oatcakes, Lemon Syllabub with Petticoat Tails, Finnan Mousse, Loch Fyne Kipper Pâté, Clapshot with Braised Leeks, Edinburgh Rock, Cockaleekie, Potted Hough, Selkirk Bannocks, Scots Flammery, Blairgowrie Foam, and Cranachan.

"I wrote it about ten years ago. It only took me two hours to write it, and so far I've made four thousand quid off it."

"That's great. You should write another one."

"Yeah, I should. But I'm retired now, and I don't have the time or the energy." Like many people, he had more time when he was working than he does now he's retired. "I'll sign it for you if you buy it." He told me he was from Cornwall, though he'd been living in Scotland for forty years.

I said, "I guess they don't let you forget you're from away, eh?"

"It's not so bad," said he. "You see, I have a passport: my wife was born here." He was a giant, full of life. He took up a lot of space, but he moved around quite well. He was like a beer truck on a single-track road, but he had no problems steering. "Write a cookbook if you want to make money," he said. "Only takes one evening to write them, and you can live off the proceeds forever." He'd written dozens of novels previously, but could never get any of them published.

There's some tourism in this area, enough to keep John's cookbook in print. But other than the local folks, nobody's interested in the Dalriada Empire or stone circles. When Mr. Leese had cleared out, the woman said, "It's the continuing presence of the people in the prehistoric past that gives this area its charming atmosphere, and such an aura of friendliness among the people."

In the pharmacy, in the large administrative town of Lochgilphead, further south from Kilmartin, a young pharmacist, about twenty-one, was engaged in a bedside-manner conversation with an extremely old woman who was walking with the aid of two crutches. Even though he had a long queue of people waiting to be served, the two of them were chatting aimlessly about the weather, the kelp on the beach, the nice new girl at the hardware store. Finally, he didn't have what I wanted: batteries for my camera. The clerk in the bookstore was helpful, and said that they, like everyone else, were out of stock of the two most important guides to the antiquities of this area. As for my batteries, I'd have to go to a smaller town a few miles further along, Ardrishaig.

Lochgilphead and Ardrishaig share a large tidal inlet called Loch Gilp, which on the map looks like a fin on the back of the shark of great leaping Loch Fyne. It's low tide at the Lochgilphead waterfront, and they're having a Saturday-afternoon festival, with balloons, and kids running around screaming with joy. Ardrishaig is bright, cheery, unneurotic, and with a standing stone, a pier, and a lighthouse. All the locals are strolling around with big smiles on their faces, enjoying the fine weather. Along comes a tall, bearded man of about fifty, and he's giving every car as it passes a friendly little salute. From the waterfront you can see Lochgilphead sparkling and tiny in the distance.

As for the camera, I didn't need batteries, and I didn't need to take this trip to Ardrishaig. "You're having a bad day," said the shy, quiet man in the camera shop, who refused to take any money for telling me my camera had become locked, and showing me how to unlock it. "I've had a call from the bookstore in Lochgilphead and you've left your books there."

As I left the second time, that bookstore clerk said, "Enjoy your holiday." A quizzical look came on her face. "If that's what it is," she added. I told her every day's a holiday when you're a travel writer. She smiled. She was a bit of an inventor. She said she was going to get a patent on a cigarette lighter with a computer chip which only let it be lit every two hours or so. One could presumably preset it to keep one's smoke intake at a reasonable level. By the time this book comes out they should be available everywhere.

At a hardware store in Lochgilphead the clerk offered me the choice of a rough-cut chamois (for cleaning my car windows) for a pound or a smooth one for eight pounds. I suggested the more expensive one was for snob appeal. "Aye," she said, "there's a lot of that around here." She had a son in British Columbia. She couldn't pronounce the name of the town so she wrote it out: VERNON. I told her I had problems myself pronouncing Lochgilphead. She said, "Oh. that's easy. Just say LOCH-*gilp-head* real fast."

When people in the west of Scotland refer to someone being "in Lochgilphead," they mean he's drying out. The town is surrounded by idyllic suburban residential areas, with historical street names such as Dunadd Place and Glassary Avenue, and it boasts a large alcohol-abuse centre.

The hill behind the old Cairnbaan Hotel, on the old narrow Crinan Canal, which connects Loch Gilp with Loch Crinan on the Sound of Jura, can be climbed simply by following the ancient drystone Pictish wall, which stands about three feet high. But the area has been crudely clear-cut, and here and there loggers have bashed in parts of the wall. The ancient footpath has been submerged under great mounds of shale, dug up when the logging roads were built. But suddenly I come across a stout standing stone pointing the way to the top of the hill, where there's a wonderful display of the mysterious cup-and-ring markings dating back to the parting of the Red Sea. These rock carvings are protected by an iron gate sturdy and well-designed. The fenced enclosure is about thirty by forty yards, and the fence has been built with care and reverence, unlike fences at other sacred spots such as Stonehenge. The fence is not intended to annoy, but rather to please people and make them glad the site is being protected.

The sign says the decorations are five thousand years old, which sounds right, though some say more like 5,500. The cup-and-ring markings have been pecked out on a series of horizontal stones lying a bit above the surface of the soil. These pre-Pictish, Neolithic markings are found throughout Ireland and Scotland – and nobody knows what they represent. Some speculate that they were carved in commemoration of different groups of people meeting at certain spots on an annual basis, but that doesn't say much about what they mean.

There is little if any moss on these stones, and, because they lie flat, they have not been weathered as badly as the standing stones would have been. As a result the markings are less eroded, fresher, more spectacular, much more so than similar markings in Ireland. The carvings are placed in what seem to be random patterns – that is, ungeometric, in a style reminiscent of the seemingly casual randomness of the aboriginal art of Australia. There appears to be no reason why any one carving should be at one spot and not at another. It suddenly hits me that they're also reminiscent of tiny crop circles carved into the stone. A good-sized orange would sit right in the middle of the largest of the cup markings, like an egg in an eggcup, and then there is a ring around it about an inch further out from the circle. Most of the cups would take an average-size plum. Occasionally, a cup will have a double ring around it. Great skill, motivation, and patience went into these designs. Some of the cups have no rings around them. So we have cups alone, cups with one ring, and cups with two rings, which is a bit reminiscent of a road map, with different symbols for different-sized cities. Could these be maps of some sort? If this was a great meeting place five millennia ago, these carvings might have shown how to get to certain settlements of varying sizes. In fact there are little paths pecked out in the rocks as well, tiny dots in a regular meandering line, linking one cup and ring with another. The dots of which these "paths" are composed are small, a wooden match could barely be inserted into them. They might represent footpaths through the forest, from one settlement to another. Some of the paths are double, with two exquisitely carved lines an inch apart travelling all over a large rock, perhaps representing a broader footpath.

The largest stone in this enclosure is about eight yards long and more than a yard wide. Along the entire length a series of paths are cut into the stone; they connect with each other in various ways, and there are crossroads. They merge, and they fork, and they go on and on. At one point there is a curving line, done in a different style, that seems to represent a river, with banks on each side. One of these roads, a double line, goes from one end of the stone to the other, the entire eight yards, and the two carved lines are so close there is the thinnest, finest ridge between them. This is truly a great work of art, a five-thousand-year-old art gallery sitting atop a windswept hill, surrounded by a rapidly disappearing forest. On one average-sized stone, chosen at random as an example, are fourteen perfectly executed cup-and-ring markings, and one that looks a bit sloppy, as if done by an apprentice.

A few miles north is Dunadd, the Fort on the River Add. It's known as the Stronghold of Dalriada, Kingdom of the Scots, and it commemorates a culture much more recent than the prehistoric carvings at Cairnbaan. Dunadd is probably the site where kings were inaugurated, the Westminster Abbey of ancient Scotland. "This is an excellent example of a Dark Age Fortification," reads the sign. Some Pictish carvings along the way to the top of the hill indicate it was originally a Pictish stronghold, but the Picts were driven out by the invaders. These Pictish carvings are recognizable as such, and are definitely of an entirely different order than those of the mysterious earlier race of people who put up the stone circles and carved the cups and rings.

Excavations here at Dunadd, a rocky hill 150 feet high, have shown it to have been not only a complex fortification but also a centre for fine metalworking. It was particularly important around AD 500, though it continued to be in use until around AD 1000. The famous Pictish Boar of Dunadd is on this hill, carved into a horizontal stone outcropping, as well as a carved Pictish footprint and a basin, all of which were thought to have some significance in the inauguration of kings. In fact the footprint is referred to as the "footprint of fealty," and the basin as the "anointing stoup." There are also some phonetical ogham carvings in an unknown language. The carved footprint was toeless, and there's a similar toeless one at the village of Kilmichael Glassary a few miles away, Glassary being an old name for this part of Argyll.

Dunadd's not as difficult a climb as Dun Bhuirg on Iona, but it's about three times as high. The boar is not as impressive as it seems to be in photos and drawings: some oaf has taken a sharp stone and tried to delineate the boar more clearly to ensure a good photo, so its natural lines have been seriously disturbed. I hope when he saw what a mess his scratchings had made he was a bit embarrassed. To make a rock carving clearer for the camera, it's perfectly okay to take a handful of grass and rub it in. That will give good definition, and will do no harm.

Two miles further north lies an extensive series of strange burial mounds from before 3000 BC, when the first dynasty in Egypt was coming to power. Cattle are bellowing in the distance. I'm alone in an immense valley of the dead, absorbing the atmosphere. The first cairn is deep enough that one can stand up straight inside it. There are three chambers, from which pottery and burnt bones were removed during an 1864 excavation.

There's also a series of baffling stone circles from the same era. Just enough is known about them to ignite the flames of our confused sense of mystery. These circles were badly tampered with during the nineteenth century: farmers clearing fields would toss their stones on top of the circles. The first is about forty-five feet in diameter, and in the centre is a well-preserved cairn about four by seven feet, and about three feet deep, though it was probably originally deeper. A small stone circle immediately surrounds the cairn, with the stones almost shoulder to shoulder. The main circle contains about sixteen stones, although a few have disappeared. On the northernmost stone are the remains of a nicely carved spiral about sixteen inches in diameter. Spirals are still being drawn today by children, and you sometimes see them on TV commercials for blow-out furniture sales. Also, we've discovered great multitudes of spiral nebulae, including our own, out there in the cosmos. But the charm of the spiral for the human mind isn't as strong as it used to be. Speculating about the symbolic meaning of the spiral also tends to cheapen its charm.

In the centre of another stone circle is a lidless box composed of six flat stones set on their sides, the largest being about three feet long and eighteen inches wide. These are surrounded by twenty-one tall standing stones in a circle. No one knows if the large outer stones came first or the small inner ones, or both at the same time. My instinct says the small inner structure was built first, to honour some great hero, and then, as his posthumous fame continued to spread, and great miracles were attributed to him, the large outer circle was built.

This civilization, which lasted for an unimaginable span of time, was a peaceful one, generally speaking. Because population pressures were non-existent, there was little warfare: much more pottery from the third millennium BC has been found than articles of war, although arrowheads, handy for hunting, are numerous. The Roman invasion would probably have been the first. There is no sign of a Pictish invasion. Perhaps the Picts seeped in without causing any fuss.

People are drawn back to these stones because of the sense they give that their builders lived in a time of peace and well-being, were deeply mystical, and had a profound vision of the universe. They were obsessed with the heavens, and probably worshipped the sun. The cairns might have been built by people other than the ones who built the stone circles, but it's generally agreed that the different kind of structures represented change in thinking rather than invasion. The antiquity of the stone circles at the time might have caused the cairn builders to build elsewhere. The circles were too sacred even for the interment of dead heroes, until a later date.

This whole area is located on a flat plateau of rich farmland, musty old greystone gabled farmhouses, and churches from the eighteenth and nineteenth centuries, with grassy areas and occasional hills to the south towards Lochgilphead. The area is criss-crossed by straight, narrow stony roads with the occasional little stone bridge. Occasional grassy knolls are covered with buttercups, daisies, clover, and thistle, and often endowed with a burial cist on top, sometimes at the foot of a great old oak tree. Also, I have discovered why the thistle is a major emblem of Scotland: step on one, while running around barefoot, and it hurts like mad.

Stone circles are rare; you have to seek them out. In a built-up area they've usually lost their power to shock and delight. Imagine my joy as I came across five great towering massive standing stones forming a giant X in the middle of a farmer's field. The farmer has left a spacious circle of fallow ground around them.

It's ecstasy being here, surrounded by these five monsters: my brain cells shiver with pleasure. The stones are arranged like the diamonds in a giant five of diamonds, and each one is about nine feet in height, and casting a shadow about twice that length. So there are two stones in each of two sets, with the sets separated by eighty yards, and each stone facing its counterpart across that distance. The fifth stone is standing precisely at centre field – forming a kind of football field with two goalposts and a lonely old player standing in the middle of the field, remembering his days of glory with downcast eyes. The one in the middle is covered with cup-and-ring markings, well preserved in the temperate climate of this valley. Instead of touching each stone, or pouring a little Scotch on each one (these deserve a case of Laphroaig each), I give each in turn a big deeply felt hug and tell them I really admire their ability to stand tall for such a length of time. There are tales of people getting severe shocks from touching a standing stone. (One, at Avebury, actually collapsed on top of a guy who was sitting there eating his lunch, and his body wasn't recovered for three centuries.) Almost hidden in the tall, wet grass surrounding the stones can be seen some short squat "recumbent" stones, in seemingly geometric relationship to the big five, including a modest circle of stones a foot or two high surrounding the one in the middle. This is a rare and original megalithic monument. I've never seen or heard of anything like it.

As for urinating on these stones, I silently ask the centre stone, with its random pattern of cup-and-ring carvings. if it would mind.

"Davy," it said. "You don't mind my calling you Davy, do you?"

"N-no sir."

"Well, Davy, I'd prefer you not to pee on me, if it's all the same with you."

"Oh, that's fine by me," I say, and reach over and give it a big hug and a soulful kiss. Some of these cup-and-ring markings, unlike the previous batch I saw, or any I've seen before, in fact, are in pairs, to form figure eights. I count five eights, each composed of two cup-and-ring markings. As I head back to the car I pass an amazing sight – a single sheep standing alone with half of the herd rushing towards it from one side and the other half rushing towards it from the other. It was . . . inexplicable.

SALTY KIPPERS AND
BLOTTING PAPER

Ford • Fearnoch • Lochgilphead

Sunday, June 23. Elizabeth had suggested I call her before nine last night if I wanted fresh monkfish, venison, pigeon breast, or roast duck à l'orange for dinner. But I neglected to do so, got back late after a hard day viewing antiquities, and ended up having a chicken sandwich and several glasses of bubbly in the kitchen with her and her convivial husband, Harry, who definitely did not fit the mould of Scottish husbands I'd been hearing about. I ordered the sandwich, and Elizabeth called me into the kitchen to eat it with them. "Sit down and have a glass," she said. By the time I left two hours later, the three of us had gone through about three bottles of champagne. They had a good working knowledge of the history of the area, and had interesting things to say about every place I'd visited. They said there were sixty thousand people living in this relatively small area when the megalithic monuments were erected five thousand years ago. This is known from observable agricultural patterns.

I mentioned having seen, in Kilmartin Church, an old high cross that had weathered in such a way that it looked as if there was an angel standing on Christ's shoulders and popping a bottle of champagne, and the champagne was curving in the air and falling all over Christ's face. He didn't appear to be enjoying it at all.

"He liked wine," said Harry. "I'd have thought he'd be holding his head up with his mouth agape."

Later at the bar, a fellow wanted to know why I was travelling alone. I told him I had a lot of annoying, irritating habits, and intimacy didn't agree with me. He said he had his share of annoying habits too, and his wife will never let him forget it. In fact, she often will spend hours pointing out ones he didn't even know he had. "She even hates the way I stir my tea," he said, "and I have to go in the other room."

Overheard in the dining room this morning:

"Was that tea you wanted?" the waiter said to an elderly man who was with his wife and their grown son.

"Coffee."

"I was close."

Laughter.

"What are yiz planning to do today?"

"Buy a paper and check the lottery results."

"Haw haw! There you go, your toast won't be long."

"How long?"

"Less than six inches."

He told me his name was Kevin Gerbil, and he started making funny little eating movements with his pursed-up lips. He had a sparse little moustache. In fact, he was a sparse little fellow, alarmingly svelte. I said, "Are you growing that moustache, or is that as big as it gets?"

"It's growing me," he said.

It's amazing how small most people are in Scotland. It seems all the big ones emigrated ages ago.

In Scotland you never see NO TRESPASSING signs. But occasionally you'll see a PUBLIC EXCLUSION ZONE sign. A big black spaniel is having a half-baked snooze right in the middle of the road. He snaps wearily to attention when he hears me coming, gets up, looks annoyed, waddles off to the side of the road. Then I go by, and through the rear-view mirror I see him go back to the same spot, smell it, then lie down again and fall asleep. I'm dying of thirst as I drive along. I should have had another pot of tea this morning. Those kippers were too salty. That's a good excuse for a pint.

In a village pub on a lonely road somewhere southeast of Ford, in Fearnoch I think it was, I got chatting with a tall, red-haired man, Josh, with a face that seemingly never stops smiling, and his short wife, Gillian, who also smiled a lot. She insisted on going home and fetching her book on the standing stones. She said they had two copies and they only needed one, and it was mine to keep. It was called *The Prehistoric Rock Art of Argyll* by Ronald W. B. Morris, published in 1977. It's full of photos. Morris lists all the "clues" that may lead to discovering the meaning behind the cup-and-ring markings, but gives no theories. In fact, he says he is publishing the book in the hope that a reader will write back with any further clues, and possible theories.

Gillian said it's a "complete fallacy" that the Scots are parsimonious pennypinchers. "It's one thing to be cautious and it's another thing to be mean," she said, "and to be mean doesn't mean to be cautious and to be cautious doesn't mean to be mean." I said she was going to have to explain that more fully, so she said the reputation for being chary cheeseparers came when the Scots used to go down into England; their pound note was worth only about a shilling, so the currency was quite different. Something that seemed inexpensive to an English person might seem expensive to a Scot, and that's how their notoriety for niggardliness arose.

"Aye, you always had to watch your pennies when you went doon to England," said Josh. Even today, with the currency the same, you sometimes have trouble in England passing a Bank of Scotland note. He handed a fiver to a cabby in London last year. "I can't take this," said the cabby, so Josh grabbed it back and jumped out of the car.

It's the English who are the real tightwads. "They coom up here and they jump aboot and dance and sing 'There'll Always Be an England' or whatever," said Josh, "and they doon't spend a damn penny ever. It's incredible. To them, they think that England is the be-all and end-all among nations. And the Scottish football fans, they're regarded as the best behaved in the whole world, but the English, they're the worst."

I said one thing about the Scots, they're the best bagpipers in the world, and they said I had a point there. Back in the days when they didn't have a car, they were hitchhiking home and were picked up by a stranger in the area. They invited him in for a drink. One drink became four and the lack of music became noticeable. "I've got my pipes in the car," said the fellow. "I'll get them."

"We groaned and wondered what we'd let ourselves in for," recalled Gillian, "but he was superb. You've never heard anything like it. Turned out he was Hector MacDonald, the famous bagpiper, and he'd been playing since he was five years old. And in our little house with this confined space and this little low ceiling you could hear your ears going *yeen yeen yeen*. And the dog fled off and everything. It was impressive."

"Were you dancing?"

"No, we were flattened against the wall with the noise. You don't understand what a volume of noise comes out of those pipes. It's all right when you're hearing them outside. He was a clever piper and he was marching around and around the couch and he played the laments and the marches both. We're no expert on the pipes, we don't know anything about it really, but he never blew a wrong note, that one."

There was reported to be a ghost in this hotel. "Sometimes people who haven't seen it believe in it more than those who have," she said.

"I know a man, he doesn't drink or anything," said Josh, "and he sees a lady ghost quite often."

"Let's have another round," I suggested.

"I don't always tend bar," said the campy and coquettish bartender, a sophisticated-looking woman of fifty or sixty.

"No," a voice piped up. "A lot of times she's in front of the bar, lying on the floor covered with vomit." She scowled.

The bar starts to fill up. There's going to be a barbecue this afternoon, and I've been invited! It's in honour of someone's eightieth birthday. It's getting crowded and noisy in here. You can hardly hear the dogs barking on adjoining farms.

Gillian Henderson is from Glasgow originally, and she is a landscape painter who shows extensively and sells well. Right now she's arguing with a gallery in Oban: they want 40 per cent, while all the other galleries take only 33 1/3. I told her I'd heard Oban was a town full of extortionists, all descended from a long line of them. She said that explained everything.

Josh is a nickname, his real name is Reinout Goodheir; he was born in Holland but moved to Scotland as a child and was raised on the Isle of Tyree. "He's been here forty-six years only, so he's still an incomer," said Gillian. "And when it comes to the crunch, aye well, he's just a big Dutchman anyway." He smiled sweetly.

I asked if she signed her paintings Henderson or Goodheir. "I was at the Glasgow School of Art, and then I never painted for a long time after that, I was teaching, and came back to it later on. By then my name was Goodheir so I just used that name."

"I inspired her," said Josh.

"Aye, he kicked me in the behind," she said.

She was teaching school, and his brother was one of the other teachers. She said the first time she saw Josh he had a huge long rope wrapped around his neck and shoulders. "He was walking up the stairs in the school in among this class of thirteen-year-olds. I said, 'What is this? Is this a new member of the class?'"

"What was the rope for?"

"I don't know. You tell him what the rope was for."

"Because my completely crazy eldest brother, who was teaching there, wanted to go to a coast town to help another brother of mine pull down a tree in his garden so it wouldna go into somebody else's garden. He was so persistent it was more convenient to do it than to keep getting these calls from him."

"So if it hadn't been for that tree, you'd have never met your wife."

"Och," he said, "the coincidences of life are just amazin'. For instance, my father and I were climbing Ben Nevis. And on the way up we met this little old man and his niece, who was just a little girl. We stopped and had tea and had a long chat with them. We'd never seen them before or anything. And that little girl grew up and married my brother."

The barbecue is also a benefit to raise money for the renal clinic. A local fellow has had two kidney transplants. He had the first one twelve years ago, and it began to fail, so they gave him another one with a newer technology, and he's fine now. He's here at the bar nursing a beer, looks perfectly okay, and seems to be having a good time. I told him, jokingly, that I was beginning to think that all these people came out specially to see the Canadian tourist. "That's part of it," he said. "They know there's a tourist in here, so they all come out so they can pretend it's like this all the time and you'll go back and tell all your friends that this part of Scotland is terrific and there'll be more tourists coming in, like. This is an area that gets bypassed by tourism in general, and this is a pub that's often empty. But there's a huge crowd here, and you're definitely the only tourist."

Kay's husband, Jock, shows up, the naked man from two nights ago. His face looks as if it hasn't cracked a smile in decades. He's an ardent falconer: his falcons will only catch birds that are in the air – and they always eat them. He looks at me with the eyes of a raptor. I was mentioning certain of his neighbours I'd met at the party. "Oh, he's an idiot, he's an absolute idiot, he's out with the fairies," he said, when I mentioned one fellow I thought was a perfectly okay guy. "I'm a practical man; they're a bunch of idiots."

He ignored me when I told him he looked terrific with no clothes on. We got talking about the problems with the pine martens. "I shoot the pine martens, I don't give a damn," he said. "Anything that comes near my fence gets shot." He looked at me menacingly. The pine martens come in and they steal all his eggs. One pine marten ate three-thousand-pounds' worth of rare falcon eggs. That gives him the right to shoot them all he wants, even if they are on the so-called endangered list. His neighbours' cats, if they come up near his fence, he knows they're going to get in and disturb his birds, so he shoots them. But after he shoots them, he takes them out on the road and runs over them. This way the neighbours won't know he shot them. This is one tough Scotsman.

"One idiot found his cat run over, so he had an X-ray done and found a bullet in it. So he came up and said, 'Did you shoot my cat?'"

"So what did you say?"

"I told him to eff off."

This tough little guy was wearing a neat little Harris tweed cap and leather leggings, jodhpurs, tight knee-high leather boots. He kept saying, "I'm a practical man. If anything comes near my fence, I shoot it. Then I take it out on the road and run over it so nobody will know I shot it."

Kay was there too. I'd had three pints and was feeling a bit woozy. She said, "If you're going to be drinking you have to take a lot of blotting paper. When did you last eat?"

"I had a salty kipper around ten."

"It's six o'clock now. You gotta have some blotting paper." So she sliced open a roll, and slapped a pile of ham in it, then handed it to me with a bag of potato chips.

"If you go to the standing stones," she said, as I negotiated a corner of the roll into my mouth, "and stand real still, you can hear them whistle." She started whistling like mad.

"You mean whistling when the wind hits them?"

"No, whistling when it's dead still."

She also said we live on light, and it's because we get so much more light in the summer in the northern climes that we feel so much healthier and alive. "It's simple," she said. "The more light we get the better it is for us."

I sighed and looked into her eyes, then Jock came over looking grouchy.

Gillian says, "See that big fellow over there? He's the biggest bloody poacher in the whole district."

I went over and said, "Any poachers around here?"

He gave me a good stare. "Poachers? Yeah, I'm a poacher."

"Ever get caught?"

"Nope."

"They used to hang people for that."

"They don't hang 'em any more, they just fine 'em. Why should the laird have all the deer? It doesn't make sense to me."

Kay comes over and puts her arm in mine: she tells the poacher what a great party we had two nights ago. "We were up till five o'clock in the morning, because it was Ladies' Night, and, boy, did I ever get in trouble when I got home."

"Yeah," I said, jokingly, "you should have seen her running around stark naked and everything."

"Oh, I've already seen you naked," he said.

"When was that?" she squeaked.

"I was over at your place once and you were in the shower naked as a jaybird. The door was open and I could see everything."

"I didn't know that," she said, blushing and smiling with pleasure. She put her head lovingly on his chest and said, with a great smile on her face, "I didn't know you saw me naked."

"It'd be wonderful to find something," I said to Josh.

"Aye, that it would," he said.

"But it's not the job of the tourist. Only the locals have the time to go looking."

I didn't mean to insult him, but he looked chastised. He said it's well known that many farmers are embarrassed when someone finds a megalithic monument on their land, because, although they think they know their land well, they've never actually noticed anything unusual. "I'm going to start looking," he vowed.

Gillian had quite a gullible streak for a well-known painter. Since I was a writer, she wanted to know if I was famous. I told her that Hollywood was planning to make a film based on my life. She went all saucer-eyed and started calling friends over.

There was a happy old fellow in the pub, and people were telling me I should really talk to him, because he was so interesting. But I didn't get a chance to. I did see one fellow go up to him and say, "Hi, Willy, how are you?"

With a big glass of whisky in one hand, a cigarette in the other, and a silly grin on his face, Willy said, "I'm surviving."

What a pleasure! Sunset on Loch Crinan, which is really a small bay off the Sound of Jura, and was said to be the probable landing place for the Scotti tribes when they launched their big invasion of the fifth century. But I'm lost somewhere in this great maze of country roads between Crinan Ferry, which is on the cape north of Crinan, and Kilmartin. When you are lost, you need not stay lost long: whenever there is a choice between two different paths or roads, you merely follow the one that is more heavily trod or better paved, and you'll soon be found.

At 11:28 p.m. I've secured a place for the night. Where? Not sure, but probably somewhere around Lochgilphead. The people have returned from a family get-together in Oban. They weren't planning on taking any guests tonight, but it was so late they took pity on me. "We thought you'd have a hard time finding a place," the wife said. She said she thought Scotland was like Canada: in the winter people say the weather's so bad they can't work and in summer they say the weather's so lovely they can't work. She has beautiful thick carpets, and though I'd been walking through cow pastures and bogs, she wouldn't hear of me taking my sneakers off.

From my window can be seen numerous Pictish walls, twisted trees, meadows, cultivated fields, smaller hills, larger hills that are heavily forested except for one giant square of complete clear-cut. And there's a big Land Rover bouncing up and down through a meadow way off in the distance: there's no road there, and it's two o'clock in the morning. Hope he's not a bewildered tourist looking for a place to stay.

CARNLIATH

Furnace • Inveraray • Oban • Boily (a.k.a. Beauly)
Dingwall • Dornoch • Brora

Monday, June 24. It'd be big news if the lovely town of Furnace burned down. The Furnace Inn, surrounded by violets and azaleas, is aptly run by Violet and Gordon Pyrie. Violet was a bit embarrassed when I asked why the village was called Furnace, because she didn't know. "There's no furnace in the village," she mused.

It's a perfect day: one can wear a shirt and light sweater without feeling hot or cold. The breeze coming up Loch Fyne is moving the trees to and fro, and there's a symphony of warbling brooks and babbling birds everywhere you turn. Finally, I find the "furnace": a huge well-constructed brick-and-stone iron smelter in ruins, its tin roof badly rusted out. The building is perfectly square, it decreases in size as it goes up, and it's topped by a wide, square chimney. It was built to last forever, and the town would have been built around it, and taken its name from it.

"Och, it'd go back to the seventeen- or eighteen-hundreds," says an old fellow strolling by. The profusion of flower gardens hereabouts, he says, is because of all the Irish soil. Ships used to bring good black Irish soil over as ballast. They'd dump the soil and load up with "iron ore and cannonballs and that kind of stuff" for the return trip to Ireland.

With Scottish place names it's important to remember that the prefix *kil* refers to a church, as in Kilmartin, the church of Saint Martin. But when *kil* is a suffix, it means a wood, or a forest, for it's a corruption of the Gaelic word *coille*.

In the centre of the town of Inveraray, on Loch Fyne where it begins to peter out among the green foothills of the Grampian Mountains, there's a tall bell tower. At each end of town is a monster sign saying VISIT THE BELL TOWER. The place is full of tourists, most of whom seem to have travelled up from the Midlands of England in great tourist buses. The residents all seem in an understandably foul mood, including an old fellow running a filling station. He might only have been irritated because, when I pulled in, I had Iain Macfadyen's bagpipe music playing full blast with both windows open. If it's one thing the Scots hate, it's bagpipe music. If there's two, it's bagpipe music and haggis. If it's three, it's bagpipe music, haggis, and tourists who pretend to like bagpipe music and haggis.

I tried to make pleasant small talk as he filled my tank, but everything I said was answered with a grunt, and when he took my money he went in his little shop, closed the door, and locked it.

Once you get on the single-track roads, people are friendlier. On these busy two-lane tourist roads you can't buy appreciation. The actual Scottish tourist traps are scarce but blatantly deceitful. An official-looking sign says SCOTTISH SALMON CENTRE: you go in expecting to see salmon leaping up artificial waterfalls, and it turns out to be a restaurant. A few miles on there's a similar fake government sign saying SCOTTISH SEA-LIFE CENTRE: when you pop in they ask if you'd like to be seated in the restaurant or the oyster bar. They count on your being too embarrassed to admit you've been fooled.

An astonishing number of road signs in Scotland have been pep-
pered with gunshot and painted over and hacked at and otherwise
defaced: this would be the work of quixotic dreamers who still think
roads are the invention of the English imperialists, with plenty of
help from Satan himself. Of course, they're right.

Oban is widely known as a serene, melancholy distillery town, where
you catch ferries for the islands. But this time it's a gridlocked zoo,
with backpackers, caravans, and holidayers thronging the roads,
stores, sidewalks. But once through town the countryside immediately seems quieter than ever. I pull into a roadside tea wagon, but
they were closing up for the day. It was ten to five. "Oh, you close at
five, do you?"

"Aye, five is the time most people like to eat, I know that, but
unfortunately so do I. I'm sorry I can't even give you a cup of coffee,
for I've just poured out my boiler."

I don't want to get anyone in trouble, but I think these roadside
tea wagons are fronts for drug-traffickers and arms-runners. As I
drove away there was a near-miss with three German motorcyclists
coming around a bend on the wrong side of the road. They zoomed
over to the left side, then slammed on their brakes and went into the
same tea wagon, probably to pick up their order of heroin. By way of
contrast, along the road a bit was a pretentious holiday hotel with a
sign saying THE ART OF EVERLASTING QUALITY, which is code for
"Stay out unless you want to spend five hundred quid a night." At
least at the tea wagon you'd probably be getting your penny's worth.

I'm soon on the other side of the country, bypassing Inverness, on
course for a counter-clockwise tour around the extreme north of
Scotland, looking forward to the great mountains of the Northwest
Highlands, which caused my spirit guide, H. V. Morton, to utter such
magnificent exclamations of wild enthusiasm. When you're in Beauly

(Boily in Morton's day), an unusually bright and sophisticated town in the Highlands, a bit northwest of Inverness, with a great square, fashionably dressed people, and spiffy restaurants, you're getting close to the Brahan Seer country. The Brahan Seer was Coinneach Odhar Fiosache, an eighteenth-century oddball from the Isle of Lewis, who used a magic stone to predict, among other things, that when nine bridges span the River Ness, the Highlands will be overrun by ministers with no grace and women with no shame. After making an inappropriate remark at a dinner party at the nearby Brahan Castle, he was burned to death in a tar barrel at the orders of Lady Seaforth. He died pronouncing numerous curses, all of which came true – unfortunately for the Seaforth family.

A town up from Beauly is Dingwall, as grey and dour as Beauly is bright and fashionable. The Station Square War Memorial was exactly as Morton described it: a tall, slender pole about twenty feet high with a crossbar. It was made in France by the villagers of Cambrai, and features a curious pair of metal wings. "This cross was brought home from France in 1924," states the plaque, "and re-erected here by the 4≤4≥h Highlanders Reunion Club 1914–1918 in memory of their beloved dead, killed at Cambray, on 21 and 22 November 1917." Among those killed were a Private J. McGravel and a Corporal A. Fridge. The Battle of Cambrai was a stupendously senseless slaughter, with ninety thousand men dying in the mud. As I'm about to start sobbing, as we rank sentimentalists tend to do at war memorials, a lorry rumbles through town with a big sign saying ANYWARE ANYWHERE, causing me to laugh.

Carnliath is a superb "iron-age broch tower" overlooking the North Sea, and is a memorial to the period when warfare was beginning to catch on in Scotland. About five hundred of these small beehive-like drystone strongholds were built throughout Scotland about the time of Christ, predating the earliest needle-like "round towers" of Ireland by eight centuries. The builders of Carnliath were farmers, growing barley, keeping cattle and sheep, and they also fished from shore. As population demands were beginning to lead to conflict, these Pictish brochs were intended to withstand sieges, but not long ones, as there was no water supply.

Carnliath's doorway is four feet high and there's a window over the lintel, so you could bend over, go in, then stand up inside and look back out. In a manner typical of brochs, a spiral staircase winds all the way around on the inside, so that one can get to the second floor on a gentle slope, and the original stone steps are completely intact. The door would have been a wooden one, but another wooden one was set further back in to foil an attack by battering ram. The clever and intricate stonework is identical to that of the old walls that snake around Scotland. The Picts seem to have built, besides the brochs, enough walls to stretch around the world if laid end to end and straightened out. The walls here are about twelve feet thick, and it's easy to climb up and walk around the top of them. They contain numerous passageways and storage areas. The stonework is done with flair and artistry. It's amazing how flat the surfaces of the walls are. The construction indicates they weren't in a rush to complete the job, and the planning that went into it before construction began must have been considerable.

My impressions are that these people had their gods, but there was a matter-of-factness about their beliefs. Their predecessors in Scotland would have been sun-worshippers: perhaps the cup-and-ring carvings represent, among other things, little suns saying hello, as a sign of great respect, to the big sun as it comes sailing through the skies. That perhaps would account for the southward slopes of most of the cup-and-ring sites, and the closeness to the sea. Although these people lived in peace, they also lived in dread of the sun going out.

But it's a different story when we get to the Pictish sites. The Picts were more secular, more strictly business, yet as I left Carnliath I became unaccountably sad. Somehow I'd identified with that broch. I was saying goodbye to it, telling it I'd remember it and tell others about it. A sense of identification with the remote past is something one looks for in one's travels, or even at home, and I certainly had a strong sense of it here. The builders of this broch weren't vicious, brutal, cruel people —but they were on their way there. Once things start changing they change fast, and the people better change fast too or they're dust. From a distance one sees the broch sitting so perfectly on its grassy mound, with the proportions of a broad, flat-brimmed Panama hat.

A silver brooch found at Carnliath is in the shape of a question mark, ironically, and was probably a clasp for fastening a tunic. (Maybe that's where brooches got their name, from brochs!) It's said that one of the reasons we know so little about the Picts is that they weren't in the habit of placing personal belongings in graves – which would go along with my sense of their having been unsentimental, no-nonsense folks. But my visit to this broch reinforces my impression that the Celtic walls all over Scotland should be called Pictish walls, for the construction techniques of this broch are identical to those used in the walls.

Dornoch, a weird old town of dark greystone buildings on the North Sea, up the coast from Carnliath, is known as the site of the final witch-burning in Scotland, in 1722. This evening it's dead quiet: everyone seems to be indoors reading the Bible. The lower town practically sits on the beach: it's the oldest part of the town, and the houses are smaller and darker. The oldest houses seem to be on Elder Street, coincidentally.

In the town square of Brora, just as old as Dornoch and a bit further north, there's a bell tower that must be the highest in the world for such a small town, and it's cracked down the middle and looks about to collapse. I better not get alarmed, for I don't want to be talked about in years to come as the amusing Canadian who came to town and woke everyone up screaming the bell tower was about to collapse. They must have it bracketed from the inside.

In *Baedeker's*, the coalmine that runs under the streets of Brora "now belongs to the miners themselves, and scarcely spoils the town's amenity." The underground activities might account for the crack in the bell tower. In the tower is an ancient bell that tolls out the hours – a real bell, not tape-recorded, and pulled by hand. The crack doesn't spoil the amenity either.

SUBTERRANEAN
MOONS

Brora • Dunbeath • Grey Cairns of Camster
Hill o' Many Stanes • Wick • Scrabster • Thurso
Knoc Freiceadain • Melvich

Tuesday, June 25. My nervous, carrot-topped hostess asks if I slept well, then leaves me alone in the ballroom-sized dining room where they have, over the bar, a series of four hunting scenes from 1807: duck shooting, grouse shooting, partridge shooting, and pheasant shooting. Then she comes back with a pot of tea and tells me they're selling up, for its time to get back to the family in Inverness. They've been in Brora four years. What's the town like here? "Oh, it's all right," she says. 'They keep to themselves quite a bit, but that's true of most small towns, isn't it?" This isn't a rhetorical question. She wants an answer. I tell her that's certainly true everywhere you go.

She leaves me alone to wonder why they'd be leaving. Are they cutting their losses or have they made their bundle? I absent-mindedly pick up an old newspaper from a stack of them on a barstool and find my answer:

A Brora hotelier broke down in tears after she described in court how she had been the victim of verbal abuse from two villagers. Winifred McDonald, 50, of the Bayview Hotel, was led weeping from the courtroom after giving evidence against Philip Corbett, 34, and Isabel Macdonald, 32, both unemployed, and both of town. It was one o'clock in the morning last August when Mrs. McDonald was taking her dog for its nightly walk. She heard voices in the carpark and somebody began shouting abuse, telling her she was uglier than her mutt. Her husband, Alistair, who had been cleaning up in the bar, came out and was challenged to a fight. Phil and Isabel told him he was a coward hiding behind his wife.

This is reminiscent of the Burgess situation, though the incomers in this case were from down the road in Inverness rather than from England. And Brora does seem innately unfriendly to outsiders. When you say good morning to a local they reply good morning, but in an unmistakably sarcastic, mocking tone.

Winifred brings in my kippers. "Was that you in the paper?" I ask. She smiles shyly and says they haven't had any more trouble, and it hasn't hurt business at all. But they're careful: when she goes down to the village she takes her car, and she hires a neighbour kid to walk the dog.

The fishing village of Dunbeath is the birthplace of Neil Gunn (1891–1973), who wrote many novels set in the area and influenced by his childhood experiences hereabouts. He worked for the civil service in Edinburgh, but he revisited Dunbeath when he had the chance. Stone slabs have been erected to prevent damage from river floods in the spring, and for a while the riverside walk, running up the glen from the village, goes along the tops of the slabs, which are about five feet high. From the suspension bridge, which is bouncy, sways alarmingly, and makes funny noises (*koo-kee, koo-kee, koo-kee*),

I had the strongest feeling of being observed through a high-power telescope in the large four-gabled house way off at the end of the glen. A farmer tells me he found a William III coin in his field one day: he was offered ten pounds for it but decided to keep it. JILL PHIPPS R.I.P. ALWAYS REMEMBERED '95 someone has scrawled on a pole. The farmer says he couldn't remember any Jill Phipps, and has no idea how she died. But he makes up for it by telling me that in Scotland the byre is where you put the cows and the barn is where you put the hay. On the front door of a cute little house at the side of the river somebody has spray-painted FUCK OFF. The poor owner has painted over it about four times but it still shines through.

In Dunbeath harbour there's a statue commemorating the centennial of Neil Gunn's birth. It shows a serious and determined little boy bending under the weight of a huge fish. He's got it over his shoulder and its tail is dragging along the ground. It's called "Kenn and the Salmon, from Neil Gunn's 'Highland River'" (1937), one of about twenty-two novels Gunn wrote, some of them published posthumously and most of them still in print.

The nearby massive Grey Cairns of Camster are billed as two of the best-preserved chambered tombs in Britain. They're almost as large as Newgrange in Ireland, but less famous and more amenable to solitary, leisurely investigation. The long cairn to the west has four humps on the top and two entranceways on the side facing the road. The older, smaller one to the east was broken into by amateur antiquarians in 1865. The entranceway had been deliberately blocked by rubble in the prehistoric era, so they found it necessary to smash the capstone in order to get in. They found the remains of two humans placed in a sitting position in the inner chamber and a mass of burned human bones, flint tools, and pottery.

The passageway is exceedingly narrow and dark; it's a long, painful squeeze into the central chamber. You have to kneel and crawl on your hands and knees, and keep your head way down. There's room to stand in the inner chamber, which is illuminated through the hole in the top where the capstone had been: a Plexiglas cover keeps things dry, and allows light in. The central chamber resembles a kind of beehive hut, but with five standing stone slabs. The most impressive is a stout slab about five feet high and almost five feet wide, standing opposite the entrance. The slab is built into a wall of much smaller stones, so you can't tell how thick it might be.

In addition to the five stones, there are two others, almost nine feet high, standing like sentinels on either side of the entrance to the chamber; they're broad at the bottom and slender at the top, so that they resemble giant arrowheads. They form a support for the lintel, which is about three feet high, and they also have a hand in supporting the high and somewhat domed ceiling.

This is a well-made and well-thought-out structure. A cup marking on a stone facing back out the passageway, in the direction of the rising sun at midsummer, has been damaged, but seems to have had three rings around it. One might expect more carvings on these stones. This might have originally been a ring of five standing stones. After burials had taken place within the ring, this massive structure began to evolve, suggesting a pattern of stone circles, which were not used for burial purposes, evolving over time into cairns, which were. At any rate, as in Newgrange, the sun rising at midsummer would make a wonderful impact on this central chamber. The passageway is so long that, when I look back from the central chamber, the initial entrance appears to be about the size of the rising sun, and in a strange but pleasing manner it is bisected neatly by the horizon. At midsummer, the broad five-by-five stone at the back of the chamber would become a mirror, a subterranean moon brilliant with light.

The larger cairn had been two round-chambered cairns, which in time became entombed in the much longer one. The original two are visible in the humps along the top of the long cairn, so that it resembles a ridge connecting two high hills. The contours seem natural and extraordinarily pleasing to the eye. Not only are these cairns built to commemorate the dead, and for astronomical purposes, but they also appear to be some kind of tribute to the earth, or an offering to the earth, as if built deliberately to achieve an intimate relationship between the structure and the surrounding natural contours.

As scary as it may be, I have to go into both of these twinned cairns as well: I'll be annoyed with myself later if I don't. The inner chambers turn out to be basically similar to the first, but with variations. One of the standing stones has an interesting natural fissure that resembles a tall mountain peak with the slope plunging down to the sea. Another smaller stone in the group looks like a sheep with its eyes closed. At the back of the third chamber, another five-by-five stone, rectangular and flaring slightly outwards towards the bottom, sits on two recumbent stones and is similarly and predictably positioned to take the full glare of the rising sun on midsummer morn. This stone is moon-like, blank, but with many natural craters and other marks, and it looks like a God that has lost its face: a face without a face. Six standing stones form a pair of arms reaching out from each side of this dormant beast. The first pair of stones on either side are just shy of five feet high, the second pair are about seven feet high and the outer pair are about four feet. This is believed to be the earliest of the three cairns. Such strange beauty!

Were these people ancestors of the Picts? Possibly, but these structures were built three thousand years before there was any historical mention of the Picts. Given that the Picts built the brochs and the so-called Celtic walls, the people who built these earlier structures certainly had a much different way of dealing with stone – their techniques were more brutal, less refined, but they had more vision and more heart and they were sun-worshippers, while the Picts had left that behind, and had a far different sense of elegance, proportion, symmetry.

As I was sitting in my car wrestling with a road map, a solitary little German fellow tapped on my window with his binoculars and asked if my map showed the Hill o' Many Stanes. I said that's where I was heading next: he could follow me if he wanted, it's just a few miles from here, south towards the North Sea coast. He said yes, but first he wanted to search out a curlew he had been hearing calling. He'd never seen a curlew before, but he soon caught it in his binoculars and was able to add it to his life list.

At the Hill, four hundred small standing stones, each no more than a metre high, had been arranged in numerous rows about 2000 BC by early Bronze Age people. Half of the stones have disappeared. They were arranged in twenty-two rows running north and south, and fanning out from each other slightly towards the south end. The structure apparently had one purpose: to serve as a practical device to chart the solar and lunar cycles and to help in normalizing and regulating the farming cycle: a calendar for people with no calendars.

I asked this likeable Bavarian student if there were antiquities in his area. "Actually, yes," he said, and then he started laughing. "There's a massive Celtic fort there. It's been visited many times, it's been well explored and excavated, and much is known about it – and I've never been there." And then he starts laughing again. As for the Hill o' Many Stanes, it's similar to a larger, more elaborate, and more famous one at Carnac in France, and my friend was saying he was disappointed in this one since the stones were so small. I suggested this might have been the forerunner of the one at Carnac. "Yeah," he said, "maybe the English built it and the French stole it off them." He said he gets the same amount of pleasure out of birdwatching as he does out of visiting the old stones. But he's doing a lot of birdwatching in Britain because where he lives in Bavaria is far from the sea, and he doesn't get to see many seabirds. We didn't exchange names, but we laughed at each other's jokes. As we shook hands in farewell a lorry went by hauling a big red float with a sign saying MERRY CHRISTMAS.

There's a stunning view of Wick on the approach from the low hills to the south, with th cx fog coming in off the North Sea. Only the spires of two churches are visible above the fog. The harbour is old and full of atmosphere. There are seamen's taverns, the Caithness Voluntary Group, the Seamen's Mission, the Harbour Fish Shop, and lots of boats bobbing in the water. Someday this will be all painted up like Tobermory. It's a powerful town, with a lot of radiance about it.

The day is cool and grey, full of the smell of burning peat all along the northern coast of Scotland. It must have been an awful shock the day the silo blew down. This fellow has a lovely modern farm, along the road from Wick to Thurso, with up-to-the-minute, dark-green metal buildings – and a green metal silo. And the silo has crashed and it's fallen in pieces in a long line between the farmhouse and the barn. You can imagine people with old stone silos snickering and/or smirking in their tea. I hope he's suing the manufacturer. It must have been terribly embarrassing. None of the ancient stone silos from hereabouts got blown down.

The clever Scots love to take single letters out of signs to make something naughty, like the L out of SWIMMING POOL or the G out of LOW BRIDGE. The woman who runs a roadside tea wagon becomes attentive when she hears my accent. "Are you from America then?" she says, for she thinks perhaps I'm associated with the eighty-year-old billionaire Yank who's buying up some castle in the vicinity. I tell her I never mess with billionaires.

In a harbour pub in Scrabster, near Thurso, I'm showing off my copy of H. V. Morton's *In Search of Scotland*, with its vivid descriptions of Scrabster and Tongue. "That ferry he's talking about isn't there any more," says the bartender. "We have a causeway now." He takes me over to the other, quieter side of the pub and introduces me to Bill MacIver, a pensioner who lives in Toronto, but makes a sentimental return to his home town of Scrabster every year. He's a time-weary, cranky, but proud seventy-one. He was in the Royal Air Force in World War II. He was a pilot at first, but they took him off before he could get killed, apparently because they found out he was a good motor mechanic, and they got him working on the engines of Spitfires and whatnot, changing engines around from one plane to another. When he was made a pilot officer, he said he wouldn't take the promotion unless they still let him go to the sergeant's mess.

After the war, Bill worked on the lifeboat out of Scrabster, then spent fifteen years in Bermuda, working on nuclear submarines "as a motor mechanic, for compressors or anything like that. And then my mother died, and so when I finished my contract, I moved to Canada."

Now he's long retired and living alone in Toronto in a senior-citizen's complex. "Kenny here" – he nudges the sleepy fellow sitting next to him – "was my assistant in them days on the lifeboat – if I could keep him awake." Thunderous laughter erupts all down the bar. Bill went to visit another old mate of his today, a local hero now fallen on bad times. "He's a great guy, just a great guy, sitting there with a smile this wide on his face, sitting on his chair – no legs or nothing. Terrible."

Everyone echoes the word *terrible* all the way down the bar. The occasional tear sparkles in the lamplight. Dark rain splatters on the front window. "There's only a couple of times I ever met him," says a guy down at the end of the bar, "but I heard a lot about him all right."

"There's a picture of him there over the bar up at the Commercial Hotel," one fellow says.

"Oh yeah, they would have, there," says another. "They go and pick him up every now and again, the Commercial."

Bill returns home once a year for a month to catch up with his old friends. They give him a room over the Old Pub. That's where they used to go in the days of the lifeboats. The lifeboat would be coming in, and all the lights would come on in the Old Pub. All the people from the lifeboat would come up to the pub, and the old lady would say, "Now, yer jis' having the one now, aren't ye, and then yer off home." Of course she wouldn't mean it, and they'd all have three or four before staggering home. Bill says she always used to make him a brown ale with a brandy poured in it. That really warmed his bones. You'd have to be out at sea rescuing people in a lifeboat in the middle of winter to get the most out of a brandy in brown ale.

As for his old comrade with no legs, when he lost his one leg he said, "Now look upon the bright side, a pair of socks will last me twice as long." Then he lost the other leg, and somebody asked him what he wanted for his birthday, and he said, "How about a pair of running shoes?" It brings tears to Bill's eyes to think of him. Diabetic? "No no, I don't think that was it. He had a lot of tuberculosis in his family, that might have had something to do with it."

I'm presented with a book, a small-type forty-eight-page *History of the Life Boats of Scrabster*, and it goes back to 1860. Bill was terribly shocked that I didn't know about the tradition of the Lifeboats of Scrabster. They have sophisticated machines now; they go flying out to sea whenever any kind of ship is in any kind of trouble. Some of the crew members are paid, but most of them are volunteers, and when they get a distress call at home, out they go.

I say to him, "It says here that in 1949 one William MacIver joined such and such a lifeboat as a motor mechanic."

He sighs. "Aye, that's me."

Mr. Morton had an eye for beautiful women. In Thurso he wrote of the numerous "good-looking young fisher lassies, wearing rough skirts and aprons, and carrying on their heads big, flat, oval-shaped wicker trays of fish." But that's not the scene here today. Old St. Peter's Kirk (founded circa 1220 by Gilbert Murray, bishop of Caithness, closed to worship 1832) is so dilapidated that, when a gull lands on one of the gables, the whole structure shivers. The main old hotel in Thurso is full of elderly English people, the men in suits and white shirts and ties, and the women in nice dresses, both sitting around quietly in couples in quiet parts of the hotel. I smiled at a man as I passed, and he glared back at me, as if to say, *How dare you smile at me, sir! Damned American customs.*

I stayed here ten years ago, but this time no dice: "No, sir, I'm sorry, sir, we're all booked up tonight, sir, but if it's a hotel you're looking for, sir, there's one over here, sir." But then I thought, Thurso in the rain? Nah, let's try to get to Tongue in the rain.

But after slogging up the muddy slopes of Knoc Freiceadain, where two large chambered tombs, both apparently unexcavated, sit among three standing stones, and from where one can catch a glimpse of Orkney on a good day, I lost interest in driving any further. The three tall stones, flecked with sheep's wool, are in alignment with each other. But then I notice they are also in alignment with a slight irregularity on the top of a distant high ridge a mile or two off to the west and to a solitary church on a similar ridge to the east. I head towards the ridge to the west first, hoping faintly that on one of the two ridges there might be a place where I could sleep for the night, in mystical alignment with three standing stones. It might have a salubrious effect on my dreams.

But on the ridge to the west there's nothing but a farmhouse, with a lot of old farm machinery rusting in the rain, three bulls with rings in their noses and numbers in their ears, a curious round barn, a phone booth, and some badly damaged old Pictish walls. On the hill to the east there's an old church and a manse. This church is at most two or three hundred years old, but like many old churches it was probably built on the site of another old church, and so on back to some site of religious import thousands of years ago. Actually it's no longer used as a church, and the manse is no longer used as a manse. The old church looks as if it's used as a storehouse/studio for the current residents of the manse, which is called Rathlin. In this fog everything looks flat; it's hard to tell the glens from the hills. But what we have here are the three stones pointing directly at this old church, and, from a different angle, an ancient Pictish wall about two miles long that is pointing right towards this church. So a line drawn from the stones and from the wall would intersect right here at the church. This would be rich terrain for ley-line enthusiasts with dowsing rods.

The Melvedge Hotel, in the village of Melvich, provides spectacular views along the rocky coastline and out over the bay, with sea lions and seals on the sandbar at low tide, dolphins, sea eagles, numerous curlews, oystercatchers, mergansers, puffins, guillemots, and gannets. The manageress was running around trying to get me a room, since I was overcome with weariness and would have to leave Tongue till tomorrow. There were no vacancies in the hotel, but she found something for me down the road a bit. When I thanked her for her trouble, she shyly lowered her head with a curious look of embarrassment, as if she might just have been in the habit of receiving kickbacks from the little neighbourhood tourist homes.

AN INNOCENT
FLIRTATION IN
TONGUE

Bettyhill • Tongue • Dun Dornaigil Broch • Ullapool
Glengarry • Invergarry

Wednesday, June 26. The northeastern chunk of Scotland is fairly flat and reminiscent of the southeastern chunk of England. But when you get to the pretty village of Bettyhill, a couple of houses and a pub, you're approaching the entrance to the amazing Northwest Highlands – that is, if you're travelling westwards. Way off on the southwest horizon are dozens of pale blue mountains, each present-ing its own perennial profile to the world. Some are rounded and high, some severely peaked and relatively low, one looks like the letter M, with straight sides and a V out of the top, another like the letter N – in fact there's probably at least one for every letter in the alphabet – and then off in the distance there's an irregular ridge that looks like a long word in Arabic script. The road takes a dip and the entire range sinks beneath the horizon: the faster you're driving the faster they sink. Roadside houses are festooned with spherical fishing buoys of all colours and sizes. Sparkling rivers pour down from great looming but somehow friendly peaks, and across yellow-brown banana-coloured sandy beaches into the grey sea under a grey sky.

Mr. Morton was enthused about Tongue. He doesn t talk at all about the area we've been through the past day or so, he saves it up for Tongue, which comes from the Gaelic *tunga*, meaning "tongue." If you believe Morton, when you approach Tongue you enter a whole other world. I don't quite see it, though there are some charming white beaches, with rocky coves and little islands offshore. A cheery little tidal river, probably called the River Tongue, flows out into Tongue Cove, and perched on the Tongue Promontory, sitting above the river, is an old wrecked castle that has an aura around it that seems to be saying, *I know I'm in ruins but I don't mind one little bit.* The Tongue Hotel looks as if it might cater exclusively to retired cabinet ministers and manufacturers of computerized showers.

There's a Bank of Scotland in Tongue, and I'm the only customer. The manager, a large man with a loud voice and dressed in a black suit, white shirt, black tie, and black shoes, barks out, "Jenny!" moments after I walk in. Then he looks at me. I have a sweet little smile on my face. He looks a bit embarrassed for having yelled so loudly in a small room.

"Good morning," I say, softly.

"Good morning," says he, even more softly.

Then Jenny came trotting out.

She gave me the cash I was after. But then she noticed the manager glaring at her meaningfully and getting ready to bark again. So she remembered to ask for some identification. I decided against embarrassing her by saying, Sorry, I've already got the money. I handed her my passport, and she looked at my photo and signature and said, "Lovely day, izzen it?"

"Yes," said I. "Is it always like this in Tongue?"

"Oh no, it's up and down " she said.

Our eyes met and we both blushed. The manager went into his office with a sigh and closed the door softly.

"Up and down, that's the way I like it," I whispered.

306 ◆ AN INNOCENT IN SCOTLAND

"Och, me too," she said.

"What time do you get off work?" I queried, admiringly.

"Och, if this was last week it'd be an entirely different story, y'see, but my husband's home from his job on the oil rigs." She reached out and lightly ran her pinky over the back of my hand.

"Nice guy?"

"Och, y'know. Nothin' I do pleases him."

"Sounds like the bank manager."

"Aye, an' I wish *he'd* git a job on the oil rigs, I do."

A magnificent sky-hugger looms south of Tongue and it's called Ben Loyal, the summit of which is only 2,509 feet above sea level, but transplant it to the Alps and it'd make the Matterhorn look like a molehill. It's nicely pointed, like a dunce's cap, and it's surrounded by lesser peaks. It's green with grass on the lower slopes and green with lichen on the upper, with plenty of white and black rocks interconnected. The birds are singing as I drive along, up and down, and the landscape is like a fugue, with the rolling countryside reaching up into higher rolling countryside and then bursting forth into great arpeggios of mountains rising up into the sky from not much above sea level.

This is the road Morton took. I could have taken the new causeway, but I wanted to be loyal to the old boy, and also to find out why he felt he had entered a new world. He was so glad the ferry of the time only took foot passengers, no vehicles, because that meant he had to motor along this interesting route. But Morton, not only does he never talk about the roads he travels on, he never talks about why he never talks about them. He was too wily not to be aware that he wasn't talking about the roads, in my opinion. Maybe his editor insisted he not talk about the roads. But the simple fact is that Morton was a born promoter: he was inventing automotive tourism, and if he talked about how bad the roads were, everybody would have stayed at home – or taken the train.

How many photographs of Ben Loyal would there be in existence right now? I bet there are photos of Ben Loyal buried in boxes or pasted in albums in every country in the world. It's a wonderful mountain, and it still will be long after all those photographs are dust. And maybe someday a fleck of dust, that was once a part of a photograph of Ben Loyal, will float around the top of the mountain and land right on its topmost peak.

Morton seems to be breathing down my neck. He's sitting quietly, reliving his experiences. His spirit is right here in the car with me.

"I don't even know your first name, sir."

"Call me Henry, or call me H. V.," he says.

"Is it okay if I call you Mr. Morton? After all, you're so much older than I am."

"Yes," he says, "but when I took this route I was younger than you."

"Much smarter, too," I declared.

"I was more professional than you. I knew what the public wanted," said he. "You're a bit out with the fairies, to use Jock's expression."

"You were *there*, too?"

"I'm not letting you out of my sight for the entire trip.'

I gave it to him straight. "Maybe I'm a rank amateur by your standards, but by mine you were a cliché-monger, a promoter, and a stereotype artist. Look at what you say about Ben Loyal: 'Ben Loyal is a hill on which Norse gods might have sharpened their swords.' I mean, yech! And you never visited the prehistoric sites at all."

"They're boring. You shouldn't visit them either."

"I don't find them boring."

"Your readers will. And look, my books outsold yours a thousand to one."

"This is true. But listen to yourself: 'Thor must have come from Thurso to use Ben Loyal as his whetstone.'"

"Oh, don't worry about it young feller. No need to be jealous. It was a different world then."

"Thanks, Mr. Morton."

"And if I were alive today, I'd have a hard time making money as a writer, believe you me."

"You did a heckuva good job with those books, Mr. Morton. We don't talk like that any more, it's true, but nevertheless your books are still an enjoyable read, even if you do go on a bit about Ben Loyal."

"Thanks, partner." Yeah, he actually called me *partner*. "I think it's known nowadays as being market-driven, of having a sincere desire to give the readers what they want. If you don't have a taste for that, you're wasting your time writing."

"I know, but what isn't a waste of time anyway? Making money can be said to be a waste of time. You gotta follow your bliss, man."

"Now who's the cliché-monger?"

After entering the stratosphere of mytholinguistic ecstasy over Ben Loyal, Mr. Morton couldn't find a place to stay in Durness (probably still couldn't), so they sent him to a crummy old fisherman's hotel, which, of course, turned out to be exactly to his liking, and he wasn't too shy to tell us. He had an interesting chat with a fisherman in the evening and an enormous breakfast in the morning.

I stop to check my map, and a car pulls up behind me. The loveliest young lady with the prettiest smile gets out of the car and proceeds to take a picture of Ben Loyal. She has a good shot too, with a lovely little loch in the medium foreground, and a small herd of Highland cattle in the immediate foreground. The entire mountain, with a wisp of mist at the peak, was framed so naturally it would seem like one of those lucky, spontaneous snapshot masterpieces. She thanked me profusely for helping with the focusing.

Dun Dornaigil Broch sits on the shore of the fast-running River Hope, which flows into Loch Hope. Dwarfed by Ben Hope (3,004 feet), the broch looks like a bishop's hat, one of those ridiculously tall hats thirty-five feet high at the front and only about twelve feet high at the sides or back. A little drawing was carved into a stone by a visitor in 1772 – at which time, before radiocarbon testing, it was thought the brochs were built by the Vikings: they even thought Stonehenge was built by the Druids. It might be interesting to adapt those miniature cameras used in medical procedures for inspecting the interior of these hollow walls. It might be amazing what could be found, and without any need to excavate. Not only was this broch meant to provide protection, it was also built to be admired. Looking closely at the walls, one can only be amazed at the delicate and thoughtful stonework, and the artful use of stacks of thin loose chippings to plug up narrow fissures in the wall, in a manner identical with Pictish walls all over Scotland.

Loch Eriboll is a sea loch with a splendid array of islands in it – whaleback islands, pyramid-shaped islands, and so on. The water is green, the beaches are white, and rocks stick up out of the sand in a manner reminiscent of the Zen gardens of Kyoto. Numerous young people are running along the beach, enjoying the warm sun. And there is one older fellow in a swimsuit, and sporting a huge belly, lying on his back on the sand, trying to heat up his metabolism a bit. Directly above him is a large basalt rock that is loose and almost wobbling in the gentle breeze.

A shepherd, four dogs, and a vast herd of sheep appear on the road. Some of the sheep are chocolate brown. The shepherd is wearing a pair of blue trousers splattered with white paint, a beige cardigan, a pale-yellow suit jacket, and he's bald on top, but his sandy-grey side hair shoots out in all directions. He's got a pair of binoculars around his neck, for locating stragglers along the strand and up the side of hills. A bottleneck in the flow of traffic has ensued, and, as I drive up, the driver stalled in front of me quickly puts his camera away. Could he have been embarrassed to have been caught taking pictures of sheep?

Cars and lorries are lining up on both sides, causing the transportation of the sheep to slow down immeasurably, since the shepherd is forced to funnel the flock along the painfully narrow gap between the cars and the side of the hill. Oh, what a headache this is becoming for him. How was he to know there'd be an unprecedented upsurge in tourist traffic just as he tries to take a short cut along the road? We all seem to know we're going to be here for a good chunk of time, so all engines are turned off. In almost every car now, tourists are taking pictures of sheep in all directions. One fellow can't be bothered getting out of his car or turning around, so he's firing off pictures through his rear-view mirror.

We are now entering SIX MILES OF ENCHANTED LOWLIFE COUNTRY. It had been "gnome-like" (whatever that means), but some spray-bomber preferred "lowlife." I stop to take a shot of Ben Arkle (2,580 feet, with peak wreathed in cloud) with the old stone Laxford Bridge in the foreground (f22 and 1/30 with camera propped against arm of the new bridge, further back and at a higher level than the old one). After getting the shot, I stepped back onto the silent road while admiring Ben Arkle's twin sister, Ben Stack (2,356 feet), and almost killed a speeding cyclist. He swerved all over the road, but finally managed to come to a stop without falling – and then he actually apologized for not having given me a warning, rather than scream at me for not watching the road. He said he was drifting when he should have been whistling. He said it was great cycling around here. You can go as slow as you want up a hill and as fast as you want down a hill. But you have to carry lots of spare parts just in case. He was from Glasgow.

Ullapool, the major town on the northwest coast, is where you get the ferry for Stornoway, on the Isle of Lewis (where I'm not going on this trip), and it has the largest expanse of tacky North American-style residential and commercial architecture imaginable. Tourists drive slowly down the main street along the harbour, trying to figure out what to do, where to go, and perhaps looking for a parking spot. Tourists already parked seem reluctant to leave their cars: they sit there taking pictures of the surrounding mountains, such as Beinn Eilidea (1,830 feet) and Benn Ghobhlach (2,082 feet). Those without parking spots drive to the end of the waterfront street, where there's a turning circle, and they turn around and creep slowly back.

It's 5:30 and all the tea wagons are being towed home. There's a big football game tonight between England and Germany, but the BBC is doing a desperately hyperbolic, Mortonesque job of promoting it. They keep saying things like, "The whole nation will grind to a halt tonight" – which is definitely not true. At least the Scotland part of the nation certainly has no intention of grinding to a halt. Nobody up here – not even the English incomers – gives a hang about who wins. It's that kind of attitude on the part of the BBC that riles the Scots and makes them consider England even more of a foreign country than they ordinarily would. Also, the sleazy English tabloids have been doing their best to whip up anti-German feeling among the British fans. The German football reporters are being interviewed, and they're being noble about it all, saying the press should be ashamed of itself for trying to exploit outdated ethnic animosities.

A couple of ancient Buddhist manuscripts have been unearthed at the British Museum. They've been dated to AD 200 and are thought to be copies of verbatim transcriptions of the Buddha's words. A phone-in show host mentions this on the air, and immediately some fellow named Martin phones in from Dundee.

"Before we get deciphering those scrolls," he says, "I'd like to offer a few thoughts of my own."

"Would these thoughts be on a par with the Buddha's?" queries the announcer.

"Why not?" says Martin.

"Do you think in centuries to come we'll be talking about the thoughts of Martin of Dundee?"

"Well, you won't know till you hear them, will you?" says Martin.

"Okay, go ahead."

Martin clears his throat, then intones dramatically: "If you can answer your own questions truthfully, then you know you're being honest with yourself."

For some reason the announcer didn't consider that remark to be all that philosophically profound. "Thank you, Martin," he said, a bit sarcastically. "I think I'll take a relaxing tablet after that one. Bye-bye." *Click*.

After a long, winding drive down the northwest coast, with plenty of stops to gawk at mountains and read historical plaques, I made another sweep around Glengarry, then stopped for the night in the good-sized town of Invergarry, which the people of the glen refer to as "the village," and where they go for supplies. The night clerk and the bartender at the Invergarry Hotel are both tall, skinny, intellectual-looking fellows with long, skinny noses. Do they get many customers from Glengarry?

"I've been here six years," says the bartender, "and we used to get a good crowd in here some nights from Glengarry, but no more."

"What's the story?"

"The story is they've pretty well all been killed in car accidents."

He then proceeds to tell me the news that Dion Alexander kindly spared me when he was lamenting the dwindling population of the glen: about one horrible car crash after another, grisly details of the deaths of Glengarry residents returning to the valley after a boozy evening in Invergarry.

"All men in their thirties. They used to come down, but there have been so many car accidents they drink at their own pub they have up there. In all of Britain, if you're a male motorist in your thirties, the Highlands is the worst possible place to be. And it's not on the single-track roads either. The big crashes are always on the A roads. The A82 is apparently the worst road in Britain for fatal accidents." He mentioned one crash a few years ago in which two guys were killed and one survived. Then the one who survived was in another accident about two years later, in which he and two friends were killed. "So we don't get people from Glengarry in here any more. There's hardly anybody left up there of that age. They've all been wiped out. What a tough-luck place."

As for the crashes, he suspects it might have something to do with the shift in traffic patterns from season to season. In the summer it can take you an hour to get onto the A82 (the main road from Inverness southwest to Fort William and beyond) from a side road, but in the winter you don't even bother stopping because there's never anyone there – or almost never.

C H A P T E R 3 O

HIGH ROAD TO
GLASGOW

Invergarry • Ben Nevis • Glasgow

Thursday, June 27. Four couples, all seemingly English holidayers, sit at four separate tables in the spacious, elegant dining room of the Invergarry Hotel. They bend discreetly and whisper so softly I have to strain to hear them: "What do you make of this bloke all by himself?" And so on. There was a time this would have been painful for me, but you reach forty and overnight you're left with the self-consciousness of a paper clip.

A woman is whispering to her male friend, "Let's get a move on, there's always the possibility my husband might pop in here for a coffee." They even whisper to the waitress when they order: "We want what the funny fellow in the corner is having."

An American woman and a Japanese man come in and sit down at the table closest to mine. They are whispering too, and shy. He looks like a teddy bear; she's a foot taller than he, cute also but in a more severe way. They look a bit confused, and obviously new to

Scotland. I lean over and say, "Try the kippers, they're great." She smiles. Then they go back to whispering away at each other. About two minutes later she leans over and says, "What are kippers?" So I explain, and we get talking. She's from Idaho; he's from Tokyo. They had each been travelling solo around the United Kingdom, then happened to meet on a tourist train in Wales, became fascinated with each other, and decided to continue their trip together. They look very pleased to be together.

People are sadly walking their dogs and looking up at the great swatches of recently clear-cut forest on the slopes of Britain's highest mountain, Ben Nevis (4,406 feet), twenty miles southwest of Invergarry. Clear-cutting a forest where large numbers of people are less likely to notice it is like beating your kids where it won't show, so here they do it out in the open. Tourists are standing on bridges looking down into the roaring mountain streams, hoping to see a salmon fling itself into the sky like a great underwater figure skater. Others gather around a Highland cow and take pictures of it through the fence.

At Ionad Nibheis, the Ben Nevis info centre, one learns that, in 1911, in a stunt promoted by a car agency in Edinburgh, a Model T Ford climbed to the summit. Could it have been driven by a youthful H. V. Morton? A film features a voice droning along about how it's "often the case, even in midsummer, when the sun is warm down here in the glen, wild arctic conditions can be experienced on the upper plateau." Quartz outcroppings near the summit are often taken, from below, to be glaciers. A hotel on the summit was opened in 1894, but it didn't prosper; it closed in 1915 and is now in ruins. Three cheery English ladies in their seventies come in just as the dreary voice on the film is saying, "Remember, it's a hard walk." "Did you hear that?" says one. "He's saying it's a hard walk. By golly, it certainly is!" I asked if they'd been up. They said yes, but not today. A

316 ♦ AN INNOCENT IN SCOTLAND

few years ago. "It felt very good when we got down," said one. "It's a real achievement," said another.

And now here I am in Glasgow, several days earlier than I expected, but nothing seemed to want to delay me, and there's a lot to explore in this famous but somehow little-known and underappreciated city. Glaswegians are wonderful: this town is a laugh a minute, and it has its serious side as well. A bylaw from the seventies states that any new building must at least have "interesting corners." There's a Nelson Mandela Place in the city centre. It's not unusual to see someone bend down, pick up a tourist-tossed banana peel, and throw it in the garbage. Cabbies point out noteworthy examples of civic architecture. They go on and on about how they've been driving for thirty years or whatever and never get tired of it: you never see anything from exactly the same angle twice.

A bagpipe-and-accordion duet is coming from a small hotel with a richly ornate lobby and winding staircases, with busts of Mozart, Wagner, and Haydn in little alcoves here and there.

"Och, it's a wedding upstairs," says the woman at the registration desk. "Go on up and listen, if you will. There's a bar right next to the room where the music is. You can have a drink in there and listen to the music."

But the ballroom is filled with people in formal kilts and evening gowns dancing the night away, and the bar next door to it is jammed with wedding guests who prefer drinking to dancing.

"Oh, I am surprised," says the woman. "I didn't realize there were so many up there."

In the bar of the old railway station I chat with two hefty female bartenders – one a bit grouchy and one very merry. The grouchy one has kicked a guy out.

"Why'd you kick that guy out? He wasn't drunk was he?"

"He was *swearing* at me, just because I was busy and hadn't gotten to him yet. So I told him to go."

"Geez, I'd hate to be a bartender."

"It's fun," says the merry one. "I'm oh so very happy today.'

"It's not fun," says the other. "I'm grouchy today."

I shoot her a line from a 1959 Clark Gable movie, *But Not for Me*. "What's the matter, did your Dexedrine wear off?"

"That's right," she says, brightly. "Got any on ye?"

Later at a pizza joint, somebody with an ear for accents stood up a couple of tables away and shouted, "Are you from Canada? I lived in Toronto for twelve years. Come over and join us. Here, have some pizza." So I sat down with the young Canadian fellow and his pretty Glaswegian girlfriend. Davy McManus was a short, lovable, curly-haired fellow of twenty-seven, and Elizabeth was a svelte and youthful blonde of thirty-five. Davy was originally from Calgary and learned the marbling and tiling trade at Red Deer College, but he makes more money here than he ever could there, he gets more work, and he loves Glasgow. "Canada has no soul," he kept saying, and, even though I'd been in Glasgow only a couple of hours, I knew exactly what he meant, though I might not have expressed it that way – for, after all, soul comes in many forms. They wanted me to go to a party with them Saturday night. Some friends were coming in from the country. Elizabeth gave me her number. "Just give me a wee call if you want to go," she said. "Ye'll really like the people. There's some really interesting people going to be there."

The three of us went out in the rain, well after midnight. Soon we were walking three abreast and singing silly old Scottish songs at the top of our lungs. People were smiling in the dark rain.

We dropped into a greasy old seamen's pub, with plenty of soul and a soulful little band – two tall guys singing and playing guitar and a short, mournful-looking guy between them playing the fiddle with great solemnity. They sang the slowest and saddest version imaginable of the saddest Scottish song of all, "Scots, Wha Hae Wi' Wallace Bled."

Elizabeth and I danced to several songs. She gave me her card: ALLURE INSTANT PHOTOS – ALL TYPES OF CELEBRATION. She goes around taking pictures of people in pubs when they're drunk, and then sells the picture to them. They of course will buy it, because they know it's the only copy, and they don't want anyone else to see it. She's just getting started, but has the feeling it's going to beat flipping burgers. I told her many of the world's greatest photographers started this way. She was born in Glasgow but has Norwegian connections, owing to her mother's new husband, who lives on an island near Oslo. Elizabeth loves Oslo. And her new dad is a great storyteller who keeps them enthralled.

I felt comfortable being the third party. At one point, when we were at the bar, Liz looked at Davy and said, "I've been in many, many, many relationships in my life. But this is by far the best." They beamed like angels at each other.

GLASWEGIAN
ATMOSPHERICS

Glasgow

F riday, June 23. I've come to a beautiful place. I'm climbing up the inside of an Irish round tower. I'm leaning out a little round window and ogling the dreamy landscape. Little people scurry around down below, and by focusing on them I can see them up close, as if there are little telescopes in my eyes, and can chat with them, as if there are little volume controls in my ears. Everybody's so beautiful and interesting. I'm making friends hand over fist. Somebody presents me with two automobile tires, gaily gift-wrapped, and they're so light I can hold them up with one finger – and then they start floating in the air, with me hanging on. When I wake up, it's my first morning in Glasgow!

If you hear someone screaming on a corner with the most anguished and mournful tones of desperation, they're probably hawking fresh fruit or newspapers. They're programmed to scream out the same horrendous sound over and over again all day and all night long. But if you stop to chat, they're quite pleasant.

Every twenty seconds an old man selling newspapers on Argyll Street, behind the train station, calls out some completely incomprehensible phrase. I buy a paper. "Oh, the *Evening Record*, that's what you were hollering. Gad, I've been in this country a month and haven't understood a word anyone's said." He wants to know where I'm from. He says he has a mess of relatives "over there." Whereabouts? "Oh, could be anywhere, out in the wilds of Canada somewhere." He shakes my hand and doesn't want to stop. When I finally get my hand back he says, "No, give me your hand again." Then he says, "What's the Canadian logger's handshake?" With that he shakes my hand back and forth like a two-man saw. I tell him I haven't heard that since I was a kid. He laughs so hard I can count his teeth – all one and a half of them. He's not an everyday shaver by any means, but he's clean and otherwise fit for heaven for sure.

"Do you know what this bridge used to be called?" I ask him. Trains stream in and out of the station across this enclosed bridge three storeys above the street. Homeless Highlanders, after the clearances, would huddle here to keep dry during storms, for want of anything better, and it became their special meeting place whatever the weather.

"Why certainly," he says. "It was called the Highland Man's Umbrella."

"How did you know that?"

"Oh, I go way back. I remember my father telling me it used to be called that. And you see that big chunk missing out of the metal there? That fell off and just about killed a man."

Three things to know about Glasgow:
1. It's fashionable for women to wear long skirts, ankle-length, with sexy slits from ankle level up to the mid-thigh, during the day, at the office, or wherever. But at night they switch to extremely short miniskirts or skin-tight jeans.

2. You can feel a high level of intelligence in the air: the whole city sparkles with a street-smart fizz of quick repartee, worldly wisdom, and bright minds

3. There's lots of traffic, but never any horn-honking, and there are lots of no-automobile sections and pedestrian areas. It's hard to dislike a city like that.

I've returned the car to the airport. People are getting out of a massive tourist bus and getting their luggage together for the flight home. "*Prego, prego, prego,*" everybody's saying. I ask the driver where he took them.

"All over," he replies. "See, we've had them for a week – a whole busload of Italian brain surgeons. They were up here for a big conference. At the end of the conference most of them went home, but forty opted for staying on and going on a tour of Scotland. So we drove them everywhere, all over Scotland, for a week."

"Get a good tip?"

"Nnnn – okay, okay. Not bad, not bad. Not as good as the Americans."

Queen Elizabeth is going to be offically opening the new Glasgow Museum of Modern Art next week. Craigie Aitchison (born in Dunbartonshire in 1926) is probably the most interesting living Scottish painter, not that I can pretend to have seen them all. He's been around, paid his dues, and is now in his seventies. He's somewhat David Hockney–Stanley Spencer-ish, but more modest, metaphysical, and minimalist in style and substance. A lamb-like Bedlington terrier is his trademark, a silent dogged witness to such things as Christ's crucifixion, the construction of the Pyramids, the aurora borealis, someone having a shower, and so on. A small fourth-floor gallery is devoted to a small, selected retrospective.

A friendly guard tells me the story of her summer vacation. "I'd just passed my driving test, and we'd bought a car, and we decided, all right, that's it, throw the kids in the car, and we decided to go and see Scotland, cuz we've never been outside Glasgow, so we thought what's the point of going south and lyin' in the sun when we could see a bit of our own country first. So we started off in Oban and worked our way up and ended up in Ullapool. And it poured every day."

This woman was guarding the Aitchison retrospective. She can't stand van Gogh, but she loves British painter Beryl Cook, and she loves Degas, Manet, and Monet. But this van Gogh is a waste of paint, she can paint better than him. I tell her I don't think Beryl Cook would agree with her on that score, and she says, "Well, that's just the way I feel."

My favourite Aitchison is about the size of a postcard showing a dead yellow bird lying on its back with its feet sticking up in the air on a green lawn. In the background there's a leafless tree – three little green brushstrokes. In the far background there's a purple pyramid outlined in yellow and faint blue against a dark night sky, with one tiny eight-pointed star. It's called *Dead Bird – 1984*. He does many crucifixion scenes, showing Jesus either trying to crawl out from inside the cross, Jesus in the shape of a cross, or Jesus resting inside a transparent cross. In one he's hanging loosely by his hands from the crossbar and seems to be blowing in the wind like a wet sheet; in the foreground is a brown sheep and a blossoming cherry tree.

Nine typical tales about Glasgow:
1. It's night, and I'm standing on the sidewalk craning my neck to look up at the domed roof of the Custom House, faintly illuminated by a small green light. Somebody goes by and says, "Drop something?" I start laughing, we look at each other, he starts laughing and continues on his way, chuckling to himself.

2. On the bus coming back from the airport, the driver has to tell a determinedly stupid woman, over and over, that he doesn't go to Aberdeen, he only goes from the airport to downtown Glasgow and back. Finally, a fellow who has been patiently waiting to buy his ticket says to the driver, "Aberdeen one way, please." The driver looks at him in astonishment: the fellow starts laughing and says he couldn't resist it. The driver starts laughing.

3. Strangers here habitually have a delicious feast on each other's faces as they pass in the street. Everybody checks out everybody, constantly, and when strangers get talking, there's a tendency to get nose to nose. You can stop for a brief chat and the person is all over you. There's nothing solipsistic about the Glasgow mindset: those people out there really exist, so let's celebrate the fact.

4. One could spend a lifetime walking around without seeing the same thing twice. I have to put my camera away. It's too much. Everywhere, photos beg to be taken.

5. Two men are walking along carrying, at shoulder height, a merrily laughing but horizontal woman in the briefest miniskirt, with her long shining legs sticking way up in the air.

6. Forty guys are milling around outside the back door of a pub at two in the morning. Some are drinking beer, others eating fish and chips wrapped in newsprint. As I pass, they all turn to look at me, and one fellow yells out, "Geez, nice specs."

7. I'm sitting at the bar of a long, narrow, crowded "Spanish–American" restaurant, with a Budweiser and a plate of rice and mushrooms. I say to the bartender, "I'm enjoying this more than I would the finest steak."

   "I know what you mean," she says. After a pause she adds, slyly, "Would you consider yourself a man of normal tastes?"

   "Perfectly normal," I say. "How about you?"

   "Hell, no," she says. "I'm half-Irish."

8. Two pubs stand side by side, with a narrow store between them. One pub has a fancy, ornate façade, while the other's rundown, with greasy artificial flowers in the grimy windows. I go into the

rundown one and ask the bartender if they're in competition with the other one. "Oh, heavens no," he says. "We go in there and drink, and they come in here and drink, and we all get along fine. We share customers, people come in here one night and go in there the next, and vice versa."

9. A poster for the rock group Missing contains an interesting quote: "Rock 'n' roll is the most brutal, ugly, vicious form of expression – sly, lewd, in fact plain dirty – a rancid-smelling aphrodisiac – the marching music of every delinquent on earth." – Frank Sinatra, 1957.

An elderly lady in a long grey coat is walking along Argyll Street behind the train station and in the shadow of the Highland Man's Umbrella. She's in an agitated state. It's late at night. She keeps turning around and walking back the way she came, then turning around and coming back. Is something wrong?

"Och, aye, I don't know what to do, it's that damned old fool, it's just terrible, what a shame."

She points down the street. Two young fellows are dragging a huge, fat, bald-headed old guy off the bus. His trousers are down around his thighs, but unlike Wally he doesn't have "builder's bum" because he's wearing a tight new pair of black underpants. He has a snow-white, carefully groomed little beard and looks rather elegant, considering the circumstances. He looks well-to-do, but he's pissed out of his everlovin' mind. He seems to weigh a ton. If the fellows let go he'll fall like a rock.

He's not slurring his words. The booze goes to his legs rather than his head. He keeps offering suggestions: "Just lean me against this and I'll be all right." He's referring to a shaky tip-bin. They lean him against it, and he holds on as if it's the mast of a ship during a typhoon, but he keeps losing his grip and sliding a bit, then getting his grip back. I feel sick. He's going to drop hard and smash his skull on the pavement. "I'll be all right," he keeps saying.

The helpful guys, their bus is coming along. They want to know where I'm from precisely. Then they feel they can trust me to do the right thing. They jump aboard. The drunk starts to slip. I run back and catch him under the arms. He's so heavy I hurt my hand. He wants me to help him back up onto the tip-bin, but he's too heavy. I insist he sit down on the pavement, it's dry and clean. But he's well-dressed and doesn't want to wreck his trousers. What would his wife think? He keeps repeating, "I'll be all right."

He wants to go to Greenock. He says he has to catch the train. I make him sit down, but sitting he's even more unsteady than while holding on to the tip-bin. I try to get him to lie down, so he won't topple over and crack his head, but he adamantly refuses. He has spunk!

Finally I have him propped into a poised sitting position; he looks fairly steady. I tell him to sit there till he gets his legs back. He seems to think that's a good idea, but he doesn't want to miss his train. A red-faced Irish businessman in a suit and tie has been keenly observing all this, but from a distance. I go up to him. Any ideas?

He seems to think I want him to help me carry the guy somewhere, perhaps all the way to the train. He says he can't get involved, because he's an alcoholic himself. "I've just been to an AA meeting. I live out of town, too, and I have to go home. So I can't get involved in this for any number of reasons."

I tell him this dead-weight bozo wants to catch the train to Greenock. He says there's a little tunnel into the train station a few steps away, and then there's a long, upwardly ramped and twisting corridor that would have to be negotiated. But would the train take him? Of course not, he says. Finally he says something helpful. He says there would be "polis" (pronounced *bollis*) in the station. By polis he means police. There were always polis patrolling the station.

So he agrees to stand by and make sure the gentleman's head doesn't hit the pavement while I go looking for the polis. Inside the station, two tattooed toughguys are making obscene gestures at the ceiling. I look up. There's a little polis TV camera up there. Glasgow's famous for having an intricate TV spy system in all the high-crime areas of town. But where was the camera outside? Were the police at the station gathered around watching our struggle and laughing their heads off?

It's all aboard for Falkirk, Kilmarnock, Oban. A giant policeman and a midget policewoman appear on the far side of the station. As if by ESP they walk straight towards me. They're bored out of their minds, and delighted to have something to do. They make me pinpoint the exact location of the drunk, then they scurry off towards the winding ramp and onto Argyll Street.

I slip into the pub for a well-deserved pint. I ask the bartender if Sub Zero's selling well. It's featured in a glittering new poster as some kind of "alcoholic" soft drink with a hint of spices and herbs. She says no, it's selling poorly. Of the few who've ordered it, only about one has actually finished it.

No way will that juicehead get back to Greenock tonight. But he'll be coherent enough to have the polis call his wife and tell her he's sleeping it off in the slammer – and she can deal with him tomorrow.

FRIENDS FROM
FALKIRK

Glasgow

Saturday, June 29. A tea room called Trees is planted on the second floor above a sporting-goods store. It's been here since the turn of the century. For breakfast, I have greasy potato scones and some beans out of a can. The guy on cash is about eighty-five and fading fast. I suggest he tell them to put oatmeal porridge on the menu.

"Oh, I don't have anything to do with the kitchen," he says. "I used to work in the kitchen, but I don't have any say any longer." He looks baffled. He says he has no idea why it's not on. Has he worked here long? "Oh, I own the place. I been here about forty years." He has no idea how it got the name Trees. That was the name when he bought it in the fifties, and he had no idea what the origin of the name might be. "Possibly there were a couple of trees in the middle of the street when it first opened."

Glasgow on a sunny afternoon is full of buskers – pipers, violinists, accordionists, all playing old Scottish songs. The Nelson Monument is a carved fountain of brown limestone, forty feet high, with Queen Victoria sitting on the top. It's bedecked with Highland chiefs, waterbearers, lions, bears, stags, mythological beings, and astrological creatures. But some malcontent has vented unimaginable frustration and rage with a sledgehammer as far as he or she could reach. It looks as if it must have been a good night's work. Now there's a fifteen-foot-high barbed-wire fence around it and some scaffolding has been erected for repairs. It's in the middle of the riverside Glasgow Green, where young people dressed in black are taking close-up photographs of dandelions and each other's noses. Also there's an impressive Sir Walter Scott drinking fountain, and someone has taken a sledgehammer and given Sir Walter a huge whack in the ear. You can still admire his profile, however.

In a nearby Irish pub there are numerous photos of the boxer Benny Lynch, said to have been a world champion way back when. "About the time of the Boer War," said the bartender.

"Did he used to drink here?"

"Oh, he might have had a pint or two here now and then, as I've been told."

Signs all over the pub say, I'M FIFTY TODAY!!!

"Who's fifty?"

"I am," says the bartender, hoping for giant gratuities.

I shake his hand. "Well, congratulations. How do you feel about it?"

"Well, I feel many a better man than me never made fifty, so I'm feeling pretty good about having made it."

He wants me to sign the book. He's got two books full of visitors' names, visitors from abroad.

"You could tell I wasn't a Glaswegian?"

"It did cross my mind, that's for sure," he said.

"How could you tell?"

"Oh, the way you look, the way you dress, the way you talk, the things you say, the way you drink . . ."

"The way I drink? What's the matter with the way I drink?"

I flip through the overseas visitors' book and it appears the bartender gets fooled occasionally. He gets people to sign it who seem to be from other countries, such as India, but actually live in Glasgow. One fellow with an Indian name and a Glasgow street address has written: "I love the Scottish people. They're so honest. They have no upper lip."

Whenever I give my name, I expect people to say, "McFadden! Not one of the McFaddens who went over the sea to Canada? Geez, my grandpa knew your family well and always told fascinating stories about them. Here, let me buy you a Laphroaig. If I'm not mistaken, the McFaddens had a weakness for Laphroaig." But nothing like that ever happens. It's a lonely old world. My anticipation of going to Glasgow and being welcomed by whole gangs of McFaddens was sentimental foolishness. Yet I somehow feel at home, as never before.

As planned, I meet Liz and Davy at Molly Molloy's Pub at nine. It's so crowded you have to fight your way to the bar. We stay close to the door to keep an eye out for Liz's friends from Falkirk. Finally they come in – a woman, her husband, and about five other guys. You have to shout to be heard because everyone else is shouting to be heard. The husband immediately starts to make himself acquainted with all the babes he can get his hands on. His wife ignores him. One of the guys is her boss, and he's looking on with an amused, detached smile. He's a Pakistani and chairs some tribunal, and with him is a friend who's just in from Saudi Arabia and is due to fly back home on Monday. The Pakistani and the Saudi are in suits and ties. They smile and watch.

We become weary of the crush, so our little party heads around the corner to the Club Victoria, which seems to be a posh nightclub.

330 + AN INNOCENT IN SCOTLAND

But the Saudi and the Pakistani are the only ones allowed in. The rest of us are deemed not to be dressed appropriately. The big, surly doorman is sizing everybody up and making slanderous comments and arbitrary judgements. He takes one look at cute little Davy and snarls, "You're not getting in."

"Why not?" says Davy.

"Too cash" (as in "casual"). Then he looks at me and says he doesn't like the look of my grey sneakers. When I protest, dropping Edward de Bono's name, he says, "There are a lot of shoe stores around here, why don't you heave a rock through the window of one and get a new pair?" He wants to know why I've come all the way across the ocean with such a nice suit and such an awful pair of sneakers.

The doorman suddenly has a change of heart and allows all of Liz's Falkirk friends in. The Pakistani must have slipped him a fiver. Liz and Davy and I head sadly off into the night. Liz keeps saying, "I didna wanna go in there anyway." She's hurt and embarrassed that her "friends" should have proven so faithless. I too am shocked, but hold my tongue.

We finally find the perfect pub for the likes of us, with a giant fat woman shaking herself like crazy atop the bar. A grungy comedian grabs the mike and starts making cheap jokes about *les anglais*. He says, "Are there any English here?"

Somebody much funnier than the so-called comedian immediately yells out, "Aye!" Everyone starts howling with glee, except for the comedian, who senses the crowd's not with him.

"Come on, come on," continues the comic, "I can smell the English, I know they're here. Stick up your hands. Who's English?"

Nobody sticks up their hand.

"Who's on the dole?" he calls out. Somebody sticks up his hand.

"Och, it's not very good being on the dole, is it?"

"It beats being English," says the poor fellow, to great laughter and applause.

All the jokes are coming from the audience, none from the comic. But he doesn't seem to notice. "Come on, stick up your hands, who's English?" And that was the extent of the comedian as far as I remember. I wish somebody had yelled out, "Get the microphone away from the xenophobe." But not me, for by now I'd drunk too much and had to excuse myself and go home, leaving Liz and Davy all by themselves. I hope that was okay.

BIGOTS BECOMING
ENLIGHTENED

Glasgow

Sunday, June 30. Sunday-morning traffic is heavy. Two workmen
on a roof are throwing old lumber down to the road below. A woman
walks by in a long black skirt with a slit open to the groin: a breeze
makes it flap shamelessly as a sheet on a clothesline. The guys on the
roof whistle.

A couple pull into the parking lot and get out of their Land Rover.
"I'm telling your wives," the husband yells up to the workmen, and
his wife looks up too, pleased to have such a thoughtful husband.

"You don't know our wives."

"That's what you think."

The Land Rover guy spots me and scurries over with a worried
look on his face and a fiver in his hand.

"You couldn't change this, could you, guv'nor?"

I look in my pocket, but can only find three pounds in change.

"I'll give you three for it."

The guy thinks about it, then says: "Uh, no. Better not. Good try though." He walks away with a big smile.

For the first time in my life I get kicked out of a cathedral. A gentleman in a tight morning coat with pinstriped trousers comes up and says, "Excuse me, sir. Would you be taking the service this morning?"

"I had been thinking of it, but no. Would it be all right if I didn't?"

"I'm afraid not. We are not allowed to have people wandering about until two p.m. – sir." He's got an Edward G. Robinson sneer on his ugly face.

"Wandering about?" I said. "That's a good phrase for it. A little patronizing, perhaps. But what can one expect from a guy dressed like a monkey?"

He flinched but he recovered nicely.

"The door is right behind you, sir," he said.

Saint Mungo introduced the ancient Glaswegians to the Blood of the Lamb and the Light of the World. He also performed four major miracles, and for centuries his tomb was a place of pilgrimage. In the little auditorium in the ultra-modern and highly ecumenical Saint Mungo's Museum of Religious Life and Art, a film shows a curly-haired fellow dressed in a black robe and with numerous rings in his ears. He is described as a Scottish Buddhist. He starts off okay by preaching the standard necessity of giving up the world, your body, all the people ye've ever known. But then he goes a bit wonky: "Keep yer feet on the ground, but don't ferget to look at the stars," he platitudinizes. "We don't know how long it is that we're going to live. So I think ye have to make the best of that. Ye only get a certain amount of time and energy. How d'ye use that time and energy?"

A whole string of people make brief cameo appearances, talking about how Christianity has helped them in their daily lives: "I always have the notion of Jesus waiting for us on the other side," says one, adding, in a rather refreshing manner, that the same could be said for the gods of other religions. The museum is full of rare old stained-glass windows, original Dalis, including the original of the ultra-famous *Christ of Saint John of the Cross*, showing Christ on the cross sailing through the sky face down. There are images of white-haired, androgynous angels playing on lutes and trumpets as they escort Mary to heaven, a Buddha-faced Shiva subduing ten thousand heretics by dancing on the demon of ignorance, and an amazing collection of other works of art and artifacts from every religious tradition and every age. Each little gallery within the museum is playing a different kind of traditional sacred music, and there's a terrific collection of photographs as well.

A dark-haired, youthful little lady with a voluptuous figure crammed into a museum uniform a tad tight sashays up to me with a friendly smile. She says, with an adorable lisp, that she's deaf, but if I look right at her as I speak, she will read my lips. I tell her I'm impressed with the museum, and I can't imagine a bigoted person coming through without becoming unbigoted.

"Can you get them to come in, though, in the first place?" she says.

This is apparently a problem. The only people who visit the museum are people in the post-bigotry stage, who have begun to see that all religions are one, to use Blake's phrase.

"If they're bigoted, they wouldn't want to come here, would they?" she adds for emphasis.

A thunderous parade of Orangemen was starting up as we spoke and would soon be marching right past the museum, without a sideways glance.

With tremendous attention to detail, she tells me the story of her hard life and how she's so happy to have such a job finally. She ends by saying she's descended from the High Kings of Scotland and Ireland. I tell her I'm not surprised.

She becomes upset when I mention being kicked out of the cathedral. She says the minister of that cathedral is a fine person, but sometimes the captain doesn't know what the sailors are doing. She'd bring this unfortunate incident to his immediate attention, and nothing I could say would stop her. She's watched the lay people over there and "I know what they're like."

I'm heading over to the famed Necropolis, on the hill behind the cathedral. She, in all her years, has never been there. She's afraid of the vagrants who break into the tombs and sleep there. They attack people and rob them – even during the day. She says she's plagued by a natural lack of fear of strangers, so she has to be careful. Also, being deaf, she can't hear villains tiptoeing up behind her.

The vandalism isn't as widespread as I feared, but it's nasty. The heads of many necrologically pompous statues have been creamed with sledgehammers. Empty bottles of White Lightning and filthy old sleeping bags are everywhere. Someone has spray-bombed the name JINX ALLAN on the Houldsworth family tomb. But it's a mournfully amazing place, acres and acres of it, something to rival Père Lachaise in Paris, after which it was modelled. In his country manner, Morton swears up and down that the "obelisks, towers, memorials and minarets" of the Necropolis comprise "the most ambitious symbols of grief erected since the Pyramids."

Back at the museum, the Orangemen go banging solemnly by in the pouring rain. They stare fiercely straight ahead and give off that peculiar sense of deep, dark unconsciousness one gets from any mob under the sway of some ideology, the crueller the better. They're focused on their blowing of horns, their fingering of flutes and saxophones, their pounding of drums, and their hatred of Catholics. They give no indication they're aware they're marching past a museum dedicated to the unity of all religions. In my mind, I write a silly little poem:

336 ◆ AN INNOCENT IN SCOTLAND

Orangemen march, it's true, they do,
But if you were orange perhaps you would too.

Much later, after a nap and a change of socks, I go for a stroll. A fellow at the entrance to a pub is openly ogling a pair of lovers locked in an intensely smouldering embrace on the pavement. It's a steamy summer night in Glasgow.

"They're no old married couple," I offer.

"I should say not."

"A pleasant way of waiting for the bus."

"I don't know what's going on. She was waiting for the bus and he came up behind her and put his arms around her and she turned around and just threw her arms around him. I don't think they know each other at all."

"This is the friendliest town in the world. Can I get a drink in here so late?"

"No, it's up shop."

"Cheerio."

E   P   I   L   O   G   U   E

GLASGOW AIRPORT

Tuesday, July 2. "I doubt the answer will be in the affirmative, but do you have any Dalwhinnie whisky?" An American woman with a loud voice, white hair, white running shoes, and a Sir Walter Scott novel under her arm is yelling across the empty departure lounge to the young lady who runs the little magazine-and-book concession at the tiny domestic-flights-only Glasgow Airport.

"No. You'll have to wait for Heathrow and get it in the duty-free there."

"But Scotland is still part of the British Empire, isn't it?" shouts the Yank.

Now it was my turn to ask stupid questions. A fellow comes by in a yellow vest with BRITISH AIRWAYS in blue on the back. I ask him for the technical name for that spinning object out there. "Where?" he says. He goes to the window. Over there against the hills. "Oh, that," he says. "That's just for local radar. It's just for planes on the ground, I suspect." At first he was worried that I might be pointing out a potential problem.

A female flight attendant in a regulation pretty dress and little black wide-brimmed bowler hat runs up to him at full speed.

"He can't get the plane going," she exclaims.

This couldn't have been some kind of patented charade for my benefit; this was definitely not her way of getting him away from bores, one of which she might have mistaken me for when she saw his eyes rolling.

"He's probably got the handbrake on again," he said, and dramatically slammed his paper down on the counter. Then the two of them went jogging along the boarding ramp.

There was a delay in taking off. A young North American couple were sitting next to me, and were tense and angry about something. They were chewing gum. They were only in their twenties, but already seemed old and stodgy, stressed to the max. An announcement came over the system asking, if anyone had accidentally picked up a handbag, would they please hand it in. The announcer gave a complete description. The plane would be a few minutes late taking off, while they searched. I kept thinking how anguished the woman must feel, having lost her handbag. But my companions lacked ordinary compassion and grumbled bitterly.

"Figgers," said the man, with terrible sarcasm.

"Yeah, figgers," said his wife.

"Dammit," said the man.

"Yeah, dammit," said his wife.

Perhaps things had not gone their way in their Scottish sojourn. Maybe they found out something about their ancestors they didn't want to know.

Last night, on the Jamaica Street Bridge (at least that's my name for it, the one with the marble railings, at the foot of Jamaica Street,

which was a little Jamaican ghetto a hundred years ago), I had
watched the River Clyde flowing to the sea, and looked at the lights
of the city, and felt a river of sorrow in my heart. But I wasn't sad
about leaving, for one can always find a way of returning to Scotland.
In fact, I didn't feel sad about anything in particular, I just felt sad,
period. Chopin-sad. Then I turned around and went up to my room
and lay awake for hours before drifting off to that other world,
the one where all the McFaddens come alive again, and all the
MacLeans, and all the dead Scotsmen who ever lived, wherever their
dust may swirl.

Maybe I was sad about the people I had met in such quantities and
of such qualities, and maybe because of this long street that crosses
the bridge here and how it has had to endure so many sad name
changes as it crosses the width of the city. It's called Union Street,
and then it's called Renfield down to Gordon Street, then it's called
Union Street for a block or two down to Argyll Street, then from
Argyll it's called Jamaica Street down to Clyde Street, then there's
Bridge Street going over the bridge. On the south side of the river it
becomes Eglinton Street, then it becomes Pollockshaws Road, and
then it becomes Kilmarnock Road, and if you follow Kilmarnock
Road all the way. I'm sure you'll actually find this road is aptly
named, and that you will in fact get to the greasy old town of
Kilmarnock, the home of Johnnie Walker, and the birthplace of my
late grandmother – old Grandma Molly MacLean! Yes, that's right,
MacLean. If she tended to be a bit on the greasy side herself, she
came by it honestly.

As the plane broke through the cloud cover, I could hear that
fellow at the Ardgour Hotel saying, clear as the turquoise sky,
"Gimme a heap o' coins will ye, Billy?"

And then I heard that poacher's voice saying: "Why should the
laird have all the deer?"

It's not easy to find the fitting ending for a travel book. But in honour of H. V. Morton, whose spirit played such a large role in this book, let's have a look at how he ends his books on Scotland.

"Good-bye, and thank you for all the good and kindly things, for friendship, for humour, for beauty," he writes at the end of *In Scotland Again*, which came out in 1933 and was in its fourth edition by the following year.

And at the end of *In Search of Scotland*, which came out in 1929 and was in its fifteenth edition by 1931, he writes: "There was a burst of laughter, a whoop or two, and a volley of good nights. Then silence. In that silence a stranger said good-bye to Scotland."

INDEX

Abbotsford, 77, 80-82
Aberdeen, 13, 26, 29,
    122-25, 206, 323
Aberfeldy, 104, 109
Aitchison, Craigie, 321-22
Alexander III, 8-9, 73, 92
Alexander, Dion, 154-58
Allen, David, 93
Amulree 104-9, 111
Annick (River), 10
Aonach Mor, 182
Arbroath, 2, 266
Arculf, 110
Ard Chonnel Castle, 264
Ardgour Hotel, 180-81,
    243-60 passim, 339
Ardnadam, 7
Ardoch (Roman fort), 102
Ardoch Old Bridge, 103
Ardmeanach Peninsula, 185
Ardrishaig, 268
Ardurd, 230
Argyll Hotel (Iona), 204
Argyll region, 7, 102,
    260-85 passim
Armadale Castle, 167-68
Arnold, Fiona, 240-43
Aros Castle, 223
Arran, Isle of, 7, 9
Atholl, Earl of, 132
Auchencairn, 39
Auchterarder, 97
Awe (Loch), 260, 262
Ayrshire, 68, 231

Ballandalloch Castle, 133

Balmoral Castle and Forest,
    122
Balvenie Castle, 129-32
Banffshire, 133
Banks East Turret, 72
Beaton clan, 181, 203, 229
Beattie, Shonaidh, 113
Beauly, 288-89
Bellachroy Pub, 212
Ben Arkle, 310
Ben Buie, 232-33
Ben Hope, 308
Ben More, 188
Ben Loyal, 306-7
Ben Nevis, 182, 255, 281,
    315
Benn Ghobhlach, 311
Ben Rinnes, 133
Ben Stack, 310
Bettyhill, 304
Bill, Major, 26-30
Birnam, 110
Black, George Fraser, 101
Blair, Evelyn, 125-41 passim
Blairgowrie, 121-22
Blind Harry, 95
Bonnie Prince Charlie, 82,
    99, 147, 171, 177
Borders Country, 70-71, 73,
    77
Boswell, James, 167
Boyd, Mr, and Mrs., 9-15
Braan (River), 104-5, 109
Braco, 102
Brahan Castle, 289
Brahan Seer, 289

Broad Cairn, 122
Brontë Charlotte, 90-91
Brora, 291-94
Bruninrgton, HMS, 31
Buchanan clan, 170
Bunessan, 192, 230
Burgess family, 250-60
    passim
Burghead, 141
Burns Robert, 11, 15, 22,
    26-29, 75, 81-82
Bute, Isle of, 7

Cairntaan, 269, 271
Cairn o' Mounth, 123
Cairngorm mountains, 132
Calgary, 211-12
Campbell clan, 132, 171,
    183 219, 264
Campbell, Donald, 171
Campbell, Sir Joan, of
    Calder, 184
Carlyle, Thomas, 22-24
Carn Liath Broch, 289-91
Carter Bar, 71, 73
Castle Douglas, 40-42
Cathrin Inn (Coupar
    Angus), 111, 114
Chalcraft, John, 240-43
Charles, Prince, 31, 257
Cherrytrees, 44-50
Cheshire, 49
Cheviot Hills, 73
Clamshell Cave 219-220
Clan Donald Museum, 167,
    175

Clark, George, 25, 33-40, 70-71

Clegg, Dr., 218, 225, 227-29, 232, 234

Cnoc Ard Annraidh, 199

Colonsay, Isle of, 156

Comet, The, 2

Comyn, Alexander "the Black," Earl of Buchan, 131

Cook, Beryl, 322

Cooke, Wally, 244-60 passim

Corran Ferry, 180-81, 243, 253

Coulter, John, 165-66

Coupar Angus, 111, 118

Craignure, 230

Cree (River), 50

Creetown, 44-50, 55, 67

Crieff, 97

Crinan Canal and Ferry, 269, 284

Croggan, 230

Croit Glack Gorm, 211, 214

Crosskeys Hotel (Kelso), 75

Cuan (Loch), 216, 229

Cuillin Hills, 173

Cuin, 216

Culloden, 82, 147, 221

Cumbria, 72

Dalbeattie, 36

Dalmally, 260

Dalriada region, 260-85 passim

de Bono, Edward, 1, 330

Dee (River), 123

Dervaig, 211, 217, 226, 229

Devil of Glenluce, 66

Diana, Princess of Wales, 31

Dick Institute (Kilmarnock), 16

Dingwall, 141, 289

Don (River), 124

Donald clan, 167-68

Dornoch, 291

Dougald, Johnny, 203

Douglas Arms Hotel (Castle Douglas), 41

Druids, 72, 193, 309

Drummond Castle, 99

Dryburgh Abbey, 79, 82-84

Duart Castle, 181-84, 233, 254

Dubh, King, 143

Dufftown, 128-30

Duirinish Peninsula, 168

Dumfries, 17, 19, 21-40, 69-71, 81, 83

Dunadd, 271

Dunbartonshire, 321

Dunbeath, 294

Dun Bhuirg, 205, 272

Dundee, 29, 119

Dun Dornaigil Broch, 308

Dunfermline, 97

Dun I, 204, 206

Dunkeld, 105, 110

Dunoon, 7

Dunrobin Castle, 120

Dunsinane, 110, 122-23

Dunvegan Castle, 161-71, 212

Dunvegan (Loch), 168

Durness, 308

Ecclefechan, 22

Edinburgh, 74, 85, 89-97, 157, 168, 294, 315

Edinburgh Evening News, 165

Edward I, 13

Edward II, 84

Eildon Hills, 73, 80

Elizabeth II, Queen, 31, 321

Elspeth of Scone, 119, 121

Erraid, Isle of, 190

Eriboll (Loch), 309

Esk (River), 71

Essex, 45, 48

European Union, 136

Evans, Sally, 90-92

Fairlie Roads, 8

Falkirk, 326, 329-30

Falklands War, 114, 129

Fearnoch, 278

Ferguson Gallery (Perth), 116

Ferguson, Louise, Sandy, and Derek, 150-54

Ferguson, Sarah, 70

Ferguson Ship Builders, 5

Findhorn, 128, 141

Fingal's Cave, 194, 197

Fionnphort, 191, 197, 230

Fishnish, 180, 185

Fitzgerald, Colin, 92

Five Sisters, 159

Flodden, Battle of, 97

Footwall, 71

Ford, 260-85 passim

Forest Commission, 45-47, 151

Forres, 141

Fort Augustus, 177-80

Fort William, 243, 313

Froach, 109

Froachie (Loch), 109

Furnace, 286

Fyne (Loch), 268, 286-87

Galloway, 17, 22, 57, 59, 81

Gatehouse of Fleet, 42-43

Gerbil, Kevin, 277

Gibson, Donald, 100

Gilp (Loch), 268

Glasgow, 7, 162, 165-66, 185, 191, 310, 316-40

Glasgow Evening Record, 320

Glasgow Green, 328

Glasgow Herald, 1, 251-52

Glasgow Museum of Modern Art, 321

Glasgow Necropolis, 335

Glasgow Royal Hospital, 163

Glasgow School of Art, 280

Glasgow University, 261

Glas Maol, 122

Glenalmond, 107

Glencoe, 260
Glenelg Ferry, 159-61
Glenfiddich Distillery, 123
Glengarry, 146-60, 177,
312-13
Glengarry Partnership
Initiative, 155
Glenlivet, Battle of, 132
Glenlivet Distillery, 129
Glenluce Abbey, 65
Glen of Strathbaan, 104
Glen Orchy, 260
Glenquaitch, 107, 109
Glenshee, 122
Globe Inn (Dumfries),
26-32
Goatfell, 7, 9
Goodheir, Reinout (Josh
and Gillian, 278-84
passim
Gordon clan, 132
Gourock, 7
Grafton-on-Spey, 247
Grampian Mountains, 287
Grant clan, 132
Great Cumbrae Island, 8
Greenblatt, Eric and Joyce,
193
Greenfield, 147
Greenock, 2, 4, 325-26
Gretna Green, 21-22
Grey Cairns of Camster,
295-97
Gruline, 185, 218, 225
Gunn, Neil, 95, 294
Gunn, Sir James, 87

Haakon, King, 8-9
Hadrian's Wall, 21-22,
71-72
Harlaw, Battle of, 167
Harris, Isle of, 29, 168
Heading Hill (Aberdeen)
123
Hebrides, the, 95, 156
Henry VII, 97
Henry VIII, 73, 84
Hertford, Earl of, 75, 84
High Crosby, 71

Highland Man's Umbrella,
320, 324
Hill o' Many Stanes, 298
Hills of Cromdale, 132
Holy Loch, 7
Hope (River), 308
Hourston of Orkney, 209
Huntly, 125

Illean Amalaig, 230
Imperial Chemical
Industries, 13
Indomitable, HMS, 54
Infirmary Museum, 209
Innis, Hector, 75
Inver, 109
Inveraray, 183, 287
Inverclyde Newark Castle
Park, 6
Invergarry Hotel, 312-14
Inverleith Terrace
(Edinburgh), 95
Inverness, 29, 144, 288-89,
293, 313
Inverurie, 125
Iona, Isle of, 110, 177,
184-85, 189-210, 225
Iona Hotel (Perth), 116
Irongray Church, 83
Irvine, 9-16
Islay, Isle of, 156
Isle of Skye Hotel (Perth),
116
Isle of Whithorn, 58, 60
Isleornsay, 162

James IV, 81, 97
James VI, 119
Jedburgh, 73-75, 77, 140
Johnson, Samuel, 167
Jura, Sound of, 269, 284

Kellet-Smith, Yerik Struan,
252
Kelso, 75-78
Kenneth II, King, 119
Kerrara, Isle of, 181
Kier, Allen, 122
Kilcreggan, 7

Kildavie, 226
Kilmarnock, 15-17, 48, 52,
119, 326
Kilmartin, 265-85 passim,
287
Kilmichael Glassary, 272
Kilninian, 217, 221
Kilwinning, 9
Kircardine O'Neil, 123
King, Ian, 90-92
King's Stables (Edinburgh),
90
Kinloch Hotel, 185
Kinloch Hourn, 158
Kintail region, 92
Kintyre region, 7, 9, 102
Kirkcudbright, 39
Kirkwall, 8
Knaik (River), 103
Knights Templar, 86
Knoc Freiceadain, 302
Knox, John, 22
Kyle of Lochalsh, 161, 174

Labour Party, 28-29
Ladder Hills, 132
Lady Maidh, 109
Lanercost Priory, 72
Largs, Battle of, 7
Laxford Bridge, 310
Lease, John, 266
Lewis, Isle of, 29, 163, 168,
289, 310
Linlithgow, 95-97, 131
Linnhe (Loch), 180-81,
243, 247
Lismore, Isle of, 181
Little Minch, 168
Liver (River), 132
Little Cumbrae Island, 8
Lochaline, 180
Locharbriggs, 37
Lochbuie, 101, 190, 222,
230-35
Lochgilphead, 265-85
passim
Lochinvar, 77
Lockerbie, 24
"Loch Lomond," 74

Loch Ness Monster, 122-23, 141, 144-46, 178-80
Lomond Hills, 94
Lord Chelsea, 108
Lorn, Firth of, 181
Lorn, Mountains of, 182
Low Crosby, 71
Low Row, 72
Lumphanan, 122-23
Lunga, Isle of, 184, 241
Lynch, Benny, 328
Lynn of Morn, 181

MacAlpine, Kenneth, 110, 143
Macbeth, 110, 122-23, 141, 193, 208-9
Macbeth's Stone, 123
MacDonald, Hector, 279
Macdonald, Sir Alexander, 168
MacDonell, Alasdair Ranaldson, of Glengarry, 156-57
Macduff, 123, 193
Macfadyen, Iain, 170-72, 180, 287
Machers, The, 53, 58, 65
MacGregor clan, 132, 165
MacGregor, Alison, 165-66
MacGregor, Simon, 246-47
Macintosh clan, 132
MacIver, Bill, 299-301
Mackenzie clan, 92
MacKnochen of Newtown, 177-178
MacLean clan, 101, 132, 181-84, 190, 223, 230, 253, 339
MacLean, Fiona, 240
MacLean, Hector, 184
MacLean, Kenneth, 234
MacLean, Lachlan Cattanach, 11th Chief, 183
MacLean, Lachlan "Lachy," 218-25
MacLean, Lady Elizabeth, 183

MacLean, Marian, 184
MacLean, Sir Fitzroy, 26th Chief, 182
Maclean, Sorley, 175-76
MacLeod, Chris, 170
MacLeod clan, 168
MacLeod, Dolly, 168
MacLeod, Norman, son of Norman, the 23rd Chief, 168
MacMhuirich, Niall Mór, and Lachlan Mór, 167
MacNab, P. A., 224
MacPhail, Dugald, 230
Magnus, King, 8
Malcolm, 123
Mallaig, 161
Man, Isle of, 9, 39, 62
Mansfield, Earl of (Scone), 120
Manson, David, of Ecclefechan, 23-24
Margaret, Queen, 97
Martyrs' Bay, 197-98, 202
Mary, Queen of Scots, 81-82, 96, 131
Mary Queen of Scots House (Jedburgh), 75
McAughtrie, Tom 28-29
McCartney, Paul, 148
McConnell, Ian, 21, 234
McElcheran, Kenny and Linda, 44-50
McFadden clan, 68, 70, 101, 139-40, 166, 174, 181-83, 190, 222-24, 230-35, 239, 329, 339
McKay, Mr., Mrs., and Marie, 162-64
McLush, Mr. and Mrs., 104
McManus, Davy and Elizabeth, 317-18, 329-31
McMaster clan, 253
McNaughton clan, 177
McNeill clan, 132
McPhail, Charlie, 203
Meal Dubh, 146
Melrose, 77-79, 82
Melvedge Hotel, 303

Mendelssohn, Felix, 194
Minigaff, 51
Mishnish (peninsula), 216-17
Mitchell, Mr. and Mrs., 148-49, 158
Molly Molloy's, 329
Monk's Meadow, 205
Mor (Castle), 233
Moray, Men of, 143
More, Fergus, 261
Mornish (peninsula), 216-17
Morris, Mr. and Mrs. Walter, 134-41
Morris, Ronald W. B., 278
Morton, H.V., 1-340 passim
Morvern Peninsula, 180
Mound, the (Edinburgh), 92
Mount Lochnagar, 122
Mount Mayar, 122
Mull, Isle of, 29, 101, 161, 177, 180-243
Mull, Ross of, 184, 191
Mull, Sound of, 180-82
Mull, Waist of, 185, 220
Museum of Science (Edinburgh), 94
Muthill, 97-102

Na Keal (Loch), 218
National Gallery of Scotland, 92-94, 157
New Abbey, 35-36
Newark Castle, 5-7
Newcastle, 34, 111
Newton Stewart, 50, 52
Newtown, 177
Nith (River), 17-19, 25, 33
Northumberland, 72
Northumbria, 57
Northwest Highlands, 146, 288, 304

Oban, 202, 203, 219, 280, 285, 288, 322, 326
Ochil Hills, 94
O'Duine, Eva, 264

Old Edinburgh Road, 50
Old Grindles Bookshop
  (Edinburgh), 90-92
Old Spittal Lane
  (Edinburgh), 90
Orchy (River), 260
Orkney Islands, 8, 86-87,
  148, 209, 302

Peel of Glenfannon, 123
Perth, 105, 111, 113,
  116-18, 121
Philip, Prince, 19, 31, 69,
  130
Pictish Boar of Dunadd,
  271
Picts, 21, 56-57, 103,
  141-43, 169, 173, 228,
  232, 258, 260-61, 269-85
  passim, 290, 297, 302, 309
Pilgrim Way, 58
Pitlochry, 121
Plockton, 67
Port Glasgow, 2
Portree, 172
Powell, Henry, 183
Prebble, John, 156
Primrose, Christine, 172,
  175
Pyrie, Violet and Gordon,
  286

Queen Charlotte, HMS, 168
Queen's Hill, 123
Quinish (peninsula),
  216-17

Raeburn, Sir Henry, 157,
  168
Rankin clan, 181
Redesdale Forest, 73
Rede Swire, 73
Reformed Baptist Church
  (Perth), 117
Reginald of Islay, King of
  the Isles, 193, 200
Richard II, 84
Ritchie, Anna, 142
Rob Roy, 165

Robin Hood Tower, 87
Rogie, Helen, 123
Roslin, 85
Rosslyn Chapel, 84-88
Rothesay, 7
Royal Air Force, 96, 241
Royal Botanical Garden
  (Edinburgh), 95
Royal Family, 130
Royal Marines, 54
Royal Mile (Edinburgh),
  89, 94
Royal Museum
  (Edinburgh), 97
Royal Palace (Linlithgow),
  96
Royal Navy, 26, 30, 148
Royal Scotsman, 174
Rubha Hunish and Rubha
  na h-Aiseig, 171
Ruthwell Church and
  Cross, 25

Saint Adamnan, 110
Saint Boswells, 79, 82
Saint Columba, 110, 193
Saint Gilda's Church
  (Lochbuie), 232
Saint Giles' Cathedral
  (Edinburgh), 94
Saint Margaret, Queen of
  Scotland, 193
Saint Michael's Church
  (Linlithgow), 96
Saint Mungo's Museum of
  Religious Life and Art,
  333
Saint Ninian, 57, 59, 61, 66
Saint Ninian's Cave, 58-59,
  66
Saint Ninian's Gardens,
  110
Saint Vernon's Church
  (Lumphanan), 123
Salen, 185, 230
Sandbank, 7
Sandyhills, 36
Scallastle, 224
Scone Abbey, 119, 219

Scone Palace, 118
Scone, Stone of, 8
Scotland on Sunday, 90
Scotsman, The, 14-, 151
Scott, Sir Walter, 31, 73,
  77, 80-84, 95, 157, 328,
  337
Scottish tribes, 142, 284
Scottish Banner, 85
Scottish Heritage, 65
Scottish Independence, 253
Scottish Nationalist Party,
  29, 53
Scott's Lookout, 79-80
Scrabster, 290
Scridain (Loch), 187, 191
Seaforth clan, 289
Seal Island, 253
Settlers' Watch, 246, 258
Sgurr Alasdair, 173
Shakespeare William, 122,
  183, 208
Sinclair, Prince Henry, of
  Orkney, 85-87
Sinclair, William, 87
Skye, Isle of, 3, 29, 67, 147,
  159-64, 168-74, 185, 190,
  204
Slamannan, 1
Sleat, Sound of, 152
Smith, John 209-10
Smugglers' Isle, 65
Snortz, Mr. and Mrs.
  Kappy, 134-141
Solway Firth, 17, 21, 36,
  44, 50, 53
Southerness 36
Spelve (Loch), 230-31
Spey (River), 133
Spittal of Glenshee, 122
Staffa, Isle of, 194-95, 197
Stenhouse, James, 82-84
Stevenson, Robert Louis,
  247-48
Stewart, Alexander, 167
Stirling, 97
Stornoway, 52, 164, 310
Stranraer, 7, 56
Strathoil, 230

Stuart, Alexander, 101
Stuart, James and Patricia, 34-40
Sueno's Stone, 141-43
Sunderland, Ian, 60-62
Sunset Boulevard Family Entertainment Centre, 124
Sutherland, 12, 120, 229
Sweetheart Abbey, 35

Tan, the, 8
Tay (River), 109, 117
Tayside region, 110, 152
Tempest, The, 200
Thom, Alexander, 225
Thom, Archibald S., 224
Thurso, 299-302
Tingle, Stewart, 26-32
Tinkers, 68, 191
Tipper, Philip and Christine, 211-38 passim
Tobermory, 32, 185, 212, 230, 239
Tomdoun Hotel (Glengarry), 147-49, 158
Tomintoul, 132
Tomnavoulin Distillery, 132

Tongue, 299, 305-6
Touch of Class, 41
Treshnish Islands, 184, 194, 241
Tullabardine, 101
Tweed (River), 80
Tyree, Isle of, 280

Uisg (Loch), 232
Uist, Isle of, 156
Ullapool, 310, 322
Ulva Ferry, 184-85
Urquhart Castle, 145

Verne, Jules, 194
Victoria, Queen, 182, 328
Vikings, 110, 197, 258-59, 309

Walby, 71
Wall, 71
Wallfoot, 71
Wallace, William, 13
Wallflower, 71
Wallhead, 71
Walmer, 71
Walton, 71-72
Water of Luce, 65

Water of Tarland, 123
Waternish (peninsula), 168
Weekly News, 250
Well of Eternal Youth, 204
Western Highlands, 264
Western Isles, 8-9, 116
West Hall, 72
White Strand, 198
Whithorn, 56-60
Wick, 299
Wicker Man, The, 67
Wigtown, 53-58
Wigtown Bay, 44, 50
Wigtown Martyrs, 53-54, 62
Wigtown Parish Church, 54
Wigtown Square, 56-57
Wilcox, Flora (née Elder), 99-102
William III, 295
Wilson, Chug, 31
Wobbly Pins Lounge Bar, 125

Yorkshire, 30, 61, 228
Yorkshire Post, 90

Zeno, Antonio, 87

Since you enjoyed *An Innocent in Scotland* . . .

Praise for *An Innocent in Ireland*

"This is a charming and quirky work, light and breezy."
– *Irish Literary Supplement*

"[This] book is centred on the personality of the writer and his explorations into all the possible ways of telling an amusing tale. Fortunately that personality is consistently engaging. McFadden's book not only gives one the feeling it would be marvellous to visit Ireland, but that it would be great fun to do so in the company of the author."
– *Toronto Star*

"This engaging and unpretentious book made me want to visit Ireland. There is no greater compliment for a book of travel than that. An old Irish proverb says a writer is a failed conversationalist. McFadden, however, is both a good writer and a splendid conversationalist, who speaks quietly but persuasively to his readers."
– *Hamilton Spectator*

"An engaging, compelling, and captivating trip."
– *Irish American News*

"What a wonderful, wonderful book! David McFadden's humour, erudition, curiosity, his poet's loving eye, his devotion to every moment and setting in which he finds himself – all these rare gifts are here in spades. I have been to Ireland, I have written about Ireland, I have family in Ireland! And now that I have read *An Innocent in Ireland* I have at long last seen the place."
– *Barbara Gowdy*

AN INNOCENT IN IRELAND

Curious Rambles and Singular Encounters

When David McFadden sets out on a tour of Ireland, he is determined to do so in a relatively innocent state. Using as a guide only *In Search of Ireland*, a 1930 title by travel writer H.V. Morton, he plans to follow the same route, to try to determine how things have changed and how they have remained the same.

This he proceeds to do – at least at first. But soon he is wandering more and more erratically around the country, poking into any corner and musing over any sight that takes his fancy – from a cosy guest house in Kilcullen to the legendary Hill of Tara, from the south-coast pub run by twin sisters to the windswept reaches of the Ballaghbeama Gap. And increasingly he is drawn to the prehistoric monuments of ancient Ireland. As he goes, he records his very personal impressions in a clear-eyed and wryly humorous way.

Wisely, McFadden also lets the many characters he meets speak for themselves; he loves a good chat and he gives ample space to the various loquacious barmen, shopkeepers, hoteliers, and passersby along the way. And of all the eccentric and appealing characters that he encounters, one of the most intriguing is his travelling companion, the mysterious Spanish chambermaid and poet, Lourdes Brasil.

Amusing, quirky, compassionate but unsentimental, *An Innocent in Ireland* is a treat for any armchair traveller.

0-7710-5527-7
Trade paper with flaps
5 1/2 x 8 1/2
304 pages
$19.99

McClelland & Stewart   **M&S**   *The Canadian Publishers*